G000160554

Dartmoor
Themes

Dartmoor Themes
A Walker's Guide

JH Powell

Illustrations by Alan Groves

The Crowood Press

First published in 1995 by
The Crowood Press Ltd
Ramsbury, Marlborough
Wiltshire SN8 2HR

© The Crowood Press Ltd 1995

All rights reserved. No part of this publication may be reproduced or transmitted in any form or by any means, electronic or mechanical, including photocopy, recording, or any information storage and retrieval system, without express permission in writing from the publishers.

British Library Cataloguing in Publication Data

A catalogue record of this book is available from the British Library.

ISBN 1 85223 915 8

Picture Credits
Unless otherwise credited the photographs are by the author.
Pen and ink illustrations are by Alan Groves except where otherwise marked.

Acknowledgements
My thanks go to all those people who have helped me with this book. Alan Groves has taken my foggy photographs of obscure objects and produced some evocative illustrations. John Craig helped me both with the layout and with the computer maps. A number of colleagues have helped me by providing aerial photographs, without which the maps and the layouts of the antiquities could not have been produced. My son, Jake, has supported me on many field trips.

Mostly I would like to thank my wife, who has met my tantrums with amused neutrality and my frustrations with understanding and undeserved sympathy. The moor is only my second love.

Front cover: Clapper bridge at Dartmeet
Back cover: Drizzlecombe Menhirs

Printed and bound by WBC Book Manufacturers, Glamorgan

Contents

Safety

In 1968 I was introduced to Dartmoor from the back of a Royal Navy truck, which opened to reveal a dark grey landscape sporadically visible underneath a stinging rain so thin that it permeated every seam in my clothing within minutes. I was given a map and a compass, and told to be back at the naval college in Dartmouth within 36 hours. The lorry drove off. They had omitted to tell me where I had been left. I decided I didn't like Dartmoor much.

Gradually I came to know the moor in different lights. It didn't always rain, the mists and fogs had a life of their own, and the challenge of navigating for miles across the great green ocean of the north moor became a fascination. Occasionally one would see great standing stones set up for no apparent reason in the middle of the wasteland. When the sun shone, great vistas would open up. Strange outcrops of granite ploughed the seaways of the upper slopes, and buzzards would sweep overhead. I could also never understand why there were bogs on the tops of the hills as well as in the valleys.

Now, twenty-five years later, I have learnt a great deal more about the moor, from the books of William Crossing, RH Worth and others, and from talking to walkers and farmers. I have spent hours, days and weeks on the moor, searching out circles and rows, deserted farmsteads, merlins and mushrooms. I have read all the books on the myths and the legends as well as the novels based on the moor.

I hope that the rest of this book will give you some insight into Dartmoor, but I must warn you of two things. First, no matter how much you know, there will always be a surprise. Every time you walk on the moor you will find something you did not expect. Equally well, if you walk a route and look in one of the well-known texts, you will find that you have missed something and you will have to retrace your route to find it! Second, be assured, Dartmoor has the power to seduce like no other place that I know. Once it has hooked you, you will have to return over and over again to the quiet complexity of England's last wilderness. I wish you as much from the moor as it has given me, and I hope that this book will help you start to understand it.

The following section gives you some basic information about how to walk in safety and how to interpret the maps that appear in the book.

Layout

This guide is different from normal walking guides. Instead of grouping walks according to region, they are grouped according to a theme, these chosen to reflect the special interests of Dartmoor. The first chapter, for example, deals with the impact of neolithic man, and so the walks take you on routes which show you well-preserved monuments of the neolithic period. Of course, on the way you will certainly pass other interesting places and objects, such as the site of an interesting myth, or an old farm. These are explained in the walk, too, even though they are not the main subject of the themed chapter.

Each chapter starts with some **background on the theme**, which gives you enough information to put into context the things you will see. The chapter on geography and geology, for example, explains the origins of granite and tors.

Each chapter has a number of walks, each with a **map** (described below), and a walk description. These walk descriptions are not written to be complete in themselves: you must follow a map. Try the excellent Outdoor Leisure Map (number 28) at a scale of 1:25,000 published by the Ordnance Survey. By the very nature of the ground on Dartmoor, the walk descriptions can never be enough on their own, and you must take an appropriate map with you.

In the walk description you will find **key items in bold text**. These are things of interest that are described in the following pages. It is a good idea to familiarize yourself with these key items before you set off, since they are not always in exactly the same order as they appear in the walk description.

Walking on the Moor

Dartmoor presents different challenges to the walker compared with other hilly areas in the UK: few parts of it are steep; none of the tops requires you to put hand to rock; and the vast majority of the walking in both north and south

Check List

Have you:
Decided your route?
Left a note in your car or with another person saying where you are going?
Packed your map and compass?
Checked the weather?
Thought when it will get dark?
Parked your car sensibly?
Locked your car and left valuables out of sight?
Packed your waterproofs?
Packed your winter spare clothing?
Got film for your camera?

moors is straightforward. There are, however, one or two things you should bear in mind, particularly if you are venturing into the heart of the north and south moors.

Weather

Dartmoor has highly variable weather. For a lot of the time the air is clear, but it is subject to sudden drops in visibility because of rain and drizzle coming in from the west, and because of the notorious mists that can envelop it. It is important that you know the weather forecast, which you can get from the tourist information offices around the moor (for example at Postbridge)

or from advertised telephone services. The latter will only cost you a few pence and could save you the very unpleasant experience of being lost in the mist.

Valley Bogs

Let's not overstate the dangers of these. You can walk for a lifetime on Dartmoor without ever falling into one. There are stories of bogs swallowing whole waggon trains of walkers and herds of ponies. Although these are exaggerations, bogs are tricky. The basic rule is look ahead of you and be aware of the ground over which you are walking. If the ground suddenly starts to shake under your feet, then stop. You are in no immediate danger, but do not go forward. Go back, walk up to higher ground, where you can see the lie of the land and then plot a path around the sludge. Valley bogs are often a bright green colour, and can be seen by the experienced eye from a distance. Remember: there is no need to smash across them; there is always a way round. If you do fall into a feather bed, as the sludgy pits are known, you will likely as not only go in as far as your hips. Take off your rucksack, put it to your side and then wiggle yourself up on to it. If you have not panicked, you will only be a step away from firmer ground, and you should crawl on to this.

Navigation

Always carry a map and a compass. Not only will they stop you missing the pub through being lost, they will also show you all sorts of interesting things on the route which are not covered in the book. The best map is the Ordnance Survey 1:25,000 Outdoor Leisure Series number 28, available at

Key to the Maps

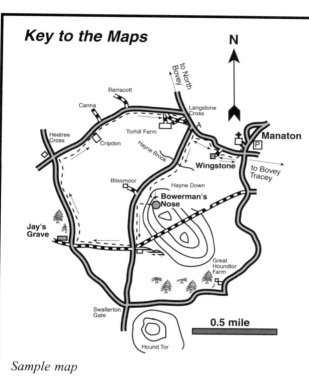

Sample map

This walk takes you into a range area. Check that no firing is planned by ringing the numbers on page 139 or by consulting a national park information centre or post office.

Do not cross the line of red and white poles if firing is planned.

This reminder appears on the map if you need to observe the range precautions. *See* pages 10, 139 and 140.

Ring: (01803) 294592 or
       (01392) 70164 or
       (01752) 701924 or
       (01837) 52939

for a recorded message telling you when it is safe to go on the ranges.

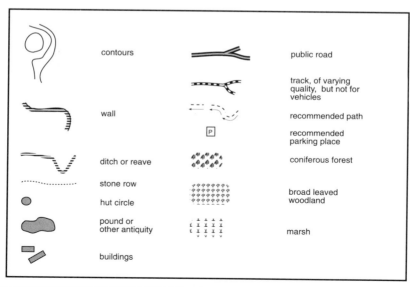

contours		public road	
wall		track, of varying quality, but not for vehicles	
ditch or reave		recommended path	
stone row		P recommended parking place	
hut circle		coniferous forest	
pound or other antiquity		broad leaved woodland	
buildings		marsh	

almost every bookshop in the area. Dartmoor does present some difficulties in navigation, since there are few features visible when the mist or rain comes in. Trust your compass and look for details like the directions of tracks and rivers. Do not follow a bearing blindly if it is leading you into a dangerous area such as a valley bog or a firing range. Try to move from feature to feature. If all else fails, follow a river downstream and you are bound to reach something you recognize.

Firing Ranges

A few parts of Dartmoor, particularly in the north moor, are subject to restrictions. You can read about these areas on pages 139 and 140. Do not cross a line of red and white poles across the moor without checking that the tors around are free of red flags or (at night) red lights. Conversely, even if there is firing you are perfectly safe as long as you stick to the correct side of the line of poles. Some of the best walking on Dartmoor is in the ranges, and you can check when firing is planned in the local post offices and tourist information centres. There is also a number you can ring to get a recorded message (*see* page 9).

Ancient Monuments

Many of the walks are centred on and around antiquities of various types. It is against the law to tamper with these in any way. You must not dig around them or use metal detectors, you must not carve or damage them, and you must not move them. Please remember that some of the antiquities on Dartmoor are of world importance (for example the Merrivale stone rows), and as such they must be protected for our children and the future.

Equipment to Take

Clearly, a short walk within sight of your car is a different prospect from an extended expedition into the middle of the high moor, but the following is a list of things you should take in summer for a full day's outing on Dartmoor.

Each person
Food and drink for the day
Whistle
Walking boots
Walking socks
Trousers — not jeans
Shirt
Sweater
Waterproofs
Rucksack

Shared (one between two)
Map
Compass
Watch

In winter you need to take a bit more equipment. The weather can change quite quickly and the days are much shorter, so you need to get out early and get back early. Aim to be back an hour before sunset in case you are delayed.

Extra winter equipment
Hot drink
Spare trousers and sweater
Hat
Gloves
Scarf
Torch

Access on the Moor

Generally speaking, access to the moor on foot is free, although sometimes it is restricted, particularly on what is known as access land. The restrictions in these areas are posted at the entrances. Access by motor vehicle is strictly limited to the public roads. If you go beyond the clearly marked limits on the smaller roads you are very likely to be seen, reported and prosecuted. Mountain bikes are limited to the bridle-ways, which are marked clearly on the maps, and the public roads. Do not risk going off the tracks either in a 4WD or on a mountain bike as you will be seen. Camping is allowed, generally speaking in the high moor, as long as you do not stay more than one night in any place, and as long as you leave no trace of your stay. Again, national park rangers will enforce the rules if you break them.

& Circles

T he stone circles and rows of Dartmoor, rising mysteriously from the hillsides and bogs of both north and south moors, represent the most obvious evidence of early man's intelligence and organization. To archaeologists they represent a fascinating set of material from which the mental abilities, social structure and organization of early man can be seen, albeit dimly, using present-day knowledge of chemistry, mathematics and astronomy, and modern techniques of recording evidence.

We see these strange, forbidding structures looming out of mists, peering over distant hillsides and silhouetted against the skyline on winter mornings and hot summer afternoons. The stone rows disappear over the green marshy horizon towards a distant join in the hills, seemingly mysterious and meaningless. Modern interpretations of the circles and rows, however, have given a fascinating insight into the uses of these megaliths, thereby helping to bring alive the activities of the early dwellers on the moor.

Two different ages of man built stone circles on the moor. Some, like Scorhill and Grey Wethers, were built by Stone Age people. Others, associated with stone rows, were built much later by Bronze Age folk. You will find more information on the way of life of the Bronze Age people as you walk the routes in the Ancient Farms and People chapter, where we visit some of the best settlements in Britain, but here we are concerned with the ritual monuments rather than the everyday life of the people. As with the other walks, of course, we come across incidental features which are explained rather more briefly than the stone rows and circles themselves.

The walks and discussions in this chapter are aimed at showing you the very best examples of well-preserved rows of standing stones and circles, and at explaining the meaning and uses of these amazing witnesses to the intelligence and ingenuity of our ancestors. Through their study we can put ourselves into the place of the Stone Age and Bronze Age farmers, who eked out a sometimes thin living on the high hills. Knowledge of the calendar was important to them, as was the maintenance of an order in their society, and the circles and rows, uniquely evocative on the unspoilt slopes of Dartmoor, can let us stand in their shoes. As you walk the routes, stop and imagine that you are a Stone Age or Bronze Age farmer, for whom the knowledge of the calendar, the best time to plant the crops, was inextricably entwined with the religion which bound your group of fellow-farmers together.

Who Built the Stone Rows and Circles?

Stalldown stone row

There are, fundamentally, four different types of Stone Age and Bronze Age remains on Dartmoor which we will visit in the walks of this chapter.

The oldest remains we shall visit are the chambered cairns of the Late Stone Age, built some 5,000 years ago by the people who lived just before the Bronze Age. We shall see an excellent example of the product of this culture when we visit the chambered tomb at Corringdon Ball. Stone Age man interred his dead in these artificial caves, which were then covered in earth. The cairns then served both to mark out a kind of church, and to provide evidence of ownership of the land.

The same people also built the splendid stone circles which we see at Scorhill and elsewhere. It is important to distinguish between these stone circles of the Stone Age and the circles which the later Bronze Age people built around their own peculiar burial mounds. The latter are often quite large, and can easily be confused with the larger megalithic monuments of the Stone Age which derive from the henge type of circular ritual monument like Stonehenge. The Stone Age circles were used for ritual purposes without question, but whether they were also used as a calendar, as many prominent astropalae-ontologists would have us believe, is very much open to doubt. Probably there is an element of truth in the suggestion that the alignment of the sun, moon or indeed stars could be used as a fairly accurate means of telling when certain festivals should take place, or when crops should be planted.

The third and fourth types of monument are distinctly younger, being Bronze Age constructions. The people whose culture is characterized by the distinctive beakers which they left their dead for use in the afterlife were accustomed to bury their dead in stone-lined holes in the ground, and above these they heaped a cairn of rocks and earth. These cairns take up prominent positions on the skyline, so as you walk the moors, keep your eyes open for the evocative silhouette of these low mounds. Many of these cairns were unfortunately robbed indiscriminately during late Victorian times, and are hence now of little use to archaeologists.

Also associated with the Bronze Age people are the dramatic stone rows whose purpose is almost certainly ritual, providing a route for processions and religious ceremonies. The first walk in this chapter takes us to one of the best of these, at Stalldown.

12

Early Man – A Rapid History of Our Ancestors

The first men (1,000,000-100,000BC) – the Palaeolithic Period

Man emerged from the shadowy ancestral home of southern Africa some million years ago. Gradually he began to distinguish himself from other apes by his ability to use tools, notably digging sticks, stone hammers and axes, and by his social behaviour. Over the subsequent millennia, man developed, at first slowly, but later more rapidly, an armoury of stone-working techniques that gave him access to sophisticated tools for cutting, killing and tool-making itself. The two illustrations of the early and late stone axes show you the difference in quality over this huge period. There is very little evidence of palaeolithic man on Dartmoor, but we do know that early ancestors of ours did live in the west of Britain.

Early palaeolithic axe

VAB

The end of the Ice Age (10,000-3500BC) – the Mesolithic People

This period of European prehistory is dominated by the changes in climate which took place as the Ice Age ended. The general warming of the climate allowed the growth of extensive light forest, with its inevitable increase in food plants and animals. As crop plants began to be domesticated, Mesolithic man adopted a more residential lifestyle, in contrast to the wandering nomadic way of life of his ancestors. These people were essentially the same as us, with very sophisticated hunting and social skills, who lived together in cooperation. There are remains, notably on the sea shore and in coastal regions, all over western Britain.

The Agricultural Revolution (4000-2000BC) – Neolithic Man and the Megaliths

The spread of agriculture through Europe from the Near East was a gradual process, diffused slowly by the twin means of physical migration of farmers and by word of mouth as trading began to establish itself.

By about 4000BC, farming had established itself as a way of life in the inhabited world: this is the period we now know as the neolithic period or New Stone Age. We see the establishment of small farming communities which, in northern Europe, are normally placed near forest lands, from where fodder could be gathered, and from where cultivated food could be supplemented by hunting and gathering of plants and berries. The dwellings of the time were wooden, with wattle and daub walls in some cases, and with thatched roofs.

Social structure by this time was well established, with a developed tribal structure, and with shamans or priests as doctors and ritual leaders. We know that there were doctors because of the incidence of certain flowers and herbal plants in burial sites, both from this period and from the earlier mesolithic period.

Finely shaped axe

VAB

It is important to remember that these people were essentially the same as us; there is less variation between modern man and neolithic man than there is between the inhabitants of a small village today. Physically and intellectually they were just like us, with the same worries, concerns, joys and preoccupations. They felt our misery in bereavement, our insecurity in conflict, our joy in love and friendship. They had a language of which we have only the faintest knowledge, this drawn from our examinations of the pre-Indo-European languages of Europe in the form of Basque and Iberian among others. But their language was rich and complex and more than adequate for the discussion of politics, abstract argument, art and aesthetics and the practicalities of government and making a living.

It is at this time that we see the remarkable rise of ritual burial in the form of megalithic tombs, also known as cromlechs or dolmens, which appeared all over Europe from about 2500BC. Why did they arise? It is unlikely that they were brought in by some large-scale invasion of a different culture; more likely that they formed a natural response to a change of lifestyle. It is probable that a more stable pattern of tribal life was needed, resulting in a greater understanding of the importance of ownership of a tribal food area, with the resulting requirement to express ownership of that area in opposition to other tribes and groups. When this is coupled with a more

13

Palaeolithic art

VAB

formalised and openly expressed structure in the tribe, we can hypothesize that a communal ritual burial would emerge naturally from the other developments going on around the tribe.

These chambered tombs, of which there are two or three on Dartmoor (including the Corringdon Ball and Spinster's Rock examples) are communal burial features, where an artificial cave is built above ground from large flat stones, and once full of remains, is then sealed by a further flat stone. The whole is then covered with a mound of stones and earth. The ones on Dartmoor are rather small, but further to the east, at West Kennet in Wiltshire in particular, the long barrow is prevalent. Here the chambered tomb is extended into a multi-chambered cave, producing the characteristic long low shape of the long barrow. There is a long barrow on Dartmoor on Brent Fore Hill. This lengthways extension of the simple chambered tomb is taken to extremes in the gallery grave, where twenty or so chambers are combined to form one feature. There are none of these gallery graves on Dartmoor.

The Beaker Folk
(2000-1000BC)

Things now get confusing, because at this time we see the influx of a people who use characteristic pottery and burial methods, while at the same time we see the continuation of the practice of erecting standing stones as ritual objects. The latter practice undoubtedly took place during neolithic times, and is connected with rituals to do with worship of the sun, moon and stars. Not surprisingly, these stones, which reach their culmination in Britain as a whole with Stonehenge and with Callanish in Scotland, and on Dartmoor with Grey Wethers and Scorhill, appear to have a combined purpose for calendar calculation and ritual. What is confusing is that these standing-stone practices and a new burial ritual (that of burying the dead singly with characteristic funnel-shaped beakers of pottery) appear to coexist for an appreciable period of time.

We call this overlapping period the LANEBA, standing for late neolithic, early Bronze Age.

Dartmoor of the LANEBA period is today considered to be extremely important, since it represents a relatively isolated and undamaged part of Britain. It is quite clear from comparisons of British LANEBA structures with those of continental Europe that the standing-stone practices here were developed in relative isolation, and

the incidence of such superb examples of stone circles and single standing stones as Scorhill and, say, Beardown Man on Dartmoor is very high. Additionally, the effect of subsequent usage by man on the moor is less than elsewhere, and this, coupled with the generally featureless terrain, makes Dartmoor *the* place in Europe to look at the remains of this period.

Bronze Age Dartmoor
(1500-750BC)

Some time before 2000BC, man discovered copper, probably by the accidental smelting of copper ores in a fire. It was some time before the addition of tin (about 10 per cent) was found to produce an alloy whose hardness and ability to hold an edge was significantly better than copper alone. By about 1200BC on the continent, everyday objects were being manufactured, and we can safely assume that the trading patterns of Europe at this time allowed the introduction of such objects into early Bronze Age British society at this time.

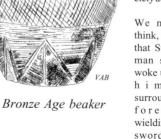
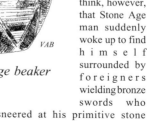

VAB

Bronze Age beaker

We must not think, however, that Stone Age man suddenly woke up to find himself surrounded by foreigners wielding bronze swords who sneered at his primitive stone weapons and then drove him out into the sea. The introduction of bronze weapons in particular was a

14

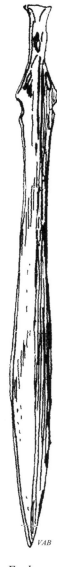

Early Bronze Age sword

gradual process, with stone tools (many of which, in the form of precisely manufactured microliths, were extremely effective and cheap) remaining in use for many hundreds of years. We have already seen how the Beaker folk, arriving about 1700BC, appeared to live in cultural harmony with the late Stone Age megalith people, and we should bear this in mind as we consider the change from an exclusively stone-tooled society to the height of the Bronze Age culture, in, say, 1000BC.

Dartmoor at this time was teeming with Bronze Age villagers living in collections of huts on the sides of the hills in relatively favourable climatic conditions. They farmed their pigs and cattle and went hunting for that little Friday night extra. We examine the way of life and huts and enclosures of these people else-where,

but it is worth noting the stone rows which these people put up with such enthusiasm on Dartmoor. These rows appear to be the extension of the late Stone Age henge features under the influence of the early Bronze Age people. They offer similar possibilities for a combination of ritual use and calendar calculation, although because of their linearity they would most likely only have been of use for telling a particular time in the calendar, as opposed to the multi-purpose stone circles. Many archaeologists have speculated over the alignments of the stone circles and rows, finding extraordinary densities of alignments of the stones with stars and planets at the time of their use. I do not intend to go into this complex and emotive subject here, save to say that it is entirely possible that the rows and circles were used for both a straightforward ritual purpose and for telling the time.

One thing is sure, however, and that is that the stone rows and the circles took huge numbers of man hours to construct. Estimates range up to a million man hours for a large monument. The Dartmoor stone rows probably needed rather less than that, but it is an indication of the available free resource of societies at the time that such public works could be undertaken.

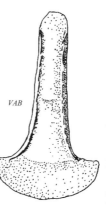

VAB

Bronze axe

Iron Age Britain (750BC-AD50)
By 1000BC Europe was beginning to see the invasion of the Bronze Age culture by a powerful integrated socially coherent wave of immigrants from the East called the Celts. These newcomers came in three separate sub-cultures, characterized by the types of art, burial, and pottery which they exhibited. They are called the Hallstatt Culture, the La Tène Culture and the Oppida Culture, the latter name taken from the Roman description of their towns. The first Celts started to arrive about 750BC.

On Dartmoor the hillforts in the north at Prestonbury and Cranbrook are the product of these artistic and civilized people, but once again we should not make the mistake of thinking that the Bronze Age people simply adopted the Celtic way of doing things suddenly. White Tor fort, for example, is very similar to an Iron Age fort, but is, in fact, dated to the late Bronze Age.

In another chapter we will look in detail at the way of life of the Bronze Age people who have left such important and accessible remains on the moor, and in yet another at the subsequent history of the moor. In the meantime, the following walks will allow you to visit the most important sites on Dartmoor over the period from the upper palaeolithic to the Bronze Age.

Bronze bracelet

VAB

15

Walk 1 – The Stone Rows of Stalldown and the Erme

Distance
About 6 miles.

Difficulty
Straightforward, with no navigational difficulties, but a map and compass must be carried if there is any possibility of poor visibility. The terrain is easy moorland at first, finishing along the sometimes marshy banks of the River Erme.

Main Features

Hillson's House	**636623**
Stalldown Stone Row	**632623**
Dancers Stone Circle	**635644**
Erme Stone Row	**635645**
Erme Plain Tinworkings	
and Blowing House	**636652**
Erme Pound	**640655**

Description of Walk
*Leave your car on the approach to New Waste Water Treatment Works near Torr (**627612**). There is usually plenty of room even on summer Sundays, and the track is good enough for all vehicles.*

*Walk roughly north-west through the Water Treatment Works until you pass on to the moorland beyond the second gate. Head up the slope to the top of Stalldown Barrow on the left until you reach the summit cairn and **Hillson's House.***

*Walk along the broad crest of the ridge to the west until you hit the top end of the **Stalldown Stone Row.***

*From the upper end of this stone row (**633625**) head northward over the moor until you reach the confluence of Bledge Brook with the larger Erme River (**634638**).*

*From here head upstream with the Erme on your right until you see the enclosure at (**635643**). From the*

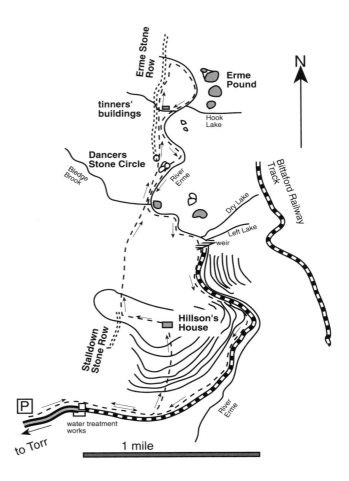

*top of this enclosure walk up the slope to reach the **Dancers Stone Circle** after only a few minutes.*

*Follow the stone row in a northerly direction until a steep river valley cuts across it at (**635651**). This is the site of the **Erme Tin Workings**. From here continue to follow the stone row as it drops down towards*

*the Erme. You will soon see on the opposite bank the enclosure called **Erme Pound**.*

*Return by walking down the Erme until you encounter a weir (**640631**). On the west bank you will find a track which curves round Stalldown Barrow and finally reaches the gate to the Water Treatment Works.*

16

Stalldown Circle and Row

Stand at the end of Stalldown Row in the centre of the circle at the north end and you are treading, with absolute certainty, where people have stood for thousands of years. Whether the weather is good or bad, whether the mist is rolling up from the south or the rain is sleeting across into your eyes, you are not the first own ancestors upon the ancient builders and users of this great stone building. At the northern end the stones are some 9 feet tall, with probably the same

Stalldown stone row looking north

cairns which mark the burial places of these unknowable people. The higher valleys were populated by farmers, who herded and protected their beasts from predators, coming into contact with their neighbours, sometimes to trade but often to fight. They honoured their dead and built meeting-places for the living.

The scene here when the row was in use is inaccessible to us today, but we can well imagine spoken prayers, ritual processions (possibly with fires) and groups chanting responses to a chief, who may or may not have been the political head of the settlement or tribe. We do know from Roman sources that the custom of the Celts, the Iron Age people who came after the builders of the stone rows, was to have a bard who was the custodian of the ritual of the tribe. It does no harm to imagine that this function extended to the users of the Stalldown Row. But the archetypal white-robed druid is a nonsense, for this is just a modern invention which does not represent any known historical fact.

to see it. As the dusk settles in winter you can feel the hand of the ancestor on your shoulder in this ancient place, used for a thousand years and then mysteriously forgotten.

Around you are the faint remains of cairns, of which the best known is the one to the east on which Hillson's House stands. We can feel the pressure of the presence of their length buried in the ground beneath, and as you walk south down the slope the stones gradually dwindle until they are about 4 feet high, to increase the effect of perspective. Since the rows were at least partially used for ceremonies, the design of this particular one is excellent. Look around. To the east is the cairn which you have just left and on all the surrounding hills you will find the

Stalldown Row is a building, a location for ceremonies, a monument to ancestors and a statement to intruders that the inhabitants' ancestors also guard their land. Stand here quietly and listen to the sounds of men who stood where you stand over the millenia, and look down the long path of history which links them with you.

Stone Rows & Circles

Hillson's House

On the summit of Langcombe Hill rests the remains of a large cairn, built in Bronze Age Britain at a time when the Greeks were at war with the Trojans. The cairn-builders were, in their own way, at least as talented, intellectual and capable as the Greeks. Probably the Greeks have had a better press, since, unlike our ancestors, their tales have ended up written down, primarily by Homer, who (if he was a single individual) took the oral tradition of the Bronze Age Greeks and recorded it formally. Homer used as a basis the tales told in the tents and in the towns, handed on from soldier to soldier and father to son. The oral tradition of the British Bronze Age people is reflected instead in the traditions of spoken poetry and story-telling in the literatures of the Welsh, Cornish and other Celtic peoples of Britain. It is the source of the Irish 'gift of the gab'.

In the cairn someone has built a rough house, using the stones found there. The local tale is that a child was once found in the vicinity, and was taken in by a man and his wife. They gave him the appropriate name of Hillson, and proceeded to bring him up. When as a grown man, Hillson discovered his roots, he built this rude house on Langcombe and lived there as a hermit, making his living by constructing, if the tale is true, eight-day clocks!

While Hillson's method of making a living may be dubious, there is a certain credibility in the story, if only because the standard of foundation and lower stonework of the House is better than the average moorland shelter. The latter were usually built either for the convenience of tinners, moormen collecting moorstone, or farmers.

The Dancers

The stone circle at the southern end of the enormous Erme Stone Row is called either The Dancers or Kiss in the Ring. The story told is that a group of young women sneaked up here one summer Sunday to dance and prance on the soft heath. All was well until they were spotted by a local godbotherer who called on the Lord to cease their unholy and disrespectful dancing on the Sabbath. The effect was spectacular, as all twenty-six girls were instantly turned to stone.

The Dancers is a Bronze Age retaining circle rather than a Stone Age megalithic circle, used more as a decoration for a cairn rather than as a ritual monument in its own right. It is similar to the walls around our churchyards or the little walls of marble we put around the graves of our own ancestors. The cairn in the centre has been robbed over the ages and gradually disappeared, possibly used as walling stone, or taken for tinners' works, although it is true to say that the tinners tended not to destroy the ancient monuments around which they worked.

The circle is about 18 yards in diameter, and has twenty-three stones standing, three of the dancers having apparently fallen down in exhaustion.

Tin-Workings near Erme Stone Row

The Erme Stone Row intersects a river at Green Bottom which comes down from the left hand bank as you go north, and jumps across a steep defile as it leaps across to the northern bank. As you cross this narrow-cut river cleft, look up and down to see some of the best tin-workings in this area.

Normally tin-workings are spread out over a considerable area, so that they do not have the impact of these. You can see here, looking up the slope, that the tinners have dug into the banks of the river to obtain ore, transported it the few hundred yards down to the buildings just below the line of the stone rows, and there have pounded it into small pieces ready for 'blowing' or smelting. The pounding machinery was driven by a water-wheel, and you can see the remains here of such a wheel in one of the houses. The other buildings around, some of which are relatively well preserved, were shelters used by the tinners who used to spend extensive periods on the moor.

You can read more about tin-mining and processing in the Tinning and Quarrying chapter, where you will also find some walks leading you to the best examples of tinners' buildings. Often, however, the extensive workings (such as those at Combeshead) are not the most evocative, simply because of their sheer size. You can stand here, however, in the mist or sunlight, at the junction of the brook and the stone row, and imagine yourself in the damp clothes of a tinner, cooking your meal, sleeping in the rudimentary shelters and counting your future wealth.

The Erme Stone Row

From the retaining circle of The Dancers stretches an enormous stone row. Look along this huge monument and you are staring at one of the most spectacular prehistoric monuments in the world. It stretches northward over the moor, and over hill and dale until it reaches a similar grave at the other end on Green Hill, which does not have a retaining circle. The Reverend Lukis in 1880 measured the row at exactly 11,239 feet and 8 inches, but let's call it two miles.

It is not precisely straight, and therefore is unlikely to have been used as a calendar measuring device. Most modern archaeologists believe that features like this are more likely to be ritual monuments for processions, but no one can know positively after so many thousands of years what the motivation was to build such structures.

We know that the construction was not casual. As we walk away from The Dancers we can see that the stones become smaller, as indeed we saw at Stalldown and although the row is by no means geometrically straight, it is clear that stones were moved to occupy their present positions. The alignment of the row is obviously more accurate where other parts of it can be seen on which to align the stones, but where the ground dips the row is quite inaccurate. Parts of the row are rather sparse because of changes in the depth of the peat. The Erme Stone Row has escaped both the vandals who have thrown down the magnificent stones of the Piles Hill Row, and the improvers who have straightened rows which were not straight, nor ever intended to be so, and inserted stones which should not have been there in the first place.

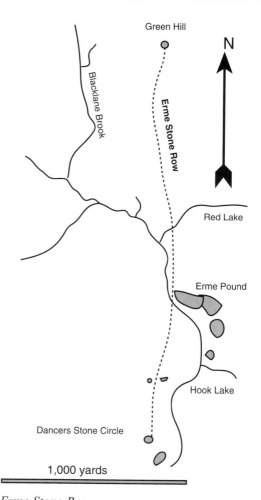

The Erme Stone Row

There is extensive tin-working here, and it is quite surprising that the stones in the row and in the circles have not been disturbed by the tinners. In fact, the tinners had great respect for the people who built the monuments, and were very superstitious about disturbing the stones. If a stone had to be moved to enable vital works to be carried out, the tinners would replace it as near to the original position as they could. They did not wish to offend the Old

Men, as they called their predecessors. As at all the other stone rows and circles, you should observe around you the dwellings, visible as circles in the moorland, of the Bronze Age dwellers on the moor who had such an intimate connection with the land and with their great ritual monuments. As you walk the Erme Stone Row, you are retreading the steps of the men and women who lived here some 3,000 years ago.

19

Walk 2 – Batworthy Corner, Scorhill Circle and Kennon Hill

Distance
About 6 miles.

Difficulty
Straightforward. Map and compass necessary. On leaving Rippon Tor care should be taken not to walk too far to the south because of the marshy ground; keep directly east onto Gidleigh Common instead.

Main Features
Teign-e-ver and W a l l a b r o o k Clapper Bridges	654871
Scorhill Stone Circle	654783
Buttern Hill	653886
Buttern Hill Stone Circle	649885
Kennon Hill Settlement	641891
Rippon (Rival) Tor	643882

Description of Walk
A good place to leave your car is at Batworthy Corner (**662865**), where the road, having passed Round Pound, stops as it enters the drive of Batworthy House. There is always room for cars here.

Leave the car-park area up the track to the south-west, keeping the boundary wall on your right. Continue round the end of the corner of the wall, keeping the wall always on your right until you are heading approximately north. Follow the wall down to the Teign River as it hammers its way over huge boulders past Scorhill Tor. The path will lead you to **Teign-e-ver clapper bridge**. If you stand on the bridge facing up slope you will see another **clapper**, over the Wallabrook to your left. From either clapper, head uphill until you see the **Scorhill Stone Circle**.

From the stone circle go north up the gentle slope of **Buttern Hill**. The top is rather flat and the summit rocks can be found at the other (northerly) end.

From the summit walk in a south-westerly direction until you reach the undistinguished saddle where the remains of the **Buttern Hill Stone Circle** lie.

From the saddle walk west and then north-west with the slope on your right until you come to the **Kennon Hill Settlement**. You will not see the settlement at first, but if you press on round the shoulder of Kennon Hill it will come into view.

From the settlement drop down to **Rippon Tor** (also known as Rival Tor) by heading back towards the dark mass of Fernworthy Forest. Rippon Tor is not very obvious from the settlement, but is the flat outcrop that lies down-slope towards the river valley.

From Rippon Tor walk in an EASTERLY direction until you are once more up slope of Scorhill Circle. The ground directly between Rippon Tor and Scorhill Circle is marshy, and, while not particularly dangerous, is nevertheless unpleasant.

From Scorhill Circle, retrace your steps back to the wall corner and from there back to your car.

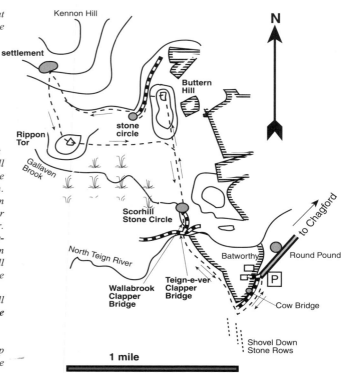

Kennon Hill

settlement

N

Buttern Hill

stone circle

Rippon Tor

Gallaven Brook

Scorhill Stone Circle

to Chagford

North Teign River

Batworthy

Round Pound

Wallabrook Clapper Bridge

Teign-e-ver Clapper Bridge

Cow Bridge

Shovel Down Stone Rows

1 mile

Buttern Hill and its Circle

On the saddle to the west of Buttern Hill lies a smaller circle than that at Scorhill, measuring about 80 feet in diameter. It is one of a set which stretches from Hound Tor down through Scorhill to Grey Wethers. It would seem that the builders of these circles established them at intervals of just over a mile and a half, although it is difficult to say what would be the purpose of such a system. Perhaps they provided cross-checking of sighting, or maybe there was some ritual purpose. In any case, the circle west of Buttern is insignificant in that the stones are all rather small, and the majority of them are recumbent. But it has a wild beauty when you come across it in the mist and rain of a winter's day, with the wind whipping up the slope to the north. Imagine the effect on the Bronze Age inhabitants of the settlement above, on Buttern Hill itself. A distance away down the valley to the north is an enclosed swamp area called the Pixies' Parlour.

As is invariably the case, the slopes around the circle are host to a number of cairns, of which two on Buttern are marked clearly on the Ordnance Survey map. If you look for these two cairns you may be disappointed, since they are just shallow mounds covered in grass, and are quite undistinguished. As they are not, in fact, cairns but hut circles, you would be doubly disappointed.

The summit of Buttern Hill is surmounted by some groups of rocks known as the Cuckoo Stone, and the view from here over what is known as the 'in-country', the outlying land of Dartmoor on the edge of the moor, is quite superb.

Buttern Hill is one of the haunted places of the moor. It appears that a man called Jan Lake got it into his head that gold was buried on Buttern Hill, and this so obsessed him that he continued to look for it after he died. When a large earthenware pot was discovered on Buttern, Jan seemed to make up his mind that it had contained the treasure, disappeared, and he never haunted the area again.

Kennon Hill Settlement

Kennon Hill contains an excellent example on its southern slopes of a multiple-enclosed Bronze Age settlement, which gives stupendous views over the valley of the Teign, fringed by the tops of Watern Tor and Kes Tor, with the dark green new Fernworthy Forest visible to the south. The river meanders its way down from the watery slopes of Watern Tor, and gathers its strength in a number of tributaries, including the Wallabrook, which makes its way down from rather further north.

A walk up the Teign is well worth while, as its upper reaches are desolate and beautiful, and the steep slopes on either side are the haunt of birds of prey, including merlin and sparrow hawks. I have also seen a peregrine here some years ago, striking a small bird in mid-air with an audible smack. On a hot summer's day the upper reaches of the Teign can be oppressively hot, with the air shimmering and curling between you and the sounds of civilization. In these conditions it is considered most reasonable to lose interest in the wealth of geological and archaeological remains in the visit, put your aesthetic sense in your rucksack, take out the cans of beer and stretch out in the heather, appearing hours later with an intense expression, talking enthusiastically about the remarkable geology of the Thirlstone or the extraordinary possible sighting of a merlin on the slopes. Kennon Hill also provides the opportunity for crashing out, with the added advantage of offering the excuse that you are imagining the late Bronze Age scene of the enclosures being full of cattle, and the few huts being peopled by your ancestors.

Rival Tor

Rival Tor (also called Rippon Tor) to the south-west of Buttern Hill takes its name from the Celtic *yr eifl* which means, not surprisingly, 'the rival'. In the Celtic languages the letter *f* is pronounced as *v*, and Crossing cites this as evidence that the Celtic derivation is wrong. In fact, the movement of consonants from hard to soft and back again is a common characteristic of Celtic speech, and can even be heard in the Devon dialect of English today, with *fen* and *ven* being the same.

From Rival Tor you can look over the Teign valley, enjoy from a distance the site of the Kennon Hill Settlement, and look at the distant Hound Tor and Steeperton Tor to the west. Imagine yourself as a shepherd on this lovely outcrop, looking over your small flock among the boulders below.

Scorhill Stone Circle

I find Scorhill Circle the most moving and evocative on the moor. Whether you are seeing it from the slopes above or below it, or standing near it looking at the strange features of the distant tors and the desolate flats of the Teign Valley below it, it stands proud and stark in memory of the remarkable people who saw fit to build it. It is meant to be either a mark of land ownership or a monument to ancestors, a church, a town hall or a meeting-place.

The circle sits on the south-facing slope near Scorhill Tor overlooking the Teign Valley and the Walla-brook, with Watern Tor winking away, the strange shapes of its laminated granite outcrops visible even at this distance. The circle has always been recognized as an important site, but surprisingly has never been 'restored' by the Victorian improvers of the moor. The circle is 27 yards in diameter, and consists of about 26 stones (one can never be entirely certain without excavating and the scores of experts who have written so authoritatively have made

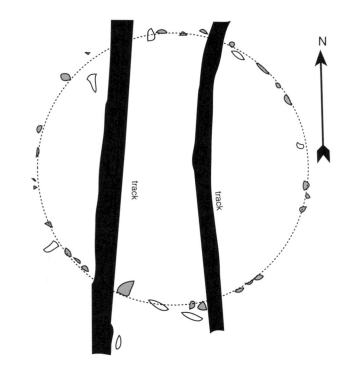

Scorhill Stone Circle

Scorhill Stone Circle

mistakes in their numbering). There is a story that some of the circles in the moor cannot be numbered because of Pixie activities; whisky is probably the more likely culprit. The largest stone lies towards the top of the slope and is over 7 feet in height.

It is possible that the circle was used for astronomical measurements. The late Stone Age builders certainly had the intelligence and the need to engage in such activities. An understanding of the passing and timing of the seasons would have been important to them for many reasons, some 3,000 years ago. The knowledge of the right times to plant and dig was held in all likelihood by a small number of priests or shamans who knew how to work the huge stone clock. In fact, the setting up of such a calendar device is not difficult and you certainly do not need a circle to do it; a number of wooden stakes in the ground would do just as well. There is something deeply satisfying about a circle though, especially one which has been as well sited as the Scorhill Stone Circle. At dusk the circle seems to come alive as the shadows grow.

Teign-e-ver Clapper

On the way to the beautiful Scorhill circle you have to cross the Teign before it cascades down finally off the high moor. The natural path takes you over one of two excellent clapper bridges of which the one over the Teign is known as Teign-e-ver. This single-span bridge, raised up above the walled edges of the stream, replaced the original one in 1826, when this was washed away in the great flood. There is also another good example of similar size near here to the north-west over the Wallabrook.

A little further downstream from Teign-e-ver is an unusual holed stone, which, like most objects with any peculiar aspect, is imbued with a mystical significance by the moor men. A common name for them is 'tolmen', which comes from the Celtic word *twll*, meaning a hole and *maen*, a stone. This particular example is said to be a christening stone, having been used by the Druids for their own fearsome and bloodthirsty ritual purposes. Another story is that you can be cured of rheumatism if you crawl down through it on to the lower ledge. In my view anyone who can do that has no need of any such cure for rheumatism! The tolmen is, of course, an example of a pot-hole. This is a cavity formed in the rock of a river bed through stones and pebbles being whirled round by the flow of a stream. The walls of any slight depression in the rock are abraded by the river and the depression is made deeper. In some cases, such as in the Teign-e-ver example, a hole can be worn right through the rock.

Walk 3 – Grey Wethers Stone Circles

Distance
About 4 miles.

Difficulty
Can be slightly wet. There are a number of confusing forest tracks but the general level of difficulty is low. Quite a safe walk.

Main Features
Grey Wethers
Stone Circles	**639831**
Sittaford Tor	**633830**
Pound	**642826**

Description of Walk
*Park your car at **Sandeman Bridge** (**657837**) near Fernworthy Forest. From the north side of Sandeman Bridge (you cannot mistake it, for it has a nameplate on it!), walk up the track away from the reservoir. Turn left immediately and cross a stream. Follow the forestry track. It turns back on itself at the end of the*

shallow valley. About a hundred yards before it begins to turn completely back on itself, there is a track on the right-hand side heading up and into the trees. It is quite difficult to see if you do not know it is there. It is not at the end of the vehicle track where it turns through 180 degrees, but is well before that.

Follow this path up through the trees. It swings to the right, and you will soon meet a gravelled track at a five-way junction. Take the track at about ten o'clock, your back being to the path you have just come out at; this is the third exit counting from left to right.

*Follow this track down, and you will see a track on your left before you come to a T-junction. Turn left here and you will soon find yourself at the edge of the forest (**646831**).*

*Wherever you come out (because you may well have been misled by new forestry tracks) turn right (north-west) and walk until you meet a wall which joins the forest boundary (**643834**). Follow this wall in a roughly westerly direction and then*

*after a few hundred yards or so you will see the **Grey Wethers Stone Circles** on the slope that faces towards the east.*

From Grey Wethers walk up the slope to the west towards Sittaford Tor.

*From the top of **Sittaford Tor** walk eastwards towards the right-hand edge of the forest. You will reach the **Pound** before the marshy ground in between you and the forest.*

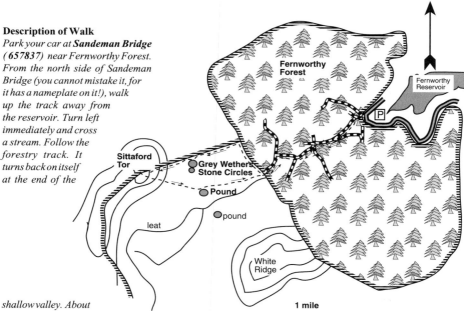

N

Fernworthy Forest

Fernworthy Reservoir

Sittaford Tor

Grey Wethers Stone Circles

Pound

pound

leat

White Ridge

1 mile

Return the same way or by following the green marked track on the Ordnance Survey map, from Grey Wethers around to the north-east and back into the forest, past Froggymead and then back to the road (not shown on diagram).

Grey Wethers Stone Circles

The two stone circles at Grey Wethers were restored in 1901 from a state where only about a third were standing. Considering the length of time which they would have been standing and their unfortunate habit of falling on unrepentant sinners (*see* page 26), this is not wholly unexpected.

The circles were built in the late Stone Age and are an example of the monumental stone circles of the period, in contrast to the other two later types of stone circles found on the moor. The latter include the circles left after a cairn has been levelled, and the retaining circle which, in the Bronze Age, was sometimes placed as an edging around a particularly important burial site. Uniquely, Grey Wethers consists of two complete circles, lying almost north-south and of approximately the same size, there being some dispute over the location of the stones in the original layout. The stones are rather regular, but the thought of some late-Victorian antiquaries that the stones had been dressed is, in fact, incorrect, and all the stones are now thought to be finished naturally.

The purpose of the circles is in dispute. Some romantics see in them Druidic cathedrals, others stone calendars and timepieces. The generally accepted explanation these days lies somewhere between the two, with the layout of the circles being primarily aesthetic and ritual, but with specific stones being used as time-markers. The circles appear to form part of a rough pattern in this north-western quadrant of the moor, the circles hereabouts occurring about every mile and a half between Grey Wethers and Hound Tor, the other side of Scorhill.

It is not unreasonable to imagine the circles, or at least the most prominent stones, being used as foresights for observations of the heavenly bodies. Such measurements would have been of some use to the farmers, but not exclusively so, since the farmer's sense of weather and climate would have meant that he would have decided when to plant crops or move stock on the state of the seasonal weather as much as on the chronological date. Timing has always had a ritual aspect, however, and a knowledge of the exact day at which the sun reached its limit of movement would have had a ritual significance.

No one knows why the builders constructed two circles at Grey Wethers. They could have been the result of an over-ambitious village leader, or a build-up of stones after some innovation in time-telling. Certainly the double circle would have provided an unusual and noteworthy site for Stone Age ritual and would have remained in use throughout the Bronze Age.

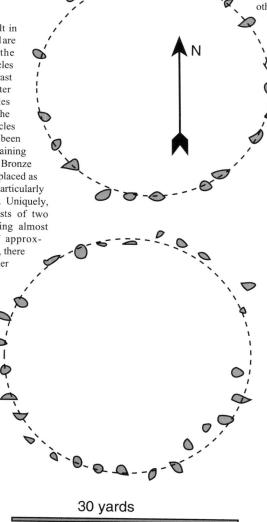

30 yards

N

Forestry Working

The old name for the region on which the national park now stands is the Forest of Dartmoor. Many people imagine that the forest was a place covered in trees, like, in the main part, the New Forest, with its beautiful beech covering. The term 'forest', in fact, referred to the use of the moor as a royal hunting ground, and the existing forestry planting, like Fernworthy, seen from all parts of this section of the moor, is indicative neither of the extent of the tree coverage, nor of the type of tree which existed on the high moor in the warmer climate of the late Stone Age and early Bronze Age.

In the following chapter, we look at the strange, twisted pedunculate oaks of Wistman's Wood and the Blackator copse, trees which have existed on the highest moorland, sheltering behind the huge boulders for many hundreds of years. Not even these trees, however, are indicative of the original main covering of the moor, since the windswept uplands were more conducive to birch and mountain ash than the slower growing oak, which tended to shelter in the upland valleys.

Fernworthy Forest is a 20th-century intrusion. Its hundreds of acres of Sitka spruce wander in a dark green rabble like some menacing crowd of Saturday afternoon thugs towards the high tors, encompassing stone circles, dells and streams in their omnivorous march. Some people say that the trees bring prosperity to the immediate region, others that they like the relief the trees bring to an otherwise boring featureless moorland. Well, the trees are not unpleasant in themselves, and they do indeed provide important jobs in an area of great and damaging unemployment, but they are foreigners none the less. As for relieving the featureless moor, Dartmoor has been called many things in its time and is indeed guilty of most sins that land is heir to, but featureless it is not, and the desolate beauty of the high moor is only marred by these dark invaders, necessary as they may be.

Sitka spruce cone

The trees are harvested every twenty years or so, and in the forest you can see three different stages of production. We start with the trenches for the young trees, dug about 2 feet deep to provide initial shelter and which are then planted with the strange plastic protectors which give the trees sunlight without exposing them to the teeth of the local sheep. Second comes the dark desert of the mature trees, supporting life largely at its edges. Last comes the sad desolation of the harvested areas, with the torn roots grasping at the sky, ripped out by the huge machines which reap the wooden harvest, the roots only to be hidden again by the cycle restarting afresh.

The Warren House Inn Con Man

William Crossing tells a story of a man by the name of Debben who sold a flock of sheep to a man at the Warren House Inn. The man, who was a stranger to the moor west of where Fernworthy Forest now lies, took it on trust that Debben's sheep were where he said they were, on the slope of Sittaford Tor. The rain trickled gently through the trees as he made his way through the woods towards what is now Fernworthy Forest, and he finally gained the open moorland in the dusk.

As he approached the flock of sheep, divided into two parts and sheltering under the lee of the tor, he gradually realized that he had been duped and that the Grey Wethers, which means the Grey Sheep, were in fact the stones of the circle.

So, don't be tempted to buy any sheep at the Warren House Inn without seeing them first!

Why the Grey Wethers Fell Over

The Grey Wethers Stone Circles have been restored – in 1891, when a survey of the original site was carried out, a number of the stones were recumbent. The story goes that if an adulterous wife wanted to absolve herself, she could carry out a number of labours, one of which was to kneel in front of one of the Grey Wethers stones. If she was truly repentant the stone would remain standing, but if there was still sin in her heart, the stone would fall over and crush her.

I don't suggest you try it – it's not worth the risk!

Walk 4 – Merrivale Stone Rows

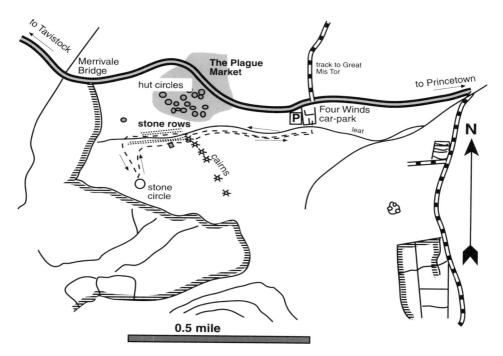

to Tavistock

Merrivale Bridge

The Plague Market

hut circles

track to Great Mis Tor

to Princetown

Four Winds car-park

stone rows

leat

cairns

N

stone circle

0.5 mile

Distance
About 2 miles.

Difficulty
No difficulties. The stone rows and other features all lie within a short distance of the main road. The ground is easy and relatively dry.

Main Features
*Merrivale Rows
  and Standing Stones* **555748**
The Plague Market **555749**

Description of Walk
The Four Winds car-park (561749) is marked on the Ordnance Survey map on the road between Two Bridges and Tavistock. It is a walled enclosure for counting sheep, and you can see the 'squeezes' through

which the sheep were forced in order to make it easier to count them. Leave your car here but ensure that it is locked and that no valuables are visible, because there have been a number of thefts from here.

Walk out of the enclosed area to the south, away from the road, and through the gap in the wall, and you will immediately come across a stream, which is, in fact, a leat. You should turn right (west) and follow the leat for about half a mile until you come across the stone rows, which lie on either side. These are magnificent examples of double stone rows, and represent the highest achievements of Bronze Age man in Britain. The hillside on which you stand is the location of the

'Plague Market', or Potato Market, although there is some dispute as to whether the area in which the dread transactions took place was, in fact, nearer the road and just up from Merrivale Bridge. The hut circles on both sides of the road here are particularly fine, being very extensive and still standing quite high above the peaty ground.

You can explore the moorland on the side furthest away from the road (the south) where you will find a number of boundary stones and menhirs, and a rather good stone circle. Make your way back to the Four Winds car-park by heading back towards the main road and turning right along it to reach the enclosure.

27

The Merrivale Stone Rows and Circles

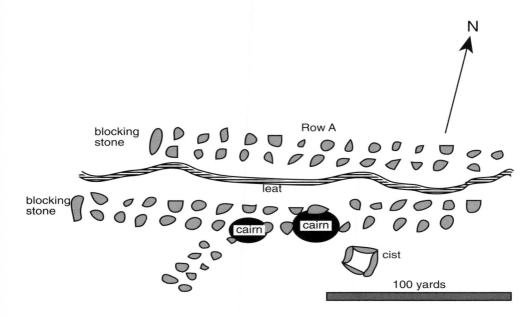

The Merrivale Stone Rows

No one really knows the purpose of Dartmoor's stone rows. Some have speculated that they are astronomical observatories, others that they are ritual pathways along which Druids and their congregation processed. We know that they were built in the Bronze Age and are associated with the cairn burials of the early Bronze Age, or LANEBA (late neolithic early Bronze Age). In many cases they lead from a cairn circle, which differ from the monumental stone circles built by the neolithic peoples in being much more intimate circles, built apparently to decorate the circular grave mounds left by these early folk. There are similar rows elsewhere in southern England, but the Dartmoor rows are unique in that they are longer and more frequent than those anywhere else in Britain. In addition, of course, Dartmoor has been less affected by modern building and development and so the rows are generally better preserved. The nearest competitor is the famous double row at West Kennet near Avebury in Wiltshire, which is generally believed to mark a processional path from Silbury Hill along which worshippers and their priests would walk. The Dartmoor rows, and the Merrivale one in particular, however, are generally felt to be too closely spaced to allow a procession between them. While this is undoubtedly true, there is nothing to stop a procession filing along both sides of the row. The double stone rows at Merrivale, which sit above the bridge on Long Ash Hill, are excellent examples of their kind. As the diagram shows there are three rows, two parallel with the leat which leads from Four Winds, and a third much shorter one which heads south-west from a cairn about two-thirds of the way along the longest row. This last row looks as though it was added on as an extension at a later date.

A very significant feature of these rows is the barrow which lies about half-way along the longest row. This is most unusual and is thought to mark the ritual burial of an important person – not because of its size, but because of its positioning in the ritual structure. Normally, a barrow which is associated with a stone row (and this is very often the case) is placed at the highest point of the row,

28

regardless of direction. This, together with the frequent shortening of the stones as the row gets further from the cairn, shows a great sense of architectural design, since the combination of the slope, the size of the stones, and frequently the narrowing of the distance between the rows all accentuate the perspective.

About 30 yards south of the longest row is a kistvaen or cist, a Bronze Age burial method which we shall talk about in more detail elsewhere, where there are better examples. Nevertheless, this one is worth looking at as it shows one of the common burial methods of the time, the other being cremation on the site of a cairn. It consists of a stone chest (whence it gets its name) with a large stone cover. The stone top of this one has been split in two, but both parts are close together in situ. You can read more about the different burial methods and the resultant remains on the moor in the introductory section. To the south of the rows you will also find a fairly low stone circle. This is a Bronze Age cairn circle rather than a neolithic monumental circle, and had a similar function to the edging of graves today, but was larger, fitting well outside the cairn perimeter. Many of the cairn circles form edging inside the mound of stones and earth, and still others are not cairn circles at all, but the inner edging of a hut circle, now eroded. This, however, in keeping with its location in this splendid ritual scene, is a true cairn circle.

Further to the south-west of the rows is what appears to be a monumental circle. It is not very spectacular since most of the stones are rather low-lying, but it does show that the site

of Long Ash Hill must have been used by peoples earlier than the early Bronze Age folk who built the stone rows. One of the hut circles near by has been excavated and stone arrowheads and tools were found there, but this is not evidence that the hut circles were inhabited by neolithic people, but rather that the early Bronze Age people found bronze expensive to use, since it required relatively rare materials and even rarer artisans to make it. In fact, a well-made stone knife is extremely sharp and serviceable, and the early Bronze Age farmers would certainly have known how to keep such a tool sharp.

All around the rows on this attractive hillside are the remains of hut circles. We do not know for sure that these

huts were contemporary with the rows, but it does no harm to people the scene with a village of Bronze Age farmers, their wives and families, guarding their beasts, seeing themselves through the winters, giving birth, growing old and dying, all in the shadow of their church, the immense stone rows. The latter connected the living with the dead, as they walked along from the burial site at one end to the open horizon at the other. Stand a while here and imagine yourself living among your ancestors without the fear we have today of the dead and the past and among your relations and friends. Think about how you would be comforted by the structure and stability of these great rows, built by the people who lie buried in them.

The Plague Market

The hill on which the Merrivale Stone Rows sit and the near by hut circles, above Merrivale Bridge, are referred to locally as the 'Plague Market', and sometimes as the 'Potato Market'. The name dates from the period just before the Black Death, when waves of the dreaded bubonic plague, spread inadvertently by trading ships, were starting to affect the densely inhabited towns and cities of western Europe. Provisions grown on the moor were placed here during plague years, and the inhabitants of Tavistock, possibly contaminated by the plague, were able to leave money in exchange without any human contact. There is some doubt about the actual location, but the theory that money and provisions were left in the stone circle associated with the row is a likely one. The moor

folk were not themselves hit hard by the plagues of the 14th century and later, but inevitably were indirectly affected because of their contact with the neighbouring towns and villages. Trade was affected, relations were killed, and the whole of Europe was decimated by this horrible disease.

Two Bridges is also known as the 'Potato Market' because potatoes from Moretonhampstead were traded there with dealers from Plymouth, Exeter and elsewhere. At the Two Bridges Hotel you can see around the entrance the original smaller building which provided refreshment for travellers. Eden Phillpotts, in his book *The River*, based in the Two Bridges area, describes the inn at Two Bridges and its patrons around the turn of the century.

Walk 5 – Piles Hill and Corringdon Ball

Distance
About 5 miles.

Difficulty
The walk is over open moorland with many features. A map and compass should be carried but the ground is firm underfoot except for a few obvious places near streams. This is a good walk for all the family.

Main Features

Spurrell's Cross	658599
The Longstone	654607
Piles Hill Stone Rows	611604
Glasscombe Corner Settlement	660610
Glazebrook Stone Rows	667613
Corringdon Ball Chambered Tomb	669613

Description of Walk

Owley village (676598) is just a small collection of houses. Above the village is a gate on to the moor marked as Owley Moor Gate. This is a convenient place to park your car; there is room for perhaps four cars, with another smaller lay-by down the slope. The roads are very narrow. Please park so as not to inconvenience other road users, and the villagers in particular.

From the gate take the right-hand track which works its way along gently upwards following the massively walled enclosures on the right. After a while the view opens up and you can see the shark's fin of Brent Hill across the valley. As you continue along the walls you will soon see a saddle in the hills ahead, with Glasscombe Ball on the right and Ugborough Beacon, with its few rocks, on the left. Although you cannot yet see it, **Spurrell's Cross** is just below the crest on the right of the cairn at the saddle as you approach it from Owley.

From Spurrell's Cross continue along in the same direction and you will come immediately to a partly paved track which winds its way across the moor for miles. This is the Bittaford Miners' Track. You will see to your left a prominent rock feature; this is Hangershell Rock. Turn right on the track and walk until you see a sharply pointed standing stone on the skyline to your left. This is **The Longstone**. Make your way to it.

From The Longstone make your way towards the track again, aiming for the point where the track enters a low cutting. Here there is a boundary stone marked 'U' on one side and 'H' on the other, These designate the parishes of Harford and Ugborough. This is the point at which the **Piles Hill Stone Row**

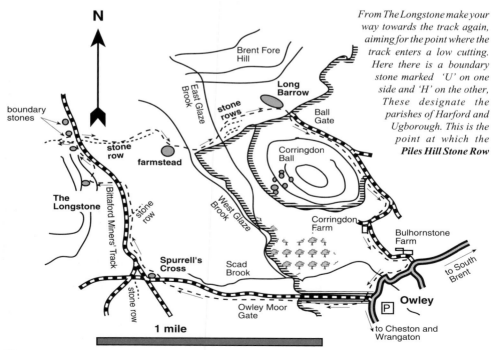

1 mile

cuts the path. To find the stones, which are recumbent (thrown down) walk directly towards the rounded hill on the right of the track. This is Corringdon Ball. Look carefully for large stones lying on the surface of the ground. Soon you should see a line of these recumbent stones which will lead you downhill and towards the left of a copse of trees which will soon become visible on the corner of an enclosure wall known as Glasscombe Corner (**663609**). The end of the stone row is above a drop into a tinners' working shortly after a cube-shaped stone before you reach the copse. From the end stone

walk at right angles to the line of the stone row until you see a roughly circular low wall of stones. This is marked on the map as **farmstead**.

From the end of the row or from the enclosure make your way to the corner of the stone walls at Glasscombe. Follow the line of the enclosure wall until, after crossing a steep-sided stream bed, you see before you the low form of the barrow, with the three large stones prominent to its right. Before you reach the chambered cairn, you will note the small stones of the remarkable stone rows at

Glasscombe called the **Glazebrook Antiquities**. Make your way to **The Corringdon Ball Chambered Tomb**.

From the chambered cairn pass through the three gates with the huge stone gate pillars topped by balls. Walk along the track, turning right whenever you are in doubt, and making your way downhill, until you reach a farmyard. Turn left here; the way is obvious. You will find yourself eventually at the Owley Bridge, from where you will have to trudge your way up until you reach the spot where you parked your car.

Piles Hill Stone Rows

Running across the Bittaford Miners' Track near the top of Piles Hill is a magnificent stone row. Admittedly it is rather spoiled by the fact that most of its stones have been thrown down at some time in the past, but the effort involved in finding and mentally re-erecting the stones is well worth while. The setting, in which the hundreds of Bronze Age huts and other remains on the hills around act as a backdrop to a great religious monument, is impressive in the extreme.

On the way up to Piles Hill after you leave Spurrell's Cross you may see on the map a stone row marked on the right of the track. It is not really worth while trying to locate this as the stones are both thrown down and small in size. The Longstone, which is so prominent on the skyline here, is the terminal stone of an enormous row which stretches up over the hill behind you on which the Bittaford Track climbs. It is in-

convenient on this walk to guide you to the Butterdon Row, so it is probably better to admire the Longstone from the track and then make your way to it in order to locate the intersection of the Piles Hill Row with the track.

Where the track goes into the low cutting at the top of the hill you can see a prominent boundary stone, put up in 1803 and marked (as described in the walk description) with U and H, representing Ugborough and Harford parishes. From here you can find the recumbent stones by walking away from the track towards the cairns up the slope. You will soon see a number of large stones in the turf, and if you look from any one you will see another row of large stones (some are missing) lying on the surface of the ground. Once you see the row you cannot miss it! Walk down as far as you wish to see the length of the row as it climbs up the side of Piles Hill.

On the other (right-hand) side the stones are probably easier to find, and it is quite easy to imagine them upright forming a feature which one writer has, perhaps rather too enthusiastically, compared with the fabulous stone rows at Carnac in Brittany. They are perhaps not quite that significant, but a double stone row of this length and context is certainly very important in Bronze Age archaeology. In terms of the great cathedrals, it is probably a Wells or a Durham rather than a York or Chartres. The row is nearly 850 yards long and contains about 150 very large stones, many of them over 6 feet in height. They were not well set up, however, and have not managed to survive the ravages of the Dartmoor cattle, which use standing stones regularly as scratching posts. Like most Dartmoor rows the Piles Hill row is not straight, but weaves about, altering its course by some 20 degrees every now and again.

Corringdon Ball Chambered Tomb

The striking silhouette of Corringdon Ball neolithic tomb

The most important feature of this part of the moor is the impressive neolithic chambered tomb on Corringdon Ball. It certainly merits a detour, as the guide books say. It stands on the gently sloped saddle between Brent Fore Hill and Corringdon Ball close to the Glazebrook triple stone rows, and in a situation of quiet beauty.

Burial practices changed from the neolithic period through the early Bronze Age, and we see here the skeleton of a burial rite older than those represented by the cairns, with their often striking retaining circles which you will have seen on this walk and on many others in the book. Dartmoor is covered in cairns and their retaining circles can often be confused with the earlier ritual stone circles. The chambered cairns

are roughly contemporaneous with stone circles, like Scorhill and with Grey Wethers, which you will have walked to see.

The tomb is very large, some 40 yards by 20 yards, with a height of 8 feet. You can see five slabs of stone sticking out from the grassy mound.

These tombs consisted of a chamber built from stone slabs into which the remains of the dead were placed. The chamber was then closed and the whole structure covered with a mound of earth, stone and turf to form the pile you can see today. This type of burial was connected with other types, notably the gallery graves and the passage graves, of which only one exists in Britain. All have the same concept of a

stone 'room' above ground, which was then covered by an earth mound.

But why should this have been done? No one really knows, but perhaps the distinction of being buried in a prominent mound was the same today as the millionaire who wants a mausoleum. Perhaps we see before us the equivalent of Lenin's Tomb. On the other hand it may have been more a defensive statement to the effect that any tribe which has the men and resources to build such a monument shouldn't be messed with. Be it St Paul's Cathedral or a Trident missile system in concept, it has certainly stood the test of time.

There are two other good examples of this type of monument at Spinster's Rock near Drewsteignton, and on Cuckoo Ball, just south of here.

Spurrell's Cross

Spurrell's cross

This cross marks the junction of two tracks which intersected near here. One ran from Buckfast Abbey to the priory at Plympton, and the other met it as it ran north – south. Crosses on paths are often placed on the crests of slopes, but this one is unusual in that respect. The shaft is newer than the head, and it could be that the cross has been moved. It is more likely that the name comes from the spurs on the cross rather than from a man's name.

Corringdon Ball and Brent Fore Hill

Because of the rough nature of the land on this rounded hill, locally known quite reasonably as a 'ball', the late arrivals of the farming community have largely left the remains of the Late Stone Age and Bronze Age people untouched. There has, of course, been some damage through natural causes, but this area is very well preserved. It is not convenient to walk around the ball as access is restricted.

There are a number of rectilinear field boundaries (which are not easy to see) on the south-easterly part of the ball, but we shall not concern ourselves particularly with these here.

Of far more interest are the extensive Bronze Age pounds and enclosures. There are a number of huts and enclosures towards the northern end of the ball. Many are built into the walls of the enclosures, showing an economy of effort and a desire to be near their beasts which we do not share today. The enclosures, of which there appear to be four, seem largely independent, as if they were four different villages within the same community. They would have afforded a degree of privacy but at the same time would have allowed for easy mutual support in case of attack. Some of the huts can be seen to have upright slabs used as an inner walling, so that the inside of the hut can be set down in the ground, providing weatherproofing and warmth. There was little problem with damp floors, mostly because there was no alternative. The largest enclosure must have presented an impressive defensive barrier, and you can imagine the effect of its steep walls by taking account of the turf which has grown upon its top and sides.

There is a larger hut near the summit of Corringdon Ball, and speculation suggests that this was the dwelling of a chief. The hut is unusual in that it has very thick (2 metre) walls and its own attached field.

Look over to Brent Fore Hill from the chambered cairn site near the gateposts. There are at least twenty more hut circles there, and the whole area must, in Bronze Age times, have been quite densely populated – in fact, more so than today. If you choose to walk over there you can find the hut circles in the main part above the leat.

There are hundreds of remains in this area, ranging from the neolithic chambered cairn to the field system, and it would be confusing to describe any of them in detail. The whole feeling of the area is that of constant and dense population during the late Stone Age and Bronze Age at least, and it is well worth while trying to imagine the smoke rising from the huts, the people going about their way, the noises of the animals and the general hubbub of a major Bronze Age upland village system.

Glazebrook Stone Rows

The row near Corringdon Ball known as the Glazebrook Group is unique in that it appears to be a seven- or eight-fold row. There are examples of double and even triple rows on Dartmoor, but only this one is so wide in its extent. Some experts now consider that the Glazebrook Group actually consists of one single row and two triple rows.

Walk 6 – Drizzlecombe and Whittenknowles

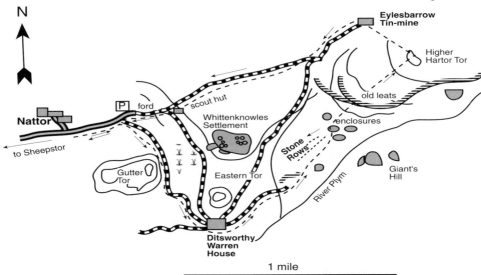

N

Eylesbarrow
Tin-mine

Higher
Hartor Tor

old leats

scout hut

Nattor

ford

P

to Sheepstor

Whittenknowles
Settlement

enclosures

Stone
Rows

Gutter
Tor

Eastern Tor

River Plym

Giant's
Hill

Ditsworthy
Warren
House

1 mile

Distance

About 3 miles.

Difficulty

Not difficult. Good tracks and plenty
of landmarks. A map and compass
must be carried.

Main Features

Ditsworthy Warren	
House	**583663**
Drizzlecombe Rows	**593670**
Eylesbarrow Tin-mine	**598682**

Description of Walk

From the road end at Nattor
(*578673*) walk along the
continuation of the road over the
ford until you see the scout hut on
your right. Go through the gate and
start walking along the track at the
front of the hut. This is *Edward's
Path*, which will lead you to
Ditsworthy Warren House quite
directly. The path is clear and
straightforward, and bends to the
right and then the left around

Eastern Tor. As you round Eastern
Tor you will see the trees at
Ditsworthy Warren House on your
left. A gravelled vehicle track joins
from the right. Follow this to your
left and you will soon reach
Ditsworthy Warren House.

Take the track behind the house and
follow it generally downwards towards the Plym, where it turns more
directly down the slope. Look up
and you should see clearly the two
huge menhirs of **Drizzlecombe**
ahead of you. Make your way directly towards them. If it is very wet
underfoot you are better going to
the right here and skirting around
an unpleasant but perfectly safe
swamp.

After investigating the stone rows
carry on up the slope to the top
menhir. Further up you will find
more remains: a huge cairn, some
hut circles, and a pound. You can
see some very distinctive field mark-

ings on the slope on the other side of
the Plym under Hen Tor, the dark
triangular tor opposite. Continue
up the slope past the cairn on the left
and keep going in the same direction, crossing two dry leats, one of
which is rather indistinct. Soon you
will see the outcrop on Higher
Hartor Tor (*599677*) ahead of you.
Make your way directly toward this.

Eylesbarrow Tin-mine can now be
seen clearly, only some 400 yards
away to the left. Make your way to it.

The route from Eylesbarrow back
to the car is straightforward.
Continue down the track towards
Sheepstor. You will see a ruined
building on the left, and a hundred
yards or so beyond this a track leaves
to the right. Take the left fork here,
past a water boundary marker.
Continue down the track and you
will soon see the trees surrounding
the scout hut. Go over the bridge by
the ford to return to your car.

34

The Drizzlecombe Stone Rows

There are three separate groups of features at Drizzlecombe. These exhibit what for Dartmoor is an unusual degree of planning, in that if you were to add another row to the north of the existing ones they would present a striking symmetrical appearance. The diagram shows the general layout.

The three superb menhirs are worth looking at, and present an impressive indication of what the Bronze Age builders were capable of erecting at their ceremonial sites. Like most Dartmoor rows the Drizzlecombe ones start at a barrow, here at the upper end of the row. Generally, the Dartmoor rows do have a cairn at their upper ends, so that we can guess that there was some significance and connection between the rows and the cairns. Other evidence of this is found in the frequency by which large retaining circles around cairns occur near the ends of the rows.

As explained elsewhere, stone circles associated with rows are quite different in nature and purpose from those built by the late Stone Age (neolithic) folk. The Bronze Age circles are always associated with cairns and often with rows, and appear to serve the purpose of decorating and making significant the burial sites associated with ritual sites. Here in Drizzlecombe we can see this quite clearly in the three barrows at the upper end of the rows.

Stand at the end of the row marked B in the diagram and look uphill. You will see that it points directly to a large cairn on the other side of the enclosure. Additionally, you can see from the diagram that there is an alignment between the cairn known as Giant's Basin, the cairn you are

looking at and the cist, or burial chest, at the bottom of the figure below.

The presence of the two enclosures at the top of the picture gives an insight into the respect which the Bronze Age people had for their ancestors. They did not choose, as we do, to place their revered forebears in separated cemeteries, but rather lived among them, or if not exactly among them, in such a

relation that they could see on the horizon and on the slopes of hills opposite where their ancestors dwelled. We see at Drizzlecombe, as at so many Bronze Age sites, the intimate connection between the farms and the ritual centres. Stop a while in the enclosures, look at the rows, and imagine yourself with your pigs and cattle around you, looking out over the scene which you and your ancestors have built out of the bare moorside.

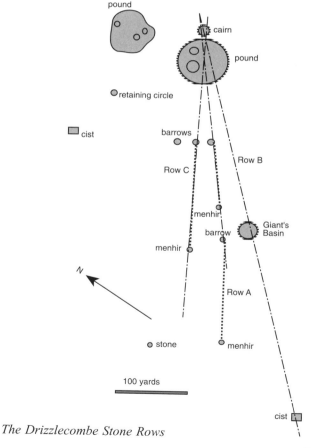

The Drizzlecombe Stone Rows

35

Ditsworthy Warren House

Ditsworthy Warren House takes its name from the practice of the farming and tin-mining communities of rearing rabbits in warrens on the moorside. These were dry areas, easy to dig into and the rabbits could colonize them thus providing a ready source of nourishing meat in all seasons. The warrens are also known as 'buries', but this name is more properly applied to the pillow mounds or artificial warrens which the farmers, and, in particular the tin-miners, used to raise to provide above-ground dry accommodation for the rabbits.

Ditsworthy Warren House used to be known as Ware's Warren, after a family of that name who lived here during the last century. It is now used as an adventure training site by the Royal Navy.

The house is rather fine, even with its blind windows and overgrown garden. You can well imagine using it as a base for farming the fertile Plym valley, and it would have been a comfortable family home for many years. It does not have the poignant quality of Brown's House in the north moor, as it has been well maintained by the owners. It has more of the character of a working moorland farm than Nun's Cross, and is altogether a more attractive building. Imagine the life you would have led out here on the moor, looking after the stock in all weathers, making your way across Ringmoor Down to market. Imagine lambing in the late winter up here on the moor, having to be out all through the night to see your flock survive the snows and the cutting wind. Then imagine the welcome which

Ditsworthy House would have given you on your return, the now blind windows shining out over the Plym to welcome you back in the early morning as the weak sunlight drifted through the spindly trees which you can still see there today.

The house overlooks the extensive tin-workings at Meavy Pool, where you can see a huge girt or tinners' gully, from which tin ore was won and then pounded and washed to pan out the valuable ore. If you choose to go on to Eylesbarrow, you can see the last site on the moor at which tin was actually smelted. There are better preserved sites where the water-wheel slot and other details, such as the mould stones into which the tin was cast, can be seen, but none the less Eylesbarrow is unique and is definitely worth a visit.

Eylesbarrow

This area in the north of the Plym valley, high up on the moor, is one of the most interesting tin-mining sites in the moor. It was still working in 1826, and was the last tin-smelting place to be operational in Dartmoor. In the Tinning & Quarrying chapter, we deal with tin-mining itself, but if you have chosen to walk to Eylesbarrow it is worth finding the leat which carried the water, the wheel-pit, the 'blowing house', and the very long flue which carried away the smelting fumes, while still retaining the tin which would otherwise be carried away wastefully. Also on the site you can see the bearing stones of a flat-rod system for carrying power from the engine house to the more distant parts of the mine. There is also a small shaft, now blocked up.

The tin-miners used to follow tin lodes from their traces on the stream beds up to the mother lode higher up. The ore was then brought back to a mill for crushing and smelting in a charcoal furnace. Water power was used to drive a wheel for the bellows. You can read more about this process in the Tinning & Quarrying chapter.

Eylesbarrow is one of the oldest names on the moor, in one form or another, and forms one of the key points on the perambulation of 1240, when it was spelled Elisboroughe. Other variations are Yelsbarrow, Ailsborough, Elysburgh, and Gyllesburgh. Take your pick! The perambulation is a definition of the divisions of the moor, noting the key points which define the parishes, owned land and so on. We know a lot about the key points on the moor from the 1240 perambulation, which is the first one to which we have extensive access today.

Drizzlecombe Menhir

This magnificent standing stone is one of the finest on the moor. It presents quite different aspects as you walk round it, looking thin and mean from one angle and fat and solid from another. The stone is more than 9 feet tall, and at least a third of its length is embedded in the earth below, making it something like three times as high as a man. It must have taken considerable effort to transport and erect the stone. As you can read elsewhere, the menhir forms part of the sighting lines of the Drizzlecombe rows.

This menhir was re-erected after it was found towards the end of the last century by the Dartmoor Exploration Committee. Two other stones in the series were also put back up at the same time, and we are fairly sure that they are now in their original positions.

The Drizzlecombe rows

Walk 7 – Down Tor

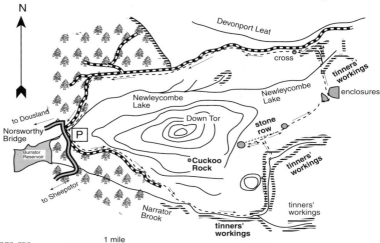

Distance
About 4 miles.

Difficulty
Combeshead tin-workings are confusing but safe. Map and compass must be carried and sensible footwear worn.

Main Features

Cuckoo Rock	**585686**
Combeshead Tin-workings	**587686**
Down Tor Circle	**588694**
Drivage Bottom Tin-workings	**597704**

Description of Walk

Norsworthy Bridge car-park (**569693**) is a suitable place to leave your vehicle but do ensure that it is locked.

Take the track which leads first south-east and then gradually turns more easterly. It will take you through the edge of the woods and eventually, after about a mile, on to the northerly banks of the Narrator Brook and into the beautiful but well worked valley called Deancombe. Up the slope on the left is a prominent rock known as **Cuckoo Rock**. Work your way gently down towards the stream which comes down Combeshead.

There is no need to go directly towards it, just follow the slope around Cuckoo Rock and drop down gradually. You will soon encounter the tributary which comes down past Combeshead Tor, the more northerly of the two tributaries. If you are lucky you will pick up a track which leads to the footbridge marked FB at **585685**. From this point work your way upstream to the east and, as you gradually rise out of the more wooded area you will find yourself in the middle of extensive tinners' piles. This is the **Combeshead Tin-Workings**.

Having explored these workings, carry on up the northern tributary past Combeshead Tor. You will find that the stream gradually works its way to the right (east) as it comes up towards the open moor. Do not turn right with it but continue north and you will bump into the **Down Tor Row** at some point towards its middle. Turn left and follow it to its cairn circle at the western end.

From the western end of the row, walk down the row to the eastern end, and then walk north-easterly until you encounter an enclosure at **591695**. From here to the settlements is about a quarter of a mile. From the enclosures walk north, crossing one stream until you reach the enclosed **Drivage Bottom Tin-Workings**.

From here go up the slope until you reach the track (if you reach the leat you have gone too far up the slope) and follow it towards the left (west) back towards Burrator. After passing Crazywell Cross (**583704**) high on the right, you will eventually come to a gateway which brings the path on to the edge of the forest. Continue down the path with the woods on your right and you will come to a junction, with a track on your right leading to Leather Tor Bridge. Go straight on here, however, and you will soon find yourself back at Norsworthy Bridge car-park.

Cuckoo Rock

Cuckoo Rock stands on the hillside facing Burrator at the end of Deancombe, and can be seen from most of the downstream end of the combe itself.

I have no idea why the outcrop is called Cuckoo Rock. I have looked at it from every direction, in most weathers and lights, and I can see no resemblance whatsoever to a cuckoo. Moreover, I have rarely heard a cuckoo in the vicinity, and have even less often seen one.

Nevertheless, Cuckoo Rock is an attractive outcrop and makes a good navigation mark for miles around. It is also well worth climbing for the view it affords over Deancombe, but as for the cuckoos – well, that's for the birds!

Combeshead Smugglers' Cave

The whole area of Deancombe is supposed to be the haunt of smugglers, and you can find many likely spots where you could hide brandy from the revenue men. Cornish smugglers would haul their illegal brandy up to the Devon hills to sell it to the tinners.

In the middle of Deancombe, below the upper tin-workings, is a ford over the river on the Cuckoo Rock side of Deancombe. From that ford go upstream until you see a valley on the right, enclosed with steep sides. Part of the way up, before this valley rejoins the stream bank on the left-hand side, is a striking cave, just big enough to stand in, which could have been used to store spirits, whisked over the border by romantic men in tricorn hats at the dead of night, swords swinging at their sides, accompanied by black-eyed beauties who said things like, 'Ah har, me hearties' and 'shiver me timbers'. Well it could have served that purpose, and there are certainly many reasons why the caves and working population of Deancombe would have proved attractive to smugglers, but this particular cave used to contain not brandy, smuggled illegally by swashbuckling smugglers and their raven-haired Cornish maidens, but — spuds!

This is, in fact, one of a large number of very effective potato-storage caves that were used by tinners and farmers to store food (root vegetables in particular) while they worked for months on end high up on the moor. Sorry to disappoint you!

Down Tor Circle and Row

The extensive stone row on Hingston Hill is invariably known as the Down Tor Row, although it does not actually lie on that tor. The row runs east–west and at the west end has a retaining circle which is well worth seeing,

juxtaposed as it is with the large stones at this end of the row.

At the other, lower end of the row is another very large cairn separated from the end of the row by a considerable distance. There are some quite large standing stones in the row at this end, too, bearing in mind that the base of the stones are buried some distance below ground for stability.

Standing at either end you can see that where the ground dips towards the middle of the 400-yard row, the stones are out of alignment. This is possibly due to slippage of the ground, but in other stone rows, there seems to be less care taken in the alignment of the row than is possible by sighting. This lends further credence to the theory that the rows were not used for any astronomical observation, but rather for ritual, processional purposes. At the eastern end is a good pound, used for keeping beasts safe from predators and away from the crops. This pound has no hut circles associated with it, which is rather unusual.

Down Tor Row is well worth a visit, as its length and the size of the stones (some are 13 feet high at the western end) make it one of the best on the moor.

Myths & Legends

Dartmoor has a wealth of stories and mysteries associated with it. Because of its deep Celtic heritage the local people have a tradition of oral story-telling, where tales are passed on from generation to generation. Tales of pixies in particular abound. Every dell and valley, every marsh and lake is inhabited by the little people, whom today we imbue with a picturesque homeliness which our recent forebears did not grant them. The stories of the pixies are often dark and frightening, but today we have sanitized them, removing the shadows from the stories since they frighten us. The pixies are not sweet little fairies who dance happily around fairy rings, smiling beneficently upon the human beings who happen to come across them; they are more real than that, with a manipulative side to them which reflects the darker side of human nature itself. The pixies engage in the theft of babies, which grow up in mysterious ways and they take their punishment upon interfering humans who dare to go too far into their little kingdom. But they do have a good side, too, and if left alone to their devices, they appear to trouble only the wicked and lazy.

In this chapter we visit the site of the death of Childe the Hunter, a real-life historical character who lived in the 11th century and whose sad death is commemorated with a fine cross and mound in the wilds of the southern moor. The high moor abounds with stories of the Devil and his hounds, too, rushing around with the wind and the hail searching for unbaptised babies and sinners all. Many of the locations which we visit on the walks in the following pages are the stalking ground of Dewer, as the Devil is known locally, who often appears in the guise of a great black dog.

It is, of course, the great black dog of the Baskervilles which draws a number of people to the moor, following as they do the dramatic story of Sir Arthur Conan Doyle. The story is set in the vicinity of Fox Tor, the Grimpen Mire of *The Hound of the Baskervilles*, and we shall visit the actual site of the final death throes of the hound.

Lastly, we look at the magical stories of Eden Phillpotts, the little-known novelist of Dartmoor who wrote so many sound stories based on the locations around the moor. I hope that the introduction given in the walks in this chapter will encourage more people to take up the books of this sensitive and realistic writer whose gripping human stories are set up in the high moors and in the woody in-country of Dartmoor.

The Devil on Dartmoor

Like most country districts, Dartmoor has its share of stories involving the Devil. On Dartmoor the Evil One is supposed to appear regularly with his black 'wisht-hounds', a fiendish pack of dogs hunting the countryside for the not-so-innocent, pulling them down in the dusk and dark, and carrying them off to Hell with cries of triumph. The pack, with its black horseman in charge, hunts the desolate areas of the moor when the wind blows. The Dewerstone (Walk 33) in the south moor provides the magnificent setting for the wisht hounds and the Devil, who hunt the area looking for a victim, whom they then hound and deceive until they drive him near the huge vertical face of the Dewerstone. The poor unfortunate eventually hurls himself over the edge, to be dashed on the jagged rocks below.

You are quite safe so long as you have never sinned – absolutely never. Think about it. Are you quite sure?

The Devil is supposed to have left many marks on the moor. One of the more interesting is the Devil's Frying Pan on Mis Tor (Walk 24). This whole area used to be named Mistor Pan, and for many years strangers to the area thought, not unreasonably, that this referred to the great marsh to the north of Mis Tor. In fact, the story goes that the Devil uses a large rock basin on the top of the tor as a frying pan to cook his breakfast after scouring the moor with his hounds. You can find it to the north of the largest tower of the tor, and quite high up. The basins form when water freezes in shallow depressions in the rock. Because of the laminar nature of the granite, the freezing can sometimes split out a thin layer of rock by cracking open a feldspar crystal. Gradually, over many years, the water eats its way down in successive freezing and thawing until the depression has steep, sometimes overhanging sides. These basins can be quite deep, often 4 inches or more, and sometimes the walls break away to produce a channel, as in Mistor Pan. There is a superb example on Kestor in the north, which is well worth seeing.

As you can imagine, there are various bloodthirsty stories of druids using them for sacrifices.

Brent Tor Church

The Devil was also busy around Brent Tor, where the impressive Brent Tor Church dominates the eastern skyline. The 40-foot tower was originally to be built at the foot of the tor, but the Devil, who did not take kindly to such things being erected in his domain, decided to frustrate the builders by moving the stone to the top of the steep tor. The solution was simple – the church was built at the top of the tor instead. You can see the pyramidal shape of Brent Tor from many of the walks in the west of the moor.

An alternative story tells of a merchant in the 14th century whose cargo was threatened by a shipwreck at sea. He prayed to St Michael, saying that if he were spared he would build a church in his name. St Michael did his stuff, the cargo was saved, and the merchant went looking for a suitable spot. He soon came across Brent Tor, and started to gather a huge pile of stones with which to build the church. After a fortnight the Evil One took notice of this and threw the stones away. The merchant, undeterred, carried on building the pile of stones, but again, after a fortnight, the Devil cast them to the four winds. By this time the merchant was getting a trifle irritated with this building and scattering, so he turned to St Michael and informed him of his difficulty. St Michael was distinctly unimpressed by this presumptuous behaviour on the part of the Evil One, and, in an attempt to protect his own investment, lay in wait for the Devil in the pile of stones. When the Devil appeared for the third time, St Michael hurled stones at him, hitting him fair and square between the horns. The Devil fled in fright, and St Michael got his church on Brent Tor, which we can all admire today.

Many stories are told in Somerset and Devon of Arthur, the legendary Iron Age chief who will return to lead the Celts to victory in the last great battle. He and the Evil One appear together in the south-east of the moor. Near Blackingstone Rock is a small tor called Heltor; both used to be bare of rock. One day Arthur was on Heltor, minding his own business and admiring the view over his kingdom, when the Devil appeared on the nearby Blacking-stone Rock, and idly lobbed a large rock in Arthur's direction. Arthur, not being one to turn the other cheek, replied with another, slightly heavier missile. The game soon got out of hand, with great rock lumps being hurled with increasing accuracy at the protagonists. Eventually reason prevailed, and both parties retreated only slightly hurt. The last rock hurled by Arthur is said to have formed what is now Blackingstone Rock, and the last hurled by the Devil formed Helston Tor.

The circles of mysterious standing stones on the moor are the subject of many myths. There are a number of tales of dancers being turned to stone because of their disrespect for the Sabbath and also of the power of the stones to protect themselves from the tampering of ne'er-do-wells out to take stone for gate-posts and the like. Some of the stones are said to turn back into people on certain nights, and in particular many of them are said to come alive on Midsummer's Eve, but the ones on Belstone Hill in the north moor are an extreme case – they are said to turn into dancing maidens every day at noon. William Crossing tells the story of a priest who opened a cist at Widecombe. He was repaid by having his house burned down mysteriously the following night.

The River Dart itself is frequently said to be a hard landlord. There is an old rhyme,

River Dart, O River Dart
Every year thou claimest a heart

and there are many of the older people who will not go near the Dart in the early part of the year for fear of being the sacrifice that year. The story was remarkably accurate for many years even in modern times, and if you count modern accidents like cars running into the steep-sided valley of the Dart, it is still so.

Some of the stories and traditions date back well beyond Christianity into the Iron Age. In particular, the stories told about wells and springs have a Celtic provenance which is well recorded, albeit orally. The Celts worshipped deities which lived underground, and wells and springs were revered as the entrances to the world of the gods. A relict of this religion can be seen in the many stories about travellers being 'pixie-led' and then finding their salvation by drinking from a pool, such as Fice's or Fitz's well near Princetown (and its namesake north of Okehampton).

John Fitz, after whom the wells are named, was the grandfather of Lady Mary Howard, of Fitzford, who lived in the 17th century. She is thought to have been confused with another Lady Howard who poisoned two of her four husbands and ended up in the Tower. Lady Mary Howard is condemned to rattle around the roads in her carriage, with a great black dog running before her and with a headless driver sitting at the front. She travels every night from Fitzford House in Tavistock through the town of Lydford to Okehampton Castle. I've never seen her – and I sincerely hope I don't!

Pixies on Dartmoor

Don't you love the sweet little pixies with their pointed hats and their funny little ways with the foxes and badgers? The only trouble they cause is the occasional drink of milk from a generous cow. Everyone loves the pixies! Let's all go out at dusk to look for their fairy lights as they prepare to dance away the summer eventide in their pretty revels, making the fairy rings in which they party away the long evenings.

Let's not. The local tales of pixies are legion, and most of them are a touch on the unpleasant side. Try this one.

A woman is sitting by her fireside in the late evening. It is a wild night, with the wind easing its fingers into the cracks under the door and the gaps in the stones of the chimney breast. Her husband has gone out and her child is sleeping gently in the next room. A knock is heard at the door, and she opens it to see a kindly-looking small middle-aged man dressed in ordinary clothes holding the reins of

a horse. 'Come with me,' he says, 'I understand that you are a midwife and my wife needs you. Her child is due soon. You must come.'

The woman tells him that she is worried about her baby and the stranger tells her that it will be perfectly safe until the husband comes home. Most reluctantly the woman is persuaded by the man's obvious distress and worry for his own wife and pulls herself up on to the horse's back. They set off into the night along a path the

woman does not recognize, even though she has lived in the area all her life. The night is dark, and the wind tugs at her hair and squeezes the tips of her fingers. She worries about her child.

Soon the couple come to a clearing where there is a small turf-roofed cottage that the woman has not seen before. The man helps her down from the horse and rushes to the door, beckoning the woman to enter. Inside the cottage the man's wife is in considerable distress, screaming for the help of the midwife. Soon it is all over. The midwife manages to save both woman and child, and the small, delicate creature is put into a rough blanket in a wicker crib at the side of the bed. The man is voluble in his gratitude, and leaves to make a hot drink for the three of them, before the horse is brought to take the woman back to her cottage.

While the man is out the strange woman asks the midwife to rub the baby's eyes with some ointment that she draws from a bedside table. The midwife rubs the baby's eyes gently with the ointment and gives the pot back to the woman. By this time the midwife is suspicious about these goings on, and before washing her hands she secretly rubs her own left eye with the traces of ointment on her fingers. To her amazement she suddenly sees that the perfectly ordinary woman who has just given birth is the most beautiful faerie creature, with golden hair and a jewelled silk dress in place of the rude sacking which she wore before. Moreover, when she sees the baby her breath is taken away – the wicker crib in which he lies has been transformed into a silver filigree basket. When the husband comes back the midwife is amazed to see that he is not an ordinary middle-aged man at all, but a lithesome fine-featured nobleman, dressed in fine clothes and with a small sword hanging at his side. She has the sense to say nothing to him nor to give away that she can see the three pixies (for that is what they are) in a different light from before.

The man gratefully returns the midwife to her cottage, where she is reunited with her own child and her husband. The man thanks her profusely for saving the life of his wife and gives her a gold coin.

The next day the midwife is in town shopping when she sees the middle-aged man of the previous night making his way through the market. Wanting to thank him for the gold coin, she follows him, stops him and kisses him on the cheek, asking how his wife and baby are.

The small man looks at her and asks, 'So you can see me. From which eye can you see the pixie kingdom?' She points to her left eye, and with one swift movement the little man reaches up and plucks her left eye from its socket. Hurling it over the buildings, with the woman lying screaming on the road, he rushes off, unseen by the rest of the population, who have not had the advantage of the pixie ointment.

There are many other tales of the pixies, some of which are quite recent in origin. There are both good and bad stories. At one extreme is the story of the pixies who cleaned the house of a poor disabled woman. The woman's house was always immaculate when no one was staying with her, but gradually became dustier and dirtier whenever her lazy relations came to stay. At the other extreme is the story above, together with the many stories from all over the moor involving men who were *pixie-led* and lost on the moor. There are two wells on the moor known as Fitz's or Fice's Well, which are said to be memorials erected by a nobleman over the first water which he found after being led by pixies over the moor for what seemed to be many days.

Many places on the moor are said to be inhabited by pixies – mostly hollows and pools – and it would be idle to attempt to document them. Besides, if you went to these places you might see the pixies and you never know what might happen. If you find yourself pixie-led, two sure-fire remedies will work. The first is to turn your coat pockets inside out as quickly as you can, and the second is to turn thirteen times anticlockwise with your eyes shut. If you are not lost before, you certainly will be after that! One of the best known locations for pixie antics is the top of Bellever Tor (Walk 28), where a local farmer was pixie-led when he came across a pixie roller-disco which lasted all night, leaving him exhausted and too frightened ever to go near the tor again.

Don't forget the Pixies' Cross near Tavistock, where, in Walk 11, you can read about a pompous parson who got his come-uppance when he tried to mess with the pixies' cross. He was marooned by a bull until his parishioners rescued him!

Some Dartmoor Superstitions

Here are a few of the hundreds of superstitions and sayings of Dartmoor:

Pixies can be deterred by the ringing of church bells.

Witches cannot talk about their powers or they will lose them.

Setting fire to green bracken produces rain.

The spirits of the dead go to rest in the bogs where they try to entice travellers into danger through the wispy light of the will'o the wisp.

Witches cannot accept money for fear of losing their powers.

A way of breaking a witch's spell is to prick her with a pin. The flowing of blood breaks the curse.

If you hear the cuckoo in July you will die before the year is out.

Wych elm is used by witches, so don't touch it.

Bringing the beautiful May-thorn into the house encourages evil spirits.

Snake bites (particularly from adders) can be cured by wearing a collar of ash twigs around the neck.

Walk 8 – Fox Tor Mires

Distance
About 5 miles.

Difficulty
A walk overlooking one of the most treacherous mires on Dartmoor. Care should be taken in navigation, and a map and compass are essential. Can be wet after rain.

Main Features

Whiteworks Tin-mine	**611709**
Nun's Cross	**605698**
Black Lane Peat Pass	**628691**
Fox Tor Tin-workings	**627696**
Fox Tor	**623699**
Childe's Tomb	**626702**

Description of Walk
From Princetown drive down the narrowish road towards the little hamlet of Whiteworks (*611709*), where you will see several cottages overlooking **Whiteworks Tin-mine**. Follow the road slightly beyond these and park wherever you can, being careful not to inconvenience the inhabitants of this remote settlement. Walk back along the road to the west until it begins to swing around to the right (north). At this point a track continues over the moor to the west and after a short distance meets another track going south towards Nun's Cross Farm (*605698*), which is reached along it in about half a mile.

Nun's Cross or Bocland Cross can be found back towards the road from the grey farm buildings, but slightly to the west. It lies on the moorland side of a stone wall.

From Nun's Cross Farm head off along the stretch of the so-called Abbot's Way towards Crane Hill, and at the point where the path turns sharply to the right to make towards Plym Ford (*614692*) keep on in an

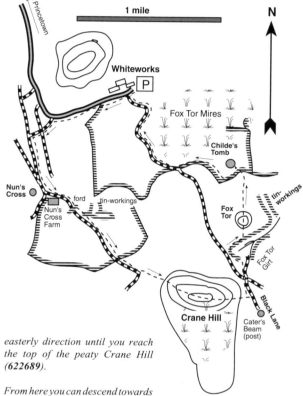

easterly direction until you reach the top of the peaty Crane Hill (*622689*).

From here you can descend towards the peat pass, marked on the map as **Black Lane (628691)**. This is a track cut down through the peat to make it easier for horse riders to traverse the soggy and deep peat.

This will lead you to tin-workings at **Fox Tor Girt (627696)**. **Fox Tor** (*623699*) is north from the top of the girt, and looks out over the formidable Fox Tor Mire, the setting for The Hound of the Baskervilles by Sir Arthur Conan Doyle.

From Fox Tor pick your way down and to the north until you meet the distinctive boundary wall. You

should now be able to see a cairn topped by a cross on the other side of the wall from Fox Tor; it lies in a partly walled enclosure. This is **Childe's Tomb (626702)**.

From Childe's Tomb retrace your steps south towards the wall and follow it to the right (east) until you meet the track near the wall junction which proceeds north and back to the Whiteworks cottages. This track skirts Fox Tor Mires, leaving them to the right.

45

Childe's Tomb

In the shadow of Fox Tor lies Childe's Tomb, its stark cross bearing witness to the tragic tale of a man called Ordulf who lived in the middle of the 11th century. He was the grandson of another Ordulf who had been a great Saxon earl in Devon earlier in the same century.

The younger Ordulf was a religious man who had bequeathed his lands to whichever church took his body when he died. Ordulf's other great interest was hunting, a common pursuit at the time on Dartmoor, and one threatening winter's day he and his band went into the high moors to hunt the deer.

slopes of Crane Hill and Green Hill, and scoured the hillsides for the deer, their great hunting dogs trotting with them. The wind cut and the deer slipped into the mist as the flurries of snow and hail veered and hauled over the rough grass and scrub.

Ordulf, a huge man over 7 feet tall, led the hunt from the front, driving onwards into the moor, always ahead and caring little for the scything

As Ordulf lay in the wet scrubby grass, he felt clinging snowflakes joining those already lying on the grass. Indifferent to the growing chill and confident in his strength, he ignored them, intent on the kill. His companions were distant cries over the wet horizon, moving northwards towards their camp and a warm fire, confident in their leader's ability and unable to keep up with his fast confident movement over the treacherous terrain.

Childe's Tomb

The men left early, the dawn lightening the sky as they left the track north of Fox Tor, and made their way south into the green and grey ocean of the great south moor. Tightening their clothing around themselves as the wind cut into them from the west, the men climbed the

wind and the numbing cold of a Dartmoor winter. On and on Ordulf pressed, sometimes riding, sometimes trotting alongside his short pony. He could see the deer tracks ahead of him as he worked his way back towards the north, and could almost taste the rank smell of the beasts as it lay trapped under the still mist in the hollows. Lost in the chase, Ordulf worked his way round in a rough circle until he lay upwind of where he suspected the group of deer to lie.

The snow grew thicker; Ordulf grew colder. As visibility grew less and less he realized that his instinct for the hunt had let him down, and he was alone in the high moor without companions and far too late in the winter's dying day. Only his pony could be heard next to him, snuffling and moving restlessly in the snow. Realizing his danger Ordulf rose and led his pony towards the north, down the slopes of the moor until they reached the treacherous mire under Fox Tor. Here he stopped, exhausted from the struggle through the deep snow that had been blown into thick drifts by the south-west wind. Darkness crept up on Ordulf like old age; he lay in the snow by his horse, sheltering from the sapping wind and the weakening snow. He would never reach his camp tonight.

Ordulf took out his short sword, and without a moment's hesitation killed the pony. As the warm corpse lay in the snow, Ordulf saw hope, and he slit open the belly of the poor animal. The entrails slithered away into the drift like a nest of snakes.

The animal's ribs were welcoming, and Ordulf, rapidly fading, crept into the belly of the horse and slept, safe from the wind, but not from the numbing cold. He would never awake from his sleep.

It was many days later when Ordulf's band of brothers found the pony's carcass. Accompanied by a party of monks from Tavistock, who had a financial interest in the search, they extracted Ordulf's body and entrusted it to the monks for safe transport to Tavistock. The monks hauled the huge body over the moor, along the rough tracks, until they could see the bridge over the river near Tavistock, known today as the Guilebridge. On the bridge, to their horror, they could see a band of Plymstock men who wanted to bury the body in their own churchyard, in order to retain control over the lands of their own parish. The Tavistock monks knew that, laden with Ordulf's heavy body, they could never beat the Plymstock men.

Quietly and quickly, two of their number went further downstream to bridge the river there, and, falling and blaspheming under the heavy weight, the Tavistock monks pulled the body on to the other side. Exhausted with panic and greed, they made it to the holy ground before the Plymstock folk knew that they had been outflanked. The land of Plymstock became the property of Tavistock.

How the present cairn and cross came to be at the supposed place of Ordulf's death is not clear, but we do know that the present cross dates from the late 19th century. In all probability it was placed over an existing Bronze Age burial chamber. The story has reasonable antecedents. The founding of the Abbey of Tavistock was greatly supported by an Ordulf, almost certainly the grandfather of the younger, frozen Ordulf, and St Eustace's church in Tavistock has a splendid arch named after him.

But why is it called Childe's Tomb, when no mention has been made of this name? There are many alternative tellings of the Childe's Tomb story. I have chosen the one that appears closest to historical fact, but others tell of a man called Amyas Childe, who is supposed to have perished in the described way. I favour the explanation that the Saxon word 'cild' meaning a lord or leader, is the source of the name. The tomb under the shadow of Fox Tor is probably the burial site of some other unfortunate who died on the moor, but it's a good story none the less!

Whiteworks

Whiteworks, which consists today of a row of cottages of varying ages, is the remains of an extensive tin-mining works on the edge of Fox Tor. The name comes from the appearance in the mine workings of the white China clay which appears when water acts upon the feldspar in granite to produce kaolinite. You can see vast quantities of this kaolin in the mounds of spoil near Cornwood in the south-west part of the moor (Walk 33).

The cottages which you see today are not the original ones, but have been erected on the site of the old dwellings put up to serve the miners. The extensive workings lie spread before you, with the green expanse of Fox Tor Mire behind them. Apparently, the area was a very busy one, with at least two wheels working away and a great deal of activity. Today it stands quiet on the edge of this inland sea of grass and water, but just settle yourself at the lower end of the row of cottages and imagine the bustle and activity of a busy mining community around you. Hear the scrape of shovel on ore, the dull thud of stones being set in place to build the retaining walls and the squeaky grind of the large waterwheels as they drove the pounding mills.

You can read more about the process of tin-mining in the Tinning & Quarrying chapter.

Nun's Cross and Farm

The gaunt grey square dwelling which you see before you at Nun's Cross is not the original farmhouse. The first Nun's Cross Farm, dating *circa* 1870, was a thatched cottage which was built to serve the lands enclosed by a John Hooper.

The name Nun's Cross appears to have nothing whatsoever to do with nuns. It comes from the Celtic word *nans,* which means a ravine or coombe, and is quite appropriate for the location, standing as it does at the head of the Swincombe valley.

The location is an important one in that it stands at the junction of two variants of the Abbot's Way, both connecting Buckfast with the west of the moor. One track goes off to Buckland Abbey (hence the word 'Boclond' on the cross) and the other to Tavistock. There are many other tracks which connect with this point – tinners' routes and farm tracks. Indeed it is a veritable Piccadilly Circus in summer, having easy access to the road at Whiteworks, and being on the route of some attractive walks up from Burrator to the west.

The cross itself is quite remarkable, standing as it does over 6 feet high. It is rectangular in cross-section, and has the word 'Siward' or perhaps 'Syward' on one side and the word 'Boclond' inscribed on the other.

For many years the cross has been significant in marking the boundary of ownership on the moor, and it is first mentioned in documents to do with the ownership of the Buckland Abbey lands in 1280, although there are other earlier references going back to 1240. The inscription 'Boclond' is almost certainly to do with the modern Buckland, but there are other sites on the moor called Buckland, which means, specifically, a place held by written permission, hence 'book-land'. The cross, referred to as *Crucem Sywardi,* marked the eastern boundary of the lands held by Buckland Abbey.

The other inscription, 'Siward', probably refers to Siward, the Earl of Northumberland, who, it is believed, held the Forest of Dartmoor from Edward the Confessor. There are other explanations, the most likely alternative being a connection with a Siward family who lived at Cholwich Town to the south of Nun's Cross.

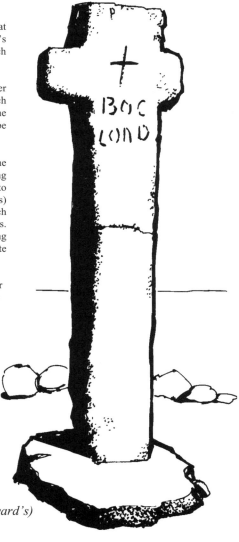

Nun's (or Siward's) Cross

Whatever the explanation, the cross is a fine one, having survived being thrown over by hooligans in 1846 and repaired by a John Newcombe. You can still see the iron band holding it together. It stands here, overlooking the desolate farmhouse, which has been uninhabited since the 1960s. Nun's Cross Farm ranks with Brown's House, built deep in the moor north of Two Bridges, as a memorial to the many people who have tried to make a living from the moor and, for one reason or another, have failed. The moor is a hard master indeed.

Fox Tor and the Hound of the Baskervilles

It is widely understood that Fox Tor Mire is the Grimpen Mire of Sir Arthur Conan Doyle's famous story, *The Hound of the Baskervilles*. Clearly, the story is set on Dartmoor, with a number of locations being easily identified – Lafter Hall, for example, where Mr Frankland lives, and Merripit House where the Stapletons reside. The main setting for the story is the area around Baskerville Hall, from which one can look across Grimpen Mire to see High Tor. Many of the other locations do not fit exactly, but allowing for a certain degree of artistic licence the reader may well choose to place Baskerville Hall near Whiteworks, and imagine looking over towards the clearly visible Fox Tor near the horizon, with the treacherous narrow path stretching out towards it.

The story of *The Hound of the Baskervilles* turns on the legend of a Sir Hugo Baskerville, owner of Baskerville Hall in 1645, who kidnapped a local girl, and, when she escaped, hunted her down. His reward was to be savaged by a huge black hound with blazing eyes, which leapt on him in the area of High Tor and left him dead.

Sherlock Holmes is visited by a Dartmoor doctor named Mortimer, who lives near the hall. Mortimer tells Holmes that he is suspicious of the death of Sir Charles Baskerville, who appears to have died of a heart attack as he was running away from something on the edge of the Moor. The footprints of a huge dog are found in the vicinity. The next day Sir Henry Baskerville, the son, is brought to Holmes's rooms. Sir Henry has received a note of warning, composed of letters cut from a newspaper, warning him to

keep away from the moor. Strangely, one of a pair of new boots has also been stolen. Holmes spots a bearded man watching him and Dr Watson, as they walk to lunch with Sir Henry.

Later, Sir Henry has another single boot stolen, this time an old one. There seems little logic in the train of circumstances. Watson is dispatched to Baskerville Hall to look after Sir Henry. As they are on their way to the hall, a soldier stops the party to tell them to take care on the moor because a murderer has escaped from the prison. Watson soon makes the acquaintance of Jack Stapleton and his sister, who live nearby. Miss Stapleton tells Watson of the story of the hound, and informs him that the locals are saying that the hound killed Sir Charles and will kill Sir Henry.

Later that night a light is seen moving on the moor near High Tor. A servant at the hall, Barrymore, is seen signalling with a candle. He looks suspiciously like the man who followed Holmes and Watson in London.

Watson and Sir Henry risk going out on to the moor and find the twisted body of Selden, the escaped murderer, at the bottom of High Tor.

In the meantime, Holmes has settled himself secretly in a farmhouse near High Tor and eventually makes contact with Watson. Holmes has seen a boy taking food and water and some letters to the escaped murderer on the moor.

The climax of the story comes when Watson, Holmes and Lestrade, a

policeman from London, go hunting for the murderer of Sir Charles on the moor the next night. They make their way out to High Tor over the narrow path through the treacherous Grimpen Mire. They look back from the Tor to see Sir Henry talking to Stapleton at his nearby house. The mist rises and thickens, and they hear the sound of a chain clinking in the thick mist.

As Sir Henry starts back towards the hall the horrifying growling noise of a huge dog is heard by the three men. As Holmes calls to Sir Henry, Lestrade sees the huge black dog, fire shining from its head. The dog leaps past him, aiming inexorably for Sir Henry. All three men fire their revolvers at the hound and kill it. All around the head is luminous paint. The hound had been used to frighten Sir Henry into leaving the path over the Grimpen Mire, so that he would drown in the liquid mud.

It turns out that Stapleton has been attempting to use the terrifying legend of the Hound of the Baskervilles to kill Sir Henry and inherit the Baskerville estates.

49

Walk 9 – Jay's Grave and Bowerman's Nose

Distance
About four miles.

Difficulty
An easy walk over gentle moorland, not far from roads. Beautiful, picturesque views of the in-country of eastern Dartmoor.

Main Features

Wingstone Farmhouse	**746811**
Bowerman's Nose	**741804**
Jay's Grave	**731799**

Description of Walk
Leave your car in the centre of Manaton village, near the church. Make sure that you secure it well from thieves.

*From the church walk south on the road until you come to a crossroads on the edge of the village. Turn right. After about half a mile you will see the **Wingstone Farmhouse** up a track on the left. After you pass Wingstone look up the slope opposite to see the huge stoned wall of Ebworthy Farm, a classic Dartmoor 'big wall'.*

*Return to the road and continue along it to the west until you come to a junction. Take the left-hand road to the south until you come out onto the moorland as you cross the Hayne Brook. You will see the prominent rock group of **Bowerman's Nose** up the slope ahead and to your left. Make your way up to it.*

From Bowerman's Nose walk down the slope towards the west until you reach the road near Blissmoor. Turn left and walk along the road until you come to Moyle's Gate. Take the track immediately after the gate, turning to your right off the road

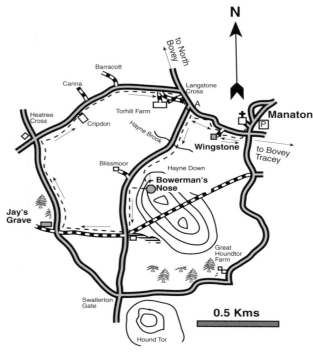

*towards the west until you come to another road, which runs between Swallerton Gate and Fordgate. At the point where the track meets the road you will find the **Kitty Jay's Grave**.*

Retrace your steps to the upper road and follow it back to Manaton, turning right at the only road junction, and passing Wingstone again on your right. Turn left into Manaton to reach your car.

Manaton Graveyard

The graveyard at Manaton houses the bones of the sad lady of Grea Tor. She used to visit the tor where she and her lover had walked before the Great War, holding hands and kissing under the green drapery that you can see there today. Soon her lover had to go to the war to fight for his country, and, ever brave, the young woman bit her lip and waved him goodbye.

Soon the letters stopped. The woman had no idea whether her lover was dead or faithless, but still she continued to go to walk under the rowans of Grea Tor, until, after many years, when the war ended, she finally came to terms with her lover's absence. Realizing that he would walk with her no more under the birches and ivy, she lay down under the rocks and died.

Bowerman's Nose

On Hayne Down you will find a most unusually shaped tor in the form of the head of a man wearing a peaked cap. The pile is some 40 feet high and has seven separate layers of rock which form the chin, mouth, nose, forehead and hat.

There are a number of theories about the origin of the name 'Bowerman'. One unlikely origin is the Celtic phrase *fawr maen,* meaning great stone. In fact, all the Celtic languages would have the adjective after the noun, giving *maen fawr,* so this is indeed unlikely.

There was, apparently, a man named Bowerman living in the area during the 11th century and this, together with a heavy helping of Dartmoor imagination, was the origin of the following story.

Bowerman was a hunter from near Manaton, who used to go alone on to the moors to kill hares and other small game for the pot. One autumn day he was lying silent in the scrubby grass of Hayne Down when he observed some people dancing on the down below him. He crept nearer, only to see that he had happened upon a coven of witches, dancing in the dusk at their yearly great festival. The dark shapes pranced and danced in front of him. He waited until the dance was at its height, and with whoops of glee, ran through the circle, scattering the witches and scaring the wits out of them.

The witches, concentrating upon their ceremony, were taken completely by surprise, and could not muster a spell to punish this infidel before he had leapt off, cheering and whooping towards his home. He was not to remain unpunished.

Bowerman's Nose on Hayne Down

Soon Bowerman was back on the hill, hunting the hares, having forgotten all about his dangerous prank. One day, as he lay under the shadow of the bushes on the down he saw before him a juicy hare bouncing about just out of bow shot. He crawled nearer, and as he did the hare bounced away up the slope. Bowerman continued to track the hare, until he was well out of sight of his home below. Soon he had it in his sights, and as he raised himself up to loose an arrow, the hare looked fully at him, and he felt frozen in its wild animal glare. Bowerman dropped his bow in the terror of the freezing gaze of the animal, and as he looked he saw the hare change gradually into a plump middle-aged matron, who looked at him in a

kindly, knowing way, seemed to check his identity, and then pointed her finger at him, laughed gently, and turned and walked away.

Bowerman did not follow her. He felt his feet sink into the peaty soil, and found it difficult to move his knees. He cried out but no sound emerged. With his last movement he bent his gaze down to where his feet were, only to see the jointed granite scuffling its way down into the subsoil. To his horror, Bowerman realized that he had been incarcerated in this stone pile, fully conscious, but unable to move a finger while his family and friends scoured the Down looking for his foolish body. His bow was never found and nor was he.

Jay's Grave

The sad story of the suicide of Kitty Jay is commemorated by a small mound with a headstone at the crossing of two paths near Hayne Down.

Kitty Jay was a young woman who fell in love with a man from the nearby farm. The two were very much in love, and, as is the way of the world, Kitty succumbed to the persuasive words of the young farm boy. They fell into one another's arms, and, confident of his love, Kitty gave herself to him willingly. After a long and fond goodbye, she crept quietly back into her own bed, dreaming of the future with her young man, and of endless similar nights of passion.

The next day Kitty called confidently upon her young man, reminding him of his promise that they would now be wed. She asked him about the ring, excited over the prospect of the wedding.

The young man rejected her, however, saying that he had no intention of marrying a worthless young woman like her, who was not only the daughter of a tenant farmer, but was clearly of low moral worth since she would sin by sleeping with a man before the marriage had been blessed by God.

Kitty said not a word and went home. All day she sat in the outhouses of Canna Farm, where she lived, and at dusk she hanged herself, without a sound save for the whispering of her lover's name.

In those times the punishment for suicide was harsh. Kitty Jay was cut down and buried without ceremony at a crossroads so that her soul would not know which way to go to haunt

the living. Her hypocritical lover was not punished, at least not in this life, and went on to make a good marriage. He lived, apparently, happily ever after, while Kitty Jay's soul wandered pathetically around the moors, looking for her faithless and heartless lover.

There is an element of truth to this story. Some time later a Mr James Bryant, of Hedge Barton, disinterred a young female body at the site, and reburied it in a box, setting up the stone that you see there now.

There is a tale that every night a bunch of fresh flowers is placed upon Kitty's grave by a spirit. It's an eerie place to spend the night, but you could camp out here looking for the ghostly visitor who comes to decorate the grave of sad young Kitty Jay, betrayed by her faithless lover.

Jay's Grave

Walk 10 – Longaford Tor and Wistman's Wood

Distance
7 miles.

Difficulty
One of the best medium-length walks on Dartmoor, this route takes you up over a long ridge which is dry and clean underfoot. Navigation is straightforward, but like all walks on the high moor, care must be taken in changeable weather. At the extremity of the walk you are approaching the most desolate part of the moor and appropriate footwear and clothing must be taken. At Crow Tor you are on the edge of a range area, but you do not actually enter into it.

Main Features

Crockern Farmhouse	**610758**
Longaford Tor	**616778**
Crow Tor	**606788**
Devonport Leat	**609779**
Wistman's Wood	**612772**

Description of Walk
The Two Bridges Hotel has opposite it an excellent parking space for about a dozen cars. Park sensibly and secure your vehicle from thieves.

Go through the gate on the moor side of the car-park and follow the track for half a mile or so up to **Crockern farmhouse**.

From Crockern go around the house to the right and continue following the track with the river below you on the left until you come to a stile over the enclosure wall. Go over the stile and head up the slope on your right until you reach the rocks of Littaford Tor *(616769)*. This is the start of a splendid ridge walk which leads eventually to Higher White Tor. You walk past a number of outcrops on the way to the triangular shape of **Longaford Tor**.

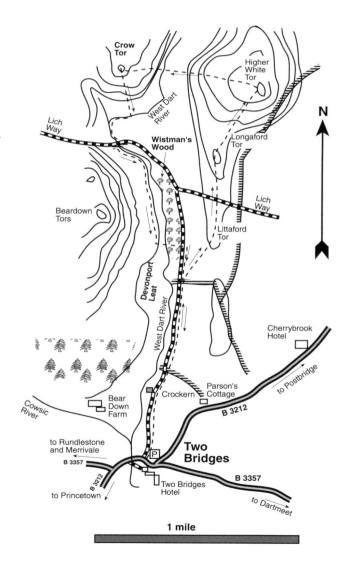

1 mile

Wistman's Wood

The Beast of Longaford can be found on the west (Wistman's Wood) side of the Tor towards the north end. It is about a third of the way up from the lowest rocks and is best seen from the same level or below and from the south side, in other words, from the direction from which you are now approaching it.

From Longaford Tor go in a northwesterly direction towards the next high tor on the ridge, dropping down a little, and then rising steadily to the rocks of Higher White Tor (619785), from which you get superb views out over the northern morass of Dartmoor.

From Higher White Tor follow the enclosure wall down towards the river in a westerly direction. This will eventually bring you to a range notice board bearing dire warnings. It is perfectly safe to continue to the top of **Crow Tor** even if the range flags are flying, but do not walk any further to the west if the ranges are being used.

From the top of Crow Tor drop down to the river and follow it until you see the point where the **Devonport leat** leaves the river, where there is a little hut on the west bank. The leat provides easy walking above a steep slope opposite **Wistman's Wood**. At any point you choose, drop down to the river and climb up through Wistman's Wood until you reach the path at the top of the wood. Take care in the wood not to do any damage either to the trees and plants or, for that matter, to yourself. The boulders can be slippery and treacherous.

Turn right on the path and follow it back down to Crockern and then to the car park.

Above Crockern on the banks of the East Dart is one of the natural wonders of Britain, Wistman's Wood. This is an ancient oak woodland of trees blasted almost horizontal by the vicious upland storms, and sheltering in the cracks between huge boulders from the wind's icy teeth.

The legends surrounding the wood are many. The Devil and his wisht hounds are supposed to find this a suitable place to hunt for errant sinners. They hunt their victims from the slopes around into the wood,

The woods have always been considered part of the great Druidic temple of the moor, a theory propounded by the Victorian antiquaries who saw each copse and wood peopled by white-bearded priests who brandished golden sickles and cut down mistletoe in preparation for their blood-thirsty rituals. Well, all right, you can find mistletoe here, and there was undoubtedly a Druidic cult which used mistletoe, a parasitic plant, in its rituals, but there is no particular reason why Wistman's Wood should be a special site above all

The Devil's black hounds haunt the stunted trees of Wistman's Wood

and force them into it. The victims, trapped in the wood, eventually fall amongst the boulders and break their legs. The hounds simply wait, closing in on their prey in silent shuffles. By the time their evil fangs sink into the flesh, the victim is mercifully insane from the horror of what is to befall him.

others. It is an evocative place, however, surrounded by hut circles and with superb views to the surrounding tors, and the Dart rushing its busy way south just below Wistman's Wood. It has a cousin in the north called Black-a-tor Wood, or Black Tor Beare, but it is not so extensive, and, being more sheltered, has larger trees. Step inside Wistman's Wood and walk around with care. The wood is a nature reserve, so you should be extremely careful not to cause damage to the rare lichens which thrive on the branches of the trees. It is remarkable how the roots of the trees have twisted their way around the huge boulders, and at first glance it seems perverse that the trees should have chosen this particularly difficult place to take seed and grow, as the boulders were even more prominent when the trees were first seeded. On reflection, of course, the boulders are the reason for the wood, since they provide protection from the grazing animals when the plants are extremely young, and from the biting winds when they are adolescents of fifty years of age or so. When the trees poke their heads up above the boulders, however, they soon learn the wisdom of being small and stunted. The evolution of such small twisted trees has taken place over many hundreds of years to produce these oaks, so well suited to their inhospitable climate. The trees are of a slightly unusual type of oak called pedunculate. The diagram shows the two different types of leaf. See if you can identify the leaves in the wood.

Inside the wood, although it is rather difficult to find, is the tomb of a terrier called Jumbo, who belonged to a master of foxhounds, one Sam Adams. The wood is a natural retreat for pursued foxes, and the terrier had made himself useful there on many a bloody occasion. Near the top edge of the wood towards the centre is another memorial, a triangular stone commemorating the cutting down of a tree for scientific purposes by Wentworth Buller in 1866. Do not even think of taking

The two types of oak leaf

Sessile Oak — Pedunculate Oak

the smallest twig from the wood; it is a site of immense importance in the study of British plants, and the authorities will lock you away if you do. I shall not visit you in prison.

There is much speculation among the experts about the origins of the name Wistman's Wood. The most commonly advanced is that it refers to a Celtic phrase *uisg maen coed*. If it were correct this would mean literally 'water stone wood', Unfortunately it is more likely that such a phrase would be *coed uisg maen* or

coed maen uisg, as the subject would normally come first in the phrase. This is nit-picking, however, and the phrase is as likely a contender as any so far.

More likely, however, is the connection between the word *wisht,* as in wisht hounds, and the name of the wood. We can, therefore, imagine Wistman's Wood to mean no more than Bogey Man Wood. And if you're ever here after dusk, you will be able to see the good reason for this particular name.

Ephraim's Pinch

Near Soussons Plantation to the south of this walk is a short, steep section of road known by all as Ephraim's Pinch.

It appears that Ephraim was an immensely strong local man who made a steady living by betting on his capacity for feats of strength, such as pulling carthorses, and lifting rocks. He met his match one day, however, when he became the subject of a bet that he could carry a sack of corn, weighing a couple of hundredweights, from the town of Widecombe to Postbridge without once dropping it.

Now this is a distance of 5 miles in anyone's atlas. Ephraim was going relatively well after he had reached the 3°- mile point when he came to the bottom of this short stretch of hill. By the time he had reached the middle of the hill, the odds had shortened, and a few yards later he became rather less popular than before, when, completely exhausted by the slope, he dropped the sack and lost all his friends their money.

Nevertheless Ephraim did win something after all, for he has been immortalized in the story of Ephraim's Pinch.

Eden Phillpotts and The River

Eden Phillpotts died in 1960 after a full life of writing novels that are set against the backdrop of Dartmoor, and that have given pleasure to thousands of readers. It is surprising that his novels, some eighteen comprising the Dartmoor Cycle, are not more popular today. In the main part they provide strong insights into the human condition, set against the scenery of specific parts of the moor. The stories are drawn with panache and skill in prose which is not overly Victorian in style, but rather simple in its language, particularly when describing the rural folk who appear within them.

Of Phillpott's novels the best known is *The River*, published in 1902 and based on the area around Wistman's Wood, Two Bridges and as far north as Devil's Tor. It concerns the lives of a rabbit-catcher, Nicholas Edgecombe, who lives in a hut near Wistman's Wood, and Hannah Bradridge, the daughter of the owner of the inn at Two Bridges. Edgecombe is a very religious man, who views the moor as an extension to his bible. One day Edgecombe is trapping rabbits on Devil's Tor when he is attacked by a white bull which breaks his leg. He is eventually found and is then taken back to the inn at Two Bridges by Hannah and her friend, Mary Merle.

Hannah and Edgecombe fall in love, and, when they meet one day on Longaford Tor, Edgecombe asks her to marry him. He is the happiest man in the world on hearing of her acceptance. They make preparations for a August wedding, and in the meantime Edgecombe carries on with his work and his devotions.

The beautiful Hannah, however, is not courted by Edgecombe alone,

and, neglected by Edgecombe through the summer, she is wooed by a ne'er-do-well, one Timothy Oldreive, who has the favour of Hannah's mother. By the time the wedding day dawns Edgecombe has left it too late. When he leaves for his wedding breakfast he is met by a friend who breaks the awful news to him that Hannah is already married. He turns around and goes back to his hut.

Eventually, Edgecombe finds solace in the love of Mary Merle, whom he clearly views as second best to Hannah. They agree to marry.

One day Edgecombe is out on the moor in a tremendous thunderstorm. Passing by the Dart he sees the shape of a small child drowning in the black waters He dives in to rescue the boy, who turns out to be the son of Hannah and Timothy Oldreive.

The climax of the drama occurs when a friend brings news to Edgecombe that Oldreive is attacking Hannah on the edge of the Dart at Two Bridges. Edgecombe hurries to the spot to assist his friend and lost lover, Hannah. In a tremendous fight Edgecombe is injured and Oldreive is drowned accidentally in the flood waters of the Dart. Hannah is free, as a widow, for Edgecombe to break his marriage vows and marry her. She has been his first love and friend for so long. He has saved her child and has even saved her from the cruelty of her

---

Phillpott's Dartmoor Cycle

Below is the list of the Dartmoor Cycle together, with each of their settings:

Children of the Mist	Chagford
Sons of the Morning	Gidleigh
The River	Two Bridges
The Secret Woman	Belstone
The Portreeve	Bridestowe
The Whirlwind	Lydford
The Mother	Merrivale
The Virgin in Judgement	Sheepstor
The Three Brothers	Shaugh Prior
The Thief of Virtue	Postbridge
Demeter's Daughter	Holne
The Beacon	South Zeal
The Forest on the Hill	Yarner Wood
Widecombe Fair	Widecombe
Brunel's Tower	Erme Valley
Miser's Money	Fox Tor
Orphan Dinah	Buckland
Children of Men	Avon Valley

The Mad Vicar of Tavistock

husband, but at the same time he is a man bound by duty and his vows to Mary. What will he do?

You will have to read the book to find out. It would be grossly unfair to reveal the denouement of this excellent story. It has high drama, action, and beautiful and accurate descriptions of the moor, and is a fitting memorial to the most prolific writer on Dartmoor. Phillpotts never brought a plot to Dartmoor, but rather sat in the moor which he loved so well and waited for the story to suggest itself from the country. This technique is extremely effective in that when one reads any of the books in the moor itself – on holiday, say – the country is made so alive and the story is so much in context that one can be sure that one is reading the work of a great story teller, and one who loved the moor deeply.

In the bed of the Cowsic river near here (not the river by Wistman's Wood – that is the Dart), can be seen evidence of one of the moor's eccentrics, a sometime vicar of Tavistock.

This individual who went by the name of Bray, had a father who had built a number of clapper bridges over the rivers in the area in order to increase the level of interest for antiquarians. The father appears to have passed his capacity for improving things without regard to antiquity down to his son. The younger Bray was very interested in the Druids, and became rather disappointed when he failed to have his theories about their habits and interests borne out by observation.

Undaunted, Bray proceeded to take a paintbrush and carefully painted letters on the large rocks in the bed of the Cowsic, dedicating them to Theocritus, Virgil and the British bards, in order to make the countryside fit in more with his expectation of it. He then obtained the services of a local labourer to carve out the letters with a pickaxe.

It was lucky that the vicar wrote down what he had done, because if the subsequent generation of Victorian antiquaries had observed them – bearing in mind that they were somewhat arbitrary in their interpretation of the features they found, we might have had all sorts of interesting theories about the Druids and their connections with the ancient Greeks!

The Beast of Longaford

High up on the north-west side of Longaford Tor is a leaping beast, trapped forever in the hard granite. Its body lies far within the tor, while its broad-jawed head looks out over Wistman's Wood to the west. The beast hunts the valley of the Dart, and it leaps down over the slope toward the ancient woodland where it lies in wait for the traveller. Many people camping in the area have heard the beast's horrible yowling roar as it attempts to terrify the intruder into leaving the relative safety of the tent and the light and into running madly towards the safety of Two Bridges.

If you stand on the west side of Longaford Tor about half-way up you can look along the side of the tor toward the north to see the dragon-like head with its nostrils and eyes defined clearly in the outline of the rock. The beast merely sleeps here, rising each night to hunt its unsuspecting prey below. Who knows how far it ranges in its travels? Maybe it can follow people to their homes and lurks, unseen, in the shadows of their children's bedrooms, waiting to make its evil meal of weak humans. Or maybe it's just a bit of rock high up on a Dartmoor hillside.

The Hairy Hands of Postbridge

The stretch of road to the west of Postbridge is the scene of a relatively modern horror story dating from just after the Great War. It involves the appearance of a pair of Hairy Hands.

A number of drivers and motor-cycle riders experienced a sudden grasp and jerk on the steering-wheel or handlebars while driving along this stretch of road on the high moor, and a number of accidents took place along the road for no apparent reason. Soon the hairy

hands became more prominent, and, gaining confidence, they began pawing at the windows of passing cars. Their fame spread, but soon they faded away and were seen no more...

...until later in the century when a number of campers reported hearing scratching sounds at the canvas, and, on pulling back the flysheet, saw in the darkness a horrible hairy hand clawing at the material. A caravanner claims to have seen the hand trying to open the catch on his van window and some girl guides are said to have run screaming from the furry fingers.

My suspicion is that it has more to do with the Two Bridges Hotel or the East Dart Inn at Postbridge than with any supernatural happening, although there could be a ghostly connection with the latter, since Post-

bridge is already known to be the haunt of a strange black dog which laps up the spilt beer in the ditch opposite the inn. Where there's one strange story, there's usually another. In this case the wife of the owner of the Inn was so scared of the black dog (a common Dartmoor euphemism for the Devil), that she made her husband turn the inn into a temperance hotel, a more horrible act than any ineffective grapplings by a so-called hairy hand!

Snaily House

Don't read this unless you have a strong stomach. In fact, it's better not to read it at all.

In the woods to the south of the Two Bridges to Postbridge road lies Snaily House. It's marked on the map. Two sisters used to live here, and were suspected of being witches since they seemed never to work in their garden nor to spend any money on food. Nevertheless, they appeared healthy and well-nourished – obviously witches. They were visited by the local 'Witch Watch', who could find no evidence that they were in league with the Devil and could find no broomsticks, black cats or suspicious, headless black cockerels.

The women were just bone idle, apparently, and had decided that in this damp and grassy part of the moor they could live perfectly well, without having to work, on...slugs.

Having been found out, and being so poor, the two sisters had no choice but to starve to death as they were overcome by the misery and shame of their poverty and idleness.

By the way, on average, five people die in Britain every year by eating slugs. They're poisonous, so don't eat them. The question I always ask is 'How do they come to eat them?' Is it a dare, or some part of a secret ritual worship of the Great Slug God? Maybe they just don't check the salad carefully enough!

Walk 11 – Windy Post and Vixen Tor

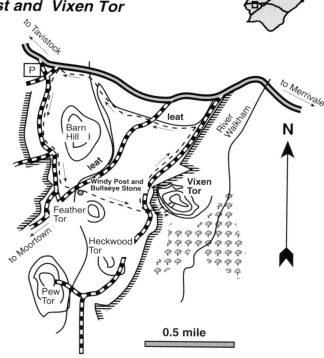

Distance

3° miles.

Difficulty

Easy. Suitable for all the family. Take care when coming down from Windy Post towards Vixen Tor that you do not walk right into Vixana's Mire.

Main Features

Windy Post	533742
Bullseye Stone	533742
Vixen Tor	542742
Grimstone Leat	543748

Description of Walk

Start at the car-park (531750) on the Merrivale–Tavistock road (the B3357) at the top of the hill on the Tavistock side of Merrivale. The Dartmoor Inn at Merrivale is an excellent place for a meal and a drink after the walk. The car-park is very large and has all the usual summer facilities of ice-cream vans, hotdog wagons and coffee stalls, but in winter is usually deserted. Please note that dogs are not allowed in the immediate area of Vixen Tor, which is private land. Dogs can be taken on the vast majority of this walk, subject to the usual precautions, but not on the enclosed land around Vixen Tor.

At the Merrivale end of the car-park you will find a concrete pipe running away from the road. This will lead you to a gully. Follow the gully, crossing an old leat. Soon you will come across a wet leat which will lead you to a large green track which cuts across the leat. This crossing is about half a mile from the car-park. Turn left at the junction and follow the track gently downhill until you see an enclosure on your right which has a right-angled corner (531745). From this corner follow the line of

the wall to another right-angled corner. Stand with your back to the corner in the wall and look towards the skyline. You will see a huge television mast ahead of you. Take the green track in that direction slightly up slope until you see the prominent shape of **Windy Post** ahead of you. Go to the post.

About 5 yards away from Windy Post you will find a **bullseye stone** in the leat. You can see the 1-inch hole clearly as it directs a limited supply of water away from the main leat.

Continue in the same direction away from the post towards the prominent tor. This is **Vixen Tor**. Make your way towards it, but do not attempt to cross the swamp on your

side of the stream unless the moor is extremely dry. It is not dangerous, but it is better to follow the line of the marsh down-stream until you meet the enclosure wall with its gate, under which the stream flows. Cross near here and make your way up slope following the wall to the stile. Climb the stile, leaving your dog on the other side.

Leave the tor enclosure by the same stile and follow the track up-slope towards the road. After some time you will encounter the leat, which runs from right to left. Follow it downstream until it crosses a steep-sided tinners' gully, and then walk up this until you meet the main road. Turn left and follow the road to the car-park. Check that Vixana has not followed you.

Vixana

The strange battleship shape of Vixen Tor looks safe enough from the roadside, but it used to hide the dark secret of the most famous witch of Dartmoor, called Vixana.

Vixana was in the habit of hiding in the great rock pile, where she would look for travellers coming down from the Windy Post (where you may well be standing). In between Windy Post and Vixen Tor is a rather difficult swamp, lying right in the path of the unwary. Nowadays it is really quite safe, but in Vixana's days it had been specially cultured by her to provide the perfect trap for the unwary – deep, thick, black liquid underneath, but green and seductive on top. Vixana loved her little swamp, and nurtured it as often as she could with the bodies of travellers, to keep it sweet and hungry for her evil purposes.

In the short winter days she would hop from crag to crag on the beautiful tor looking expectantly towards Windy Post in the hope of catching some unfortunate. As the victim started down the slope towards the tor, which was the next obvious waymark on the track, Vixana would start her mist-making. At first the mist would be thin and meagre, wafting around the tufts of moor grass and weaving its way gently, almost welcomingly towards the traveller. Then, inexorably, the mist would thicken behind him, cutting off the line of retreat towards

Windy Post. Of course, there was nothing to worry about, because the path to the tor was clear, if a little twisted.

Soon the mist would thicken ahead of the victim, and disorientation would set in. The traveller knew that it was impossible to go directly towards the tor, so he would turn on the various false paths until ...

... he took one step into the green welcoming swamp. Vixana would then shriek in anticipation as first one foot then the other became sodden with the horrible green slime. The traveller struggled like a fly in honey. In struggling, the knees became wet, then the chest became sodden with the treacherous green muck. After a while the mouth became full of sphagnum and mud. The death was horrible, more suffocation than drowning, and the twisted limbs of the terrified traveller

would flail in ineffective railing against the black terror of the swamp.

There was one traveller, however, who was not frightened of mists in the slightest. He had once had the good fortune to lift a pixie from a 'feather-bed' (a Dartmoor valley bog). This pixie was of an honourable disposition and in gratitude to the human for saving

his life, gave him a gold ring which, when worn, allowed the bearer to see through mists and to become invisible if it was turned on the finger. Our hero set off one horrible winter afternoon from Tavistock on the well-worn path and soon found himself at Windy Post. Without hesitation he set off down the slope which you are about to descend, and aimed straight for the twisty path. He noticed that the afternoon was getting dark, but he was untroubled.

Vixen Tor is the hunting ground of the evil Vixana

As our traveller approached the tricky part of the twisty path he noticed, as many had before him, that the mist was rising and getting thicker, and he thought – or perhaps he just imagined – that he could see a figure leaping about on the top of the distant crag. He decided to press on.

As the mist got thicker the traveller slipped on his ring. Suddenly his vision cleared, and he could see that he was a little way from the correct track. He immediately turned back towards the maze of paths and wound his way to the bottom of the valley where, as you did, he gained the gate and the easier ground without difficulty. It was here that he noticed the human fingers sticking up from the muddy pool next to him.

The man's blood ran cold, only to freeze as he heard the vile cackling of the evil witch on the slope above. He turned the ring on his finger and immediately felt the strange prickle of the cloak of invisibility as it slipped like a shroud over him.

Quietly he made his way up to the top of the crag, working his way round from the Merrivale side. As he climbed the rocks, the mist grew thicker. He drew nearer to the voice of Vixana, cackling as she waited for the mist to clear.

The traveller clambered silently up the last slope and to his horror saw the back of the cackling witch, chewing on the rotten finger-bone of a victim, as she awaited her next fresh meal. As he waited for inspiration, he saw the witch turn and look through him. He could see her nose twitch as the hairs in it sought for the smell she found so strange.

Was it sheep? Was it a wandering tasteless cow? Surely not this high up. At last she identified it as a human, and turned to despatch, with one snap of her unpleasant jaws, the victim who had inadvertently crept up on her. But there was nothing to be seen. Her jaws snapped at the mist.

Our hero leapt forward and with one push, hurled her off the crag. An eldritch scream pierced the granite of the tor. As she fell, the swamp opposite came alive with the fingers and arms of the doomed travellers waving defiantly as the witch was dashed, bloody and screaming, on the rocks opposite the swamp. As Vixana's dying gasp echoed round the valley our hero looked out over the swamp, now clear of mist, to see the spirits of the dead making their way along the path from Windy Post on their final journey, now made safe by a pixie's ring.

Witches on Dartmoor

As you might imagine, Dartmoor has its fair share of witches. Tales abound of these beings who, by skill and cunning, can transmogrify themselves from human to animal form and (usually!) back again. They often seem to take up the form of hares, usually in threes, and the symbol of the tinners was a circle of three hares, representing both themselves and a token against the forces of the dark. You can see examples of this symbol in the decoration of the churches at Widecombe and North Bovey.

One story is quite common on the moor, of a poor old woman who offered a service to the huntsmen, who paid a silver coin to anyone who could put up a hare for their chase. The woman was infallible and made a comfortable living, producing hares on demand. There was only one problem, however. The hares could never actually be caught, and while this was good sport it did not provide for the pot. Soon one huntsman decided to make an all out effort to catch the hare. He lay in wait all night, and managed to loose

off an arrow which hit the hare in the left shoulder. The next day the old woman was found in her cottage nursing a wounded shoulder.

The popular theory is that witchcraft represents an earlier religion that was suppressed by Christianity. In fact, the early Christian churches were far more pragmatic than that, and simply absorbed the practices and most of the beliefs into the local variation of their belief. Witchcraft today, called Wicca by its exponents, is a relatively young religion compared with the beliefs of, say, the Stone Age or Bronze Age people. It appears to be a variant of beliefs which worship not the Devil but the natural features and spirits of the world, just as the Romans had a multitude of gods for each aspect of life.

There are, of course, some people who have in the past and do today attempt to worship the Devil, and I suppose that the stone circles of Dartmoor are as evocative a place and as secluded as one could wish for such activities.

The Preacher on Pixies' Cross

On the down you can see a number of prominent standing stones, many of which are associated with interesting stories. The best tale is told about the Pixies' Cross, a crooked cross of a substantial size which lies on the golf-course between here and Tavistock. You can't see the cross from here, but it's such a good story, I think it should be told anyway.

The Windy Post, like many old standing stones, has been the subject of much speculation over its purpose. After the Civil War a local minister of religion was replaced by a churchman of extremely Puritanical beliefs, who set about converting the local population to a fundamentalism in which they did not believe. He became very unpopular, but because of the political connections of the ministry and their respect for the Church, they could do nothing about it. The minister changed everything. There was no dancing, no music, no hymn singing – no enjoying oneself at all. The congregation turned against their preacher.

One day the minister's attention was drawn towards the ancient standing stones around the moor in that area. He decided that the Windy Post, which was and still is a striking stone, was a pagan site which was a clear affront to the stark religion Cromwell's men had brought in with them. He therefore made his way to the stone to rescue his congregation from eternal damnation by carving a cross in its surface.

Off he set with his hammer and chisel, and started chipping away. The stone was extremely hard Dartmoor granite, however, and the preacher was a poor mason. The afternoon grew hot and the preacher grew tired. Sweating from his work, the preacher turned and leaned against the pagan memorial. He wiped his brow with his handkerchief and looked up into the sun to see a huge bull some 30 yards away, snorting and pawing the ground. Without a moment's hesitation the minister climbed the stout stone and perched himself upon the top, safe from the bull below.

The bull circled the stone. The preacher gripped the tip of the monument and gripped his faith equally firmly for protection. He prayed devoutly for the bull to go away. It did not. In fact, the bull decided that this intruder was definitely not to be trusted and settled down for a night of sentry duty to protect his herd from this dangerous black-gowned predator.

Come the morning the preacher was still up the stone, his hands frozen in a rictus of cold horror at the thought of falling down to meet the bull pawing the ground gently below.

It was some hours into the next day before the congregation thought to go looking for their preacher. When they finally found him, stranded at the top of the stone, he was a gibbering wreck, and the bull was walking away from the cross in a docile fashion. The preacher was rescued by his doughty congregation, and as a result was made a laughing stock of not only his parish but also of the parishes all around.

From then on, the preacher took care not to mess with the pagan stones, and took a more enlightened view of dancing and hymn-singing.

Bullseye stone

A bullseye stone is a device for ensuring that farmers do not take off more water than they are entitled to from the watercourses. The 1-inch hole drilled in the flat stone laid across the leat regulates the flow of water into a subsidiary waterway. The penalties for fiddling with the size of the hole were quite severe, as the consequences of a lack of water to cattle and crops lower down could be most serious.

Walk 12 – Sharp Tor, Leather Tor, Crazywell Pool

Distance
5 miles.

Difficulty
No great difficulty. You follow defined features all the way.

Main Features
Sharp Tor	**560703**
Devonport Leat	**561694**
Potato Cave	**565695**
Crazywell Pool	**582704**
Crazywell Cross	**583704**
Aqueduct and Cascade	**572714**

Description of Walk
Leave the car at the car-park on the B3212 north-west of Sharp Tor (**561709**).

From the car-park climb **Sharp Tor** to the south-west and admire the view over Burrator and the South Moor.

From Sharp Tor follow the wall towards Leather Tor and then make your way down the west side of Leather Tor (leaving it on your left-hand side). Join the track at the bottom running west to east across your path. At the time of writing the forest marked on the map which you are expecting to see on your right-hand side as you come down was about 12 inches high.

From the road at the foot of Leather Tor turn left up the track past the cross, and follow the vehicle track to the right and down across a modern clapper bridge over the **Devonport leat** before the khaki hut. After some buildings on the left part of the way down a steep section, you will see on the left a cave in the granite subsoil. This is a **potato cave**. Cross Leather Tor Bridge over the Meavy and continue up the slope bearing right at the Y-junction.

After a left-hand bend a lane goes off to the left. You should carry straight on here, but at the T-junction turn left. Soon the forest on your right disappears, and you get a superb view back down to Burrator Reservoir. You can see Newleycombe tin-workings in the valley between you and Down Tor opposite.

Soon you pass through a gateway onto the open moor. Continue along the track until you come across a stream crossing your path, coming down from the left from some old workings. Follow the stream up and you will soon enter the workings; after climbing the steep slope at the end, you will come across **Crazywell Pool** at the top. **Crazywell Cross** can be seen clearly from the track below the workings. It is at the east end, on the right as you look up the slope.

From Crazywell Pool continue up the slope until you come to the leat. Turn left along the leat.

From the cross climb up the slope until you meet the leat, a deep artificial watercourse running from right to left, and contouring across the hillside. Follow the leat until you reach the **aqueduct** after the **cascade**.

Climb down to rejoin the leat below the aqueduct.

Make your way up the slope opposite, aiming towards the gate in the enclosure wall. Continue to climb up in order to rejoin the main road. Turn left and make your way back to the car-park.

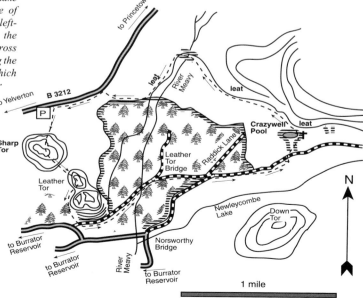

Drake's Leat and Drake's Drum

The leat above the Crazywell Pool is a part of Drake's Leat (properly known as the Devonport Leat), which extends today from the Dart above Wistman's Wood to Burrator Reservoir near here. The leat was constructed in the main part by prisoners captured in the Napoleonic Wars, but the concept of a leat carrying water from the high parts of Dartmoor to the rapidly growing port of Devonport was that of Sir Francis Drake. Although it is not described in this book, the walk along the course of Drake's Leat from Burrator to Wistman's Wood is highly recommended.

Drake, as befits the saviour of the kingdom, has a number of super-normal stories associated with him. He is supposed to have met and made a pact with the Devil on Devil's Point near Devonport, exchanging his soul for a storm which drove the Spanish fleet away from its track to the north-east, scattering it and causing the ultimate destruction of that great weapon of war. The savagery of the storm which hit the Spanish Armada was terrible. The Armada was driven eventually into the far northern waters of the Pentland Firth, followed by the weakened but courageous British fleet. The equally brave Spanish captains, unused to the ferocity of the northern British seas in winter, were unable to keep their squadrons together. Isolated one from the other at night in the horrific winter storms, the individual captains lost their ships to the rocks. The toll of men and ships ensured the safety of the British realm. The Spanish fleet never came again.

Another story is that Drake once sat upon the cliffs near Devonport, whittling a stick. Each piece of wood that fell from his whittling turned into a fully armed man-of-war.

Drake's Drum is housed in the abbey at Buckland, where Drake lived for a time. The abbey is open to visitors, and makes a good day away from the moors when the weather is foul. The grounds contain workshops where craftsmen make fine artefacts such as bellows, pottery and textiles. The story is that the drum will sound whenever England is threatened. Drake is not dead but merely sleeping, and he will awake at the sound of the drum to save his beloved country. When the German fleet surrendered in 1918, it is said that Drake's Drum was heard.

The story is very similar to those told about King Arthur, who sleeps under every prominent rock, waiting to rise and save the Celtic nation from its oppressors.

Crazywell Pool

This tinners' pool lies below the leat some way upstream from the aqueduct near Burrator. There are several stories associated with it, many of them to do with the supernatural.

The best known story is that the pool reflects the face of the next person to die in the parish if you look into it at midnight on Midsummer's Eve. Two young motorcyclists decided to test out the theory some years ago and rode out to the pool before midnight, settled down with a few bottles of beer and waited for midnight. They looked into the pool and, of course, saw nothing but their own reflections lit by the moon. They packed their bags and left, chuckling at how brave they were and how foolish were the inhabitants of the parish. They could take the mickey out of the locals the next night at the pub. On the way back to their lodgings they left the road and crashed into a tree. Both of them were killed outright. They were indeed the next people to die in the parish.

The local people say that the pool is bottomless. A party of locals is supposed to have tied all the bellropes of a nearby church together and they still did not reach the bottom.

Lastly, if you stay near the pool on Midsummer's Eve you can hear the bells of a church pealing gently below the surface. I suppose they are the bells of a pixie church.

The Cameo

Near the aqueduct over the river north-west of Burrator there used to be a remarkable work of art set in the side of the stone-block walls of the leat. If you walked about 100 yards downstream from the aqueduct and peered over on to the steep wall beneath you could see a superb cameo set into the stone. It depicted the sweetheart of a Napoleonic prisoner of war who spent his time when not working on the leat making this superbly detailed cameo from what appeared to be bone. The lady was fine-featured and had a high hairstyle, typical of the time.

I returned to the site in the 1980s to find that some 'art-lover' has hacked it out of the wall. You can still see the site if you look carefully, but what is saddest of all is that in removing it the vandal has clearly destroyed it, so that no one has the pleasure of it anymore.

& People

T he uplands of Dartmoor have, at various times in the history of man, presented a hospitable climate away from the malarial valleys below, and a wintry, windswept environment inhospitable to man and his animals. Farming as an occupation can be said to have been 'invented' in the late Stone Age, and by the early Bronze Age was in full flood. The Dartmoor climate was relatively good, and the clean air, fertility of the ground, opportunities for hunting and for gathering berries and roots to supplement the more usual farmed fare was an attractive combination for the Bronze Age farmer.

At the height of the Bronze Age occupation, at the time when the enclosures were being built and used, and the stone rows and circles were in full use, it has been estimated that there were some 1,500 – 2,000 huts on Dartmoor. These are spread unevenly around the moor, as one might expect, with the more fertile valleys having a greater proportion than the windswept, barren wilderness of parts of the swampy north moor. This represents perhaps 5,000–7,000 inhabitants of the upper moor, far more than are actually living in the same area today.

Certain sections of the moor – for example near Erme Pound and Legis Tor – must have been fairly heavily inhabited, with a village culture and a relatively high level of social and cultural activity. Other places represented isolated farming communities, trading lack of social contact for the advantages of an absence of interference from undesirable neighbours. Mostly, however, the small communities gathered themselves together for mutual protection, for social contact, and for efficiency of shepherding the farm animals.

We will look at a lot of the dwellings of these people in this chapter, seeing how they built their houses, how they kept warm and how they cooked. We can see how they kept their food stores free from vermin, and we can see how they protected their animals in enclosures or pounds. Above all, we will be able to catch a more than superficial glimpse of what it must have been like to be a Bronze Age farmer on the moor.

While we shall concentrate upon the Bronze Age, since that is the greatest attraction of Dartmoor in this respect, we shall also be able to take a look at the later Iron Age farmers, about whose stock we know so much through the work of the Rare Breeds Centre at Bovey Tracey.

Late Stone Age Farming and Life

It does not do to think of the late Stone Age folk as savages. They had a sophisticated set of tools and they had developed farming practices of breeding and crop cultivation which we follow today to a degree. They were instrumental in selecting and, at first accidentally, breeding wheats which gave full-bodied grain and stood away from the ground for easy harvesting. It was a Stone Age genius who decided to capture live wild boars and tether them to provide fresh meat without having to hunt his prey. As soon as he realized that two or more could breed, and how to feed them, pastoral farming had been invented.

The first farmers invented themselves around 6500BC in Greece. They spread by a process of diffusion until they reached the British Isles by about 4500BC. Generation by generation, without the need for any theories of massive and sudden invasion, the farming way of life spread north and west. The actual detail of the process by which farming is supposed to have entered Britain is under debate. Some archaeologists think that colonists from the Continent gradually set up their farms in Britain, while others think that the meso-lithic people of Britain travelled to the Continent and learned how to farm there. It really does not concern us here. Pigs, sheep and cattle do not occur naturally in Britain, and so the process of development of farming must have meant that these beasts would have had to have been transported by sea from the Continent. It must have been awful to transport great beasts in small boats over the notoriously stormy English Channel, and it is easy to visualize the chaos in the small vessels if they got loose at sea.

Stone scraper

VAB

The process of land development in neolithic times was straightforward. A farmer would clear a forest area, using the timber as he could, and then burn the remains, including the stumps. This would provide a good basis for the growing of crops after the land had been further enriched by animal manure and by the rotting of the stumps. From this time on the land could be ploughed with a primitive plough called an *ard*.

Villages at this time tended to be small, with either a long-house or a small number of rectangular dwellings grouped together. There is no example of a neolithic rectangular house on Dartmoor itself, but there is one at Haldon in Devon. The house was built of timber with a stone base. It measures about 8 by 5 yards. These farming practices and architectures were gradually replaced by the Beaker-derived equivalents from about 2500BC onwards.

Arrow head

VAB

Beaker Folk

In Britain around 2500BC there appeared a new type of pottery, representing a race of people who were quite different in physical structure to the late Stone Age, long-skulled people already here. These people seem to have arrived from two separate regions, evidenced by two slightly but significantly different pottery types. The first type originated from the northern European area, where the influence of incomers from the steppes brought about a change in physical and cultural characteristics. The second type, bearing the so-called 'maritime beakers', originated in the Iberian Peninsula. Both types of beakers were funnel-shaped pots quite different from the coarse pots used previously. They appear to be drinking vessels, and the fact that the Beaker Folk who brought them grew a greater proportion of barley (which can be used for the preparation of beer) indicates that the drinking of beer was a significant part of the way of life and possibly the religion of the Beaker Folk. The beakers themselves come in various types, some bell-shaped, some tall, and many covered with a pattern formed from impressing a cord into the wet surface to create the so-called corded ware.

In the south-west, the dominant culture soon became what is known as the Wessex Culture. This is characterized by a number of very rich burials with large quantities of gold interred with the body. It would appear that for the first time we see in British society the emergence of a dominant class of individuals who held sway over relatively large areas of land. Prior to this there is no evidence that there were any chiefs or kings with an influence wider than their immediate village.

Enclosures

In fact, there was no Wessex culture as such. The original people continued to use stone tools to carry out their own religious practices, and it was only gradually that the way of life changed.

The Beaker people brought with them at first only the ability to work copper, which was used to make knives and other cutting tools, and to work gold, which was used to make the most fabulous artefacts, such as the *lunulae* (gold chest decorations probably passed from one generation to another as symbols of status). It is surprising that the late Stone Age people either had no knowledge of gold or did not value it since it is the only metal which occurs in a substantially pure form in the environment. It can be found on the surface in Ireland and South Wales as well as in Scotland, all areas with which trading was carried out. Copper, however, is rather unusual, and requires the sort of temperatures which occur in pottery kilns, as opposed to open domestic fires, to purify it, but it was also available by trade with Cornwall and Ireland.

Gradually the knowledge of how to mix the alloy known as bronze began to spread, and the Bronze Age proper began in Britain. However, bronze and copper were still relatively uncommon, and stone tools continued to be used, albeit ones which were rather cruder than those of the Stone Age. Weapons of the time were quite sophisticated, with very attractive daggers being made, probably for ritual or ceremonial purposes from bronze blades with handles of bone and ivory. Other weapons included a rapier-like sword (later changing to a more conventional edged weapon) and a

succession of axes and spears, some of which were cast and worked with attractive patterns and animal shapes in the handles.

Present theories discount the possibility of a massive invasion of Beaker Folk from the sea, rampaging through Britain and imposing the use of their strange cooking pots on a frightened population. More likely is the idea of inculturation, a ten-dollar word for the simple idea that good new ideas do tend to catch on. Gradually the way of life of people changes as their hearts and minds are captured by a collection of ideas, artefacts and habits which constitute a culture.

In fact, modern man owes a lot to these rather mysterious Beaker Folk. They changed the way we bury our dead, which in the main part we do, just as they, in coffins in the ground. They brought with them metal-working, and trading in order to provide the raw materials for their tools, weapons and decorative artefacts. Lastly, they brought us beer, ale and mead, which we have, over the years, managed to change from a natural wholesome drink providing healthy relaxation from the rigours and stresses of looking after wayward cattle, into keg beer and tinned lager.

Or, on the other hand, it could just be that the Beaker Folk were just the first lager louts!

Early Bronze Age beaker

Most of the sites which we will be visiting in this chapter are associated with enclosures, often known as pounds. These are stone walls, usually about 3–4 feet high and substantially thick, which appear usually in the vicinity of huts in the areas where Bronze Age man was known to have stock. They are invariably placed near a supply of water for the animals to have something to drink. They are quite definitely not intended as defensive structures, as the Iron Age forts of 500BC onwards were, since in no case is the position defensible in the military sense. Grimspound, for example, while having a splendid view, is in such a position that defenders could be surprised from two different directions. Try it!

There are two possible purposes for these pounds. Until recently it was believed that they were primarily

Bronze Age Huts

used to keep cattle, sheep, goats and pigs in safety near the huts in times of danger. This is, of course, still possible as an explanation, but recently an alternative has been put forward to the effect that the stone walls were built to prevent cattle and other stock stomping all over the crops grown near the hut groups. The counter-argument is that some pounds were banked up on the outside with earth and small stones, which might have allowed animals to enter. Animals are quite agile – as one farmer said to me on the moor, – 'I reckon a fully fit ewe could enter the Olympics.' Generally speaking, though, even this arrangement would have kept the sheep and cattle, if not the goats, from the Bronze Age chrys-anthemums. On balance we can probably assume that the pounds were for both purposes, since in times of threat from either human or animal predators, the stock could be kept close to the huts while the animals were kept from the crops by wattle or other wooden fences.

The enclosures must have taken considerable effort to build. In many cases the walls are 7 feet wide. One of the explanations for this undue size is that they were also handy for using up the surface stone from inside the pound so that the ground could then be tilled more easily. You can see this very clearly as you walk down to the settlement at Walkham in Walk 19. The areas inside the pounds are quite free from small stones, although there are still the enormous lumps of moorstone cluttering up the insides of the enclosures. Generally, the outer walls were built with large stones and filled with smaller stuff. The builders used material close to hand, and used it without working it in any way. If you compare the stone used

at Grimspound in Walk 14 with that at Rider's Rings in Walk 15, for example, you can see that it is quite different, each being the local stone.

Some enclosures, such as Legis Tor, are built up of many smaller pounds, and you can work out which one was built first. In the Legis Tor example, the small pound marked A was the first, then B, then D then C. You can tell this because each successive one looks as if it has been nibbled into by the former. Many of the pounds use the hut walls as part of the enclosure wall, – you can see this at Legis Tor and at Rider's Rings. In others the main hut was in the centre, the striking example being at Round Pound. Sometimes the pounds are not connected to huts, and again, we can imagine that these were either for crops or for safety, although one would expect the enclosures for the safety of stock to be near the huts rather than isolated from them.

In most of Britain Bronze Age huts were constructed of wood in the main part, with wattle and daub walls and a thatched roof. On Dartmoor, however, where there was a shortage of timber, the huts were constructed with stone walls on the same general design.

A typical hut consisted of a substantial wall, some 3 feet thick, its centre filled with small stones. A conical roof was erected over this, and the whole was then roofed with turf or thatch where this was available. The roof appears to have drained out and down into the central cavity of the wall as far as we can tell, since this allowed the best structural arrangement for the roof. Excavation shows that the most usual arrangement was a central pole and a circular set of supports half-way along the length of the roof poles. This would have made a very substantial structure. A hole at the centre of the hut would have been

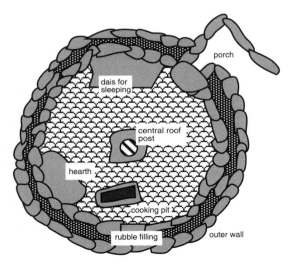

Plan view of a typical Bronze Age hut

porch

dais for sleeping

central roof post

hearth

cooking pit

rubble filling

outer wall

useful, but the likelihood is that enough ventilation was provided naturally for there to be no need for artificially made holes. The hearth was set to one side of the hut. There has been some suggestion that the large flat stones found in the centre of the ruined huts were originally used to block off a central chimney. All I can say is that you would not find me walking around a hut where a hundredweight slab of stone was likely to fall through the roof-hole and land in my wild boar supper. More likely is that these stones formed hearths or paving.

The doors in the latter parts of the Bronze Age were wooden, but animal skins would have been quite satisfactory. Latterly, windscreens were built to protect the doors from the prevailing winds, and many huts exhibit porches around their substantial stone door-frames. The ones at Grimspound, which are late Bronze Age huts, are good examples. The entrances, which must have become very damp in wet weather, were often cobbled and were dug out to provide a natural fall towards the entrance usually located downhill.

The huts were of varying sizes, from 8 feet to 30 or so feet in diameter. There was often a hut in an enclosure which was more

substantial than the others, and this is usually taken to be the dwelling of the local chief. You can see examples of such huts at most of the sites, but particularly at Legis Tor, Rider's Rings and Grimspound.

The hut interiors were excavated to about 2 feet, and then lined with stone slabs or drystone walling. The earth was removed until, in the Dartmoor huts, the growan, or underlying gravelly layer was reached.

By no means all the huts were used for accommodation. There were numbers of huts used for cooking, storing food, or for storing crops, or for animal accommodation. Some were not even roofed, but provided shelter from the cold winds for animals or while working outside.

The huts were usually grouped, often with a pound or enclosure associated with them. Pounds are described on pages 67–68, but here we should note that in some cases the hut was actually built into the pound wall, to avoid wasted effort.

Two other arrangements are noted on Dartmoor in addition to the pounds. These are farmsteads and villages. In the case of the villages, – for example at Standon Down, on Walk 16 – you can see a large number of huts apparently placed at random, but linked by wandering walls. The farmsteads, on the other hand, consist of a small number of isolated huts, together with a recti-linear field system. Kes Tor, which you visit in Walk 17 is a good example of a well-developed settlement of this type. Here you can see tremendous lines of Bronze Age (and later) field systems stretching into the middle distance. All you have to do to get an immediate impression of the farming industry of Dartmoor in 1800BC is to imagine these fields peopled by men and women tending their crops, chasing away stray cattle and sheep, and keeping watch for predators, both human and animal.

All in all, then, a Bronze Age hut, particularly one with the later refinements, would have provided a warm and comfortable home high up in the moors. It would have been straightforward to construct, and both practical and easy to maintain.

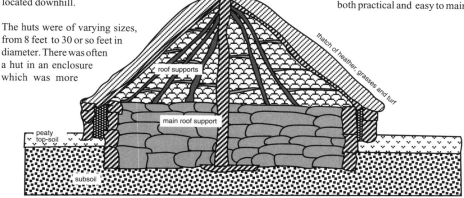

Cross-section of a typical Bronze Age hut

Dress in the Bronze Age

The materials available in the early Bronze Age were rather limited. Animal skins were still used extensively, and felted and woven materials made from wool were available. Sheep were being bred and kept as much for their wool as for their meat. Some unusual materials were made from tree bark which was broken apart and beaten to produce a felt-like material. Dyes were available from heather and fruit juices and these were used to produce an attractive range of subtle and hard wearing colours, many of which are still in use in the Highlands of Scotland today for the dying of woollen garments. The materials could be stitched with a thread and hole-maker to produce quite modern-looking garments. *Haute couture* they were not, but they were practical and attractive to the people.

Fastenings were a problem. The Beaker Folk did not bring the zip fastener with them, but they did have the use of stone and bone buttons. Jet was a popular material at the time, and the buttons were used in the same fashion as today. Also available were metal safety pins, often ornate in pattern, which served both as decoration and as a fastening, much like the kilt pins of today. Hats were probably felted or sewn roughly into conical or cylindrical shapes.

The likely pattern of dress was of a kilt and tunic, shorter for use when working in the field or hunting, and longer when practical in colder weather. There is no need to be concerned that the Bronze Age people suffered unduly from the cold for it is very likely that they had enough warm clothing and furs to withstand the winter weather of the time.

There was a substantial trade in decorative objects; we have already mentioned the kilt pins and buttons, but gold was used by the upper classes in the form of roundels (probably badges of rank), and as gorgets or neck decorations. Men wore decorative wrist guards for protecting the lower arm against the lash of a bow string, and the daggers which were worn could also be considered as decorative.

Bronze Age Religion

As the song says, 'Gimme that old time religion'. The Bronze Age folk of Dartmoor and south-west Britain had a religion older than Christianity, and we can construct a little of what they believed from the buildings, signs and artefacts they left behind. Of course we have no religious books like the Talmud or the Bible on which to base any philosophical definition of what these intelligent and capable people believed, but some of their rituals, particularly those to do with the ancestors and burials are really quite accessible to us today.

We are concerned here with the population of Dartmoor from the late Stone Age, through the arrival of Beaker Folk from about 2000 BC, into the late Bronze Age from 1400 BC and into the Iron Age from, say 500 BC.

During the earliest part of this period, Britain was populated by a race of men who had long skulls, used stone tools and buried their dead in impressive artificial caves above ground. These chambered cairns, as they are known, vary greatly in design, but many of them appear to have an element of design that allowed a funeral rite to take place at the entrance. The chambers were reused, and when full they were covered over with a mound of earth and stone to form the characteristic long shapes we associate with this period. We know that these people buried human and animal corpses in the foundations of ritual monuments, but whether these were sacrifices in the active sense we cannot know. The burial rites are rather disturbing to us today, although the Zoroastrians would recognize the procedures much more easily. When a person died their body was left in the chamber so that the flesh decayed. When the bones alone were left they were dismembered and put together, often apparently quite carelessly in one of the chambers. The bones were often placed indiscriminately among those of previous burials. From this we can infer that the late Stone Age people believed that the power of the body lay in the flesh rather than in the bones, so that when the flesh was gone the person had gone with it.

There is evidence, too, that the late Stone Age people had a particular religious interest in the sky,

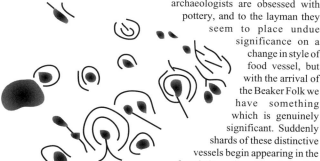

Cup and ring markings

stemming from the influence of the seasons upon them. This is shown by the alignment of certain monuments to the rising sun, which shines down the corridor leading to the central burial place. You may be familiar with this idea from reading about the Egyptian pyramids. In addition the stone circles of the time have some ability to measure the calendar, and we can safely assume that there would have been seasonal ritual activity at harvest time, and probably in midwinter as well.

Around 2000 BC, however, a new fashion arrived in Britain, with the gradual appearance of short-skulled people bearing with them a particular and quite new burial rite, and the ability to work metal. These are known as the Beaker Folk. The transition from late Stone Age to Early Bronze Age is so gradual and subtle that we refer to the period as a whole as the LANEBA, or late neolithic Early Bronze Age.

Quite suddenly we see the appearance of these characteristic beakers in all sorts of important situations. We all know that archaeologists are obsessed with pottery, and to the layman they seem to place undue significance on a change in style of food vessel, but with the arrival of the Beaker Folk we have something which is genuinely significant. Suddenly shards of these distinctive vessels begin appearing in the foundations of monuments; burials occur near large tombs, for example at Marden, where a young girl was buried with beaker pots; the major tomb at West Kennet is shut off with earth containing beaker shards. It was almost as if the old style of burial has suddenly become redundant and old-fashioned, and having beaker pots was the done thing. Because a beaker discovered in Scotland has traces of mead in it, it is possible that one of the attractions of the new Beaker rites to the existing population was that it had as part of it the need to drink intoxicating beverages, possibly with a hallucinatory effect. This would account for the position accorded the special beakers, which would have been used only for this ritual purpose.

Very significantly, the dead were buried singly in stone coffins in the ground. Beakers were buried along with the bodies and a mound was raised over them.

Gradually, cremation came to be popular. As the Bronze Age

who buried their dead. Some of the barrows dug out in the last century have yielded tremendous finds of bronze weapons and occasionally gold, since this was also imported by the Beaker Folk.

We can tell a certain amount from the archaeology of these sites. One particular site exhibits a succession of activities. Firstly a man was cremated, and his ashes put in an urn. A long pit was dug and filled with stones and the burnt bones of a

probably by dancers. Finally, that autumn, a pit was dug in front of the burial and wheat and barley were burnt in front of the grave.

We cannot know, of course, whether rituals were to honour the dead man or whether they were essentially seasonal in nature, but it is now easy to imagine the scene at the burials. We can gain another insight into the religious practices of these Bronze Age folk by examining the limited art which they have left. Most

Bronze Age burial – a cist

continued beakers became associated with the cremation rite, whereas the part of the population which continued to prefer burying their dead used a different design of vessel to place with the dead person, called a food vessel. It would seem that the beaker-users were of a different class, able to dispose of much more valuable goods with their loved ones than the lower classes

child. Then the pit was covered in clay and the man's urn was put on top. Next, another pit was dug and filled with stone, charcoal, a sheep's tooth and bits of bone. The urn was covered in rocks and turf and left until the following summer, when a ring of stones was raised around an ash-covered mound. The circle of earth between the mound and the ring of stones was then stamped flat,

prominent of the symbols used at this time is a version of the Celtic cross, which was carried over into the Iron Age religious practices and which at that time was used to represent the sun. Other marks are found on stones, notably the cup and ring markings that appear on standing stones. Unfortunately, we have no inkling of the purpose of these symbols, some of which represent parts of the body, others of which are swastika-like in design. An axe-like symbol appears in many places. The most likely story is that the cup shapes represent the moon, the rings the sun, and the axe shapes are symbols of wealth or power.

Some of the Bronze Age burials show evidence that certain individuals had the status of medicine man, or shaman, since they are buried with collections of herbs and charms such as animal teeth.

From about 1400BC in what is termed the late Bronze Age, religious practice seemed to decline, with more emphasis being put upon warlike behaviour than on ritual. With the arrival of the Iron Age Celtic people, Bronze Age religion became transmuted into a more understandable and accessible form which we know something about from the writings of the later Roman invaders.

In summary then, what do we know about Bronze Age religious life? We know how they buried their dead. We know that they worshipped the seasons and the sun and moon. We

know that certain members of society were shamans or medicine men, and that the ceremonies associated with death and the seasons were long and complicated, stretching over many seasons. Most likely is that death and the seasons themselves were inextricably bound together, with the death of the year and the birth of the growing season directly related to the equivalent events in human life. Certainly dancing was a part of the ritual. We suspect that there was an upper class Bronze Age people who continued to use Beakers in their rites and who had access to more attractive grave goods to send with their loved ones on their final journey.

Stand at the entrance to the huts on Grimspound and on Rider's Rings and try to put yourself in the shoes of a Bronze Age man or woman, perhaps preparing yourself to go with your family and relations to a seasonal ritual at one of the large barrows on the adjacent hilltops. Follow the shaman with sacrifices of wheat and barley, and imagine what it must have been like to dance with a score or more of other people at the burial site of your ancestors.

Cooking Methods

In your Bronze Age hut you have an open fire, some large stones and some small stones (fist-sized) and you have built yourself a hearth on which the fire sits. Near the side-wall you have built yourself a hole in the ground and lined it with four smooth slabs of stone, a fifth one forming the bottom. You have pots of varying sizes, but unfortunately, if you try putting one on the fire to boil water or make a stew or soup, it has an irritating habit of shattering, because it is slightly porous. So how exactly do you manage to cook yourself something to eat?

Let's take this a step at a time. You have a joint of meat and an open fire. The first method you can use is spit roasting. Wood is plentiful, and meat tastes delicious cooked over an open fire. You can also roast tubers and roots in the fire, as we sometimes do on Guy Fawkes Night.

A hot drink would be good. We can heat water by dropping red-hot stones into a pitcher. We sometimes use this method today – mulled wine is traditionally made by plunging a poker into the wine, which is effectively the same thing. There are, of course, certain disadvantages to this method. The sudden cooling of the stone does tend to make bits drop off it into the hot water, thus wearing out the teeth rather quickly. Until recently archaeologists thought that the wearing down of the teeth which is seen in Bronze Age skeletons was as a result of poor grain, but it is just as likely that it is from small pieces of stone in the soup.

Baking is a little more tricky. The Celtic lands today have a tradition of cooking grain over a fire on a griddle, and with a little imagination and a hot flat stone we can

Food pots

VAB

Tools and Weapons

certainly cook pancakes and flat breads. We cannot tell whether yeast was available, but unleavened bread is perfectly acceptable.

More prolonged cooking of a stew or a large joint of meat could be accomplished in the cooking hole. We do not know exactly what these devices were for, but they could have been used in two separate ways. First, they could have been heated up by lighting a fire in them, and then clearing it out, leaving an extremely hot space into which bread, meats or indeed stews in pots could have been put. Second, the dishes could have been put in the hole and hot stone heaped on top of them. In either case the cooking hole can be shown to be a very reasonable way of cooking.

So, there you are. With an open fire, water pots and a cooking hole you could have conjured up soup, roast meat with tubers, boiled wild cabbage leaves, and stewed fruit for the hut in no time at all. Hawaiian pizzas could have been a bit more difficult, though – no pineapples!

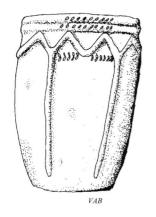

VAB

Cooking pot

As the Beaker influence began to affect the way of life in Britain around 2500–2000BC, the effect on the tools and weapons in use was small. The people continued to use the sophisticated and effective stone tools which their fathers and grandfathers had used before them. These tools were exactly what one would expect in a farming society. There were axes for chopping trees, adzes for trimming it and sickles for cutting crops. There were knives for defence and for working on skins and material, and there were daggers for self-defence. There were, naturally, no Stone Age swords, but there were spears and axes and war-axes. Many of these artefacts served a ritual or ceremonial purpose also. The skill used to make these tools, most of which were very small, is almost incredible. Early Bronze Age stone arrowheads, of which a few have been found on Dartmoor, are intricately worked pieces of flint with tangs and sharp edges that were cleverly attached to arrow shafts. If you try to make a stone tool, be careful as the pieces can be very sharp, but at the same time you will

Mould for bronze axes

be amazed just how difficult it is to exert any degree of control over the shape of what you produce. Not to put too fine a point on it (!) you are exhibiting about the same level of skill as your ancestors of a million years ago. The Bronze Age folk we are considering at the moment were as sophisticated at working their environment as you are your own, and you would be as unsuited for theirs as they would be to a modern city.

As copper came into use, knives and daggers gradually became available through trade. The cutting edge of copper is not very hard, and it must have been difficult to keep an edge. The daggers and knives were kept in scabbards, often lined with fur to protect the edge.

The most striking artefacts of this period are the swords and axes, which are works of art of a striking practicality. They vary greatly throughout the period, from simple axes which were not attached to the shaft in any way, through to the later Bronze Age axes which show an artistry and effectiveness which still appeals today. Early in the period the axes were cast in open (one-sided) moulds but later they were cast in a double mould which gave much more room for improvement

on the design. The swords begin with a rapier without a cutting edge, but which must have appeared a formidable weapon to a stone-axe-wielding late neolithic. Later the swords developed cutting edges and also had decorative handles of great and simple beauty.

Many of these tools and weapons were produced far away from the British Isles, notably in the Balkans and in the Iberian Peninsula. Travelling smiths went from area to area buying up broken tools and producing new ones from the remains. They would hide their stock in hoards which sometimes come to light today, giving some extraordinary examples and mixtures of tools. Metal-working was not a common skill among the farming folk.

VAB

Late Bronze Age sword

Disease

Life in 2000BC was not particularly healthy. Burials that have been examined have shown evidence of rickets, malnutrition and genetic diseases. Most common were tooth abscesses, caused by the wearing down of the protective enamel by poorly ground grain and the stone dust from using cooking stones to heat liquids.

Malaria was common in the early part of the Bronze Age, before the climate started to cool. Arthritis and rheumatics were usual, as the huts were very damp. It is likely that the common diseases of a hundred years ago, namely measles, smallpox, and diphtheria, were just as common in ancient times. At least one settlement was completely wiped out by an epidemic, possibly of the dreaded pneumonic plague.

On the other hand, there were no stress-related illnesses, traffic accidents were almost unknown, and the open-air life and food were very healthy in terms of heart disease and obesity. The high amount of roughage was also beneficial.

The big drawback in health terms of living in the Bronze Age was that in spite of what could have been quite effective plant-derived medicines, some of the disorders which today we would view as trivial, such as an infected cut or a broken limb, could be very serious and lead to permanent damage or even death. Mental disorders were not uncommon, and the operation known as trepanning (where a hole is cut in the skull to relieve pressure or to release an evil spirit) was often applied. The evidence of an over-ambitious trepanning appears in one of the Bronze Age graves. On balance I would prefer to be ill now rather than then.

Furniture

Very little remains of the furniture inside Bronze Age huts. We know that these people used both wood and stone to provide themselves with cupboards (actually freestanding shelves) and with a dais on which they could sit and sleep away from the damp floor. The bed platform for the man of the hut was always on the right as you entered the door, and that of the woman was usually on the left, although sometimes it was near the back. Bedding would certainly have been animal skins and spare clothing.

A hearth was provided for the fire, which was not near the centre of the hut but rather to one side. Associated with this was the cooking hole of which you sometimes see traces on the moor today, and in which dishes could be put to roast using hot stones or an overlaid fire. Cooking pots and drinking vessels would be placed on the floor or on low stone- or wood-built shelves around the hut.

It is easy to imagine tools and weapons being laid ready to hand round the hut.

From the remarkably well-preserved stone-built huts of this period in the northern Hebrides, we have an excellent idea of the requirements of these people, although it is obviously important not to assume that the way of life in the far north was exactly the same as that in the southwest. We can see there, however, that great stone slabs were piled one on top of the other, with smaller flat blocks between them to produce a kind of sideboard on which food could be prepared and stored. Food was also stored in large, conical, food vessels which formed the basis of the poor people's burial rites.

Trade

Looking at Dartmoor today we can easily get the idea that these communities were isolated from the rest of the world. This would be a mistaken view; some of the remains found in the huts show that there was a relatively well-developed network of trade throughout the ancient world. On one of the sites on Dartmoor, for example, a bead of a pottery type known as faience has been found, which at that time was only known in Egypt and the near-East. This must mean that such rare objects were available by trade from at least that distance.

Raw materials such as gold and copper were transported great distances by boat and man power. There were also thriving factories for the production of, at first, copper, and then later bronze tools and weapons from Iberia and the Balkans. We know from two huge dug-out canoes found in Norfolk that there was extensive river travel, and navigation around the seas of the British Isles, while risky, would have been eminently possible.

The hidden industry of the time is quite surprising. Salt for preserving food and for seasoning was being produced on the south coast, and rare, useful stones such as shale and jet were being exported, often in worked form, to the Continent. Bronze axes were being made in Brittany and were imported into Britain, as we know from some excavations of a wreck. Tin was being mined in Cornwall and copper in many sites in Britain. The inhabitants of Dartmoor would have been familiar with the sight of a travelling tradesman selling his wares amidst the substantial population of the moor, before he disappeared over the hill to the next settlement.

Stock

None of the traditional farm animals we associate with ancient farming were indigenous to Britain. Sheep and goats, cattle and the domesticated pig were all brought from the continent of Europe. Although we cannot obtain an exact picture of the stock at that time, we can get close to it by observing the differences between the Iron Age pigs and the modern pigs at the Rare Breeds Centre in Bovey Tracey.

We see that the 'back-bred' Iron Age pigs are smaller, more wiry, more athletic and generally more muscular than the modern pigs. They tend to be more active and responsive to their environment, and tend to go towards new experiences rather aggressively, generally presenting a more wild approach to life. We can imagine that keeping control of these sorts of animal would be rather more trouble than present-day animals, and this probably extends to the cattle and sheep which the Bronze Age farmers had to look after. I can imagine that the ability of a Bronze Age goat to get among the household vegetable crops would have been quite impressive!

Goats like this were common in Bronze Age times

Iron Age and Celtic Farming

During the period around the end of the Bronze Age, about 800BC, the climate was gradually deteriorating and the conditions which made Dartmoor so favourable for the Bronze Age farmers no longer pertained. We thus see little evidence of the isolated Iron Age farms which you can see in South Wales and elsewhere in Britain. The main Iron Age remains in the Dartmoor area are those of the hillforts at Drewsteignton and, in Walk 19 in this chapter, at White Tor, which appears to have been in use for a very long period before the Iron Age. In a similar way to the infusion of Beaker culture at the beginning of the Bronze Age, Celtic cultures began to eat their way into the Bronze Age peoples of Britain from about 800BC until the Iron Age proper from 500BC onward. The influx of more advanced and effective metal-working meant that farming methods became much more efficient, and the mere passage of time meant that the stock had

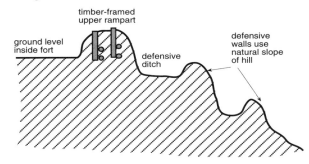

Cross-section through walls of hillfort

improved through selective breeding. Forest clearing was made a great deal easier with the newer iron blades in the form of axes and adzes, which had more effective cutting surfaces and durable heads.

Iron Age farms were larger than those of the Bronze Age, and were usually surrounded by a wooden palisade. One at least is shown to have been in use for over a hundred years, so the local societies were relatively stable.

The same could not be said, however, for society at large. As the Bronze Age continued in Britain the desirability of raw materials became a cause for open warfare, and we see in the Iron Age a further deterioration of the stability. Hence the need for the hillforts, which were always in evidence before that time, but which reached their height in the Iron Age. This was a time of warring tribes, equipped with weapons of certain destruction; the relatively peaceful life of the early Bronze Age had come to an end and was lost in time.

Nevertheless, the Iron Age farmers still continued the round of the seasons, raising crops, breeding and slaughtering stock and living their lives. Because of the presence of literate observers in the form of the Roman invaders of the first century AD, we can see quite clearly their motivations, their social structure, and their emotions and feelings. But that way of life is the subject of another chapter.

You can see the remarkable Iron Age pigs at Bovey Tracey in the Rare Breeds Centre, which are 'back-bred' to show the distinctive markings. See the pigs, observe the sty – smell the Iron Age!

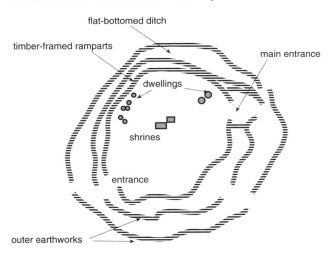

Typical Iron Age hillfort

77

Walk 13 – Ringmoor Down and Legis Tor

Distance
About 6 miles.

Difficulty
Many navigational features but does require care. Although you will not be on the highest open moor, the onset of mist and rain can prove disorientating. A map and compass are required for safety.

Main Features
Ringmoor Down Stone
  Rows and Cairn Circles **563658**
Legis Tor Pound   **570652**
Pillow Mounds   **570652**
Ditsworthy Warren House **583662**

Description of Walk
Park near Ringmoor Cottage **(558666)**. Do not obstruct the road and leave your car secure. Walk down the slope from Ringmoor Cottage and you will immediately see a green track going off to the left. This follows a wire fence and old enclosure wall until it reaches the edge of Brisworthy Plantation. Turn left over a stile and walk up the slope towards the top corner of the plantation.

Continue in the same direction over the brow of the hill. Note the reaves on your left, and a number of cairns towards the top of the hill. When you reach the brow of the hill, continue in the same direction towards Legis Tor. The **Ringmoor Down Stone Row** and its terminal circle are off to the left. Go to the stone circle.

From the circle continue down the slope to the left of Legis Tor, to where a wall crosses the stream **(567658)**. Cross the stream. Some 20 yards upstream is a stile on your right. Cross the stile and continue in the same direction towards Great Trowlesworthy Tor. Note the tin-workings on your right. Before you reach the Plym you will encounter the superb **Legis Tor Pound**. The **pillow mounds** can be seen just over the wall of the enclosure on the left as you face the River Plym, although they are not easy to locate.

Turn left upstream and follow the Plym along the same bank until you reach, after some time, a right-hand bend in the river. **Ditsworthy Warren House** can be found up the slope ahead of you and is easily visible (See page 36).

Return to Ringmoor Cottage over the clear track to the right as you retrace your steps towards the Plym. The track climbs a steep slope after crossing some tin-workings about 100 yards from the river.

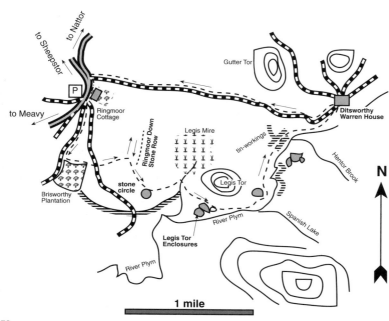

1 mile

Ringmoor Stone Circle

Ringmoor Down used to be known as Ryde Moor, and there is a story, told by William Crossing and others, that buried treasure lies below this part of the moor. The story is that if it could be found 'all England could plough with a golden share'. Please don't go looking for it as, first, it is illegal to disturb any antiquities; second, it's only a story; third, it's buried too far underground; and fourth, the proceeds are in my account in Zurich.

What you can do instead is to go and look at the nice stone circle on Ringmoor. It lies at the south end of a very long stone row, marked on the Ordnance Survey map. The row is some 300 yards long and has been restored. In fact five stones have been brought in to replace missing ones. Nevertheless it is still worth seeking out.

You can imagine the inhabitants of the large farmstead at Legis Tor and the surrounding downs using this stone row and circle for their social and religious activities. It is beautifully placed in what I consider to be one of the best scenes on the moor, with the dramatic and similar shapes of the tors around, over the Plym. It is a shame that the disused kaolin works rather spoil the effect, but with a bit of imagination it is easy to picture the scene populated by Bronze Age farmers and their stock. On the brow of the hill you can see the low, rounded shapes of a number of quite good undecorated cairns. These formed a cemetery for the area and also provided a warning to other groups that as they were powerful enough to be able to expend effort in creating the row, the circle and the extensive burial features of the cairns silhouetted all around, they should not be messed with!

Ringmoor Down Circle and Row

Pillow Mounds

Geographers apparently refer to some moraine features left by glaciers as pillow mounds, but those pillow mounds on Dartmoor marked on the Ordnance Survey map were made by warreners, or rabbit farmers. The name Ditsworthy Warren is derived from this practice. By raising a roughly dome-shaped mound above the sometimes damp earth they could make attractive and healthy homes for the local rabbits. Then they snared the rabbits and made them into nourishing stew for the tin-miners and farmers of the area. You can see at least two pillow mounds on the side of the Legis Tor enclosure to the left as you look at the Plym.

Spanish Lake

Spanish Lake is the river valley that lies opposite you as you look out from Legis Tor over the Plym. The word 'lake' on Dartmoor does not refer to an open sheet of water, but to a tributary of a river (often used by tinners), here the Plym. The name probably refers to prisoners of war who were employed extensively on the moor to build leats and other supporting features – notably Drake's Leat which links the high moor with the busy town of Devonport.

The name 'Spain' actually means 'place of the rabbits'. Maybe there's a connection between the warrens and the Spanish Lake.

Legis Tor Settlement

Legis Tor lies on the bank of the River Plym as it busies its way down towards Cadover Bridge and Plympton and a brief acquaintance with civilization before it loses itself in the English Channel. Here, however, the water is sweet and peaty, providing perfect watering for cattle. On the slopes of the Plym, on top of a small cliff, Bronze Age farmers had an extensive farming settlement, consisting of accommodation huts and outhouses, a boundary wall or pound, and an interesting vermin trap.

There are actually four enclosures, marked in the diagram as A, B, C and D. It is quite clear that enclosure A was built first, followed by B then C, and, lastly, the little corner enclosure marked D was added. The walls of the pound were originally about 5 feet thick, and seem to have been used to get rid of a lot of the surface stone which is lying around the general area – mostly clitter from the remains of Legis Tor itself. In the main part the builders managed to avoid the clitter areas, but in a place like this where the convenience of the water supply outweighs the difficulty of the ground, substantial amounts of rock had to be removed.

The ten or so huts in the compound enclosure are not all for accommodation; many are for the storing of crops or tools, or indeed for the winter protection of beasts. Each of the huts exhibits the characteristics of this type of Bronze Age dwelling. They are circular, with stone walls which were originally about 3 feet in height, with a dug floor sunk down about 18 inches into the ground until the solid subsoil was

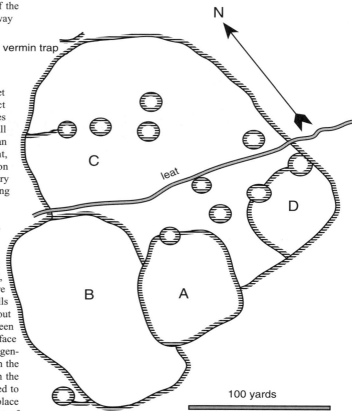

Legis Tor pound

reached. Today, of course, turf has reclaimed this central part, but you can easily imagine the hut walls as they were.

The entrances would have been rather low, and you would have had to stoop to get into the warm, thatched hut. Generally, the entrances were facing south-west or south, which is slightly surprising since that is the direction of the prevailing wind. The builders obviously preferred the more

frequent but warmer draughts from the south-west to the bitter winds blowing down from the north.

Stand in the middle of the pound or, if you prefer, on the upper slopes towards Legis Tor itself. Imagine the scene as the cattle are drinking by the Plym, with smoke rising from perhaps five huts in or near the enclosure. The women of the settlement are going about their daily chores of feeding young or sick animals, repairing the thatch

Legis Tor pound

and making or maintaining fires ready for the cooking of the evening meal. Some women are off gathering fruit or roots, depending on the season, and some of the men are guarding the cattle and searching for the odd sheep which has made a bid for freedom. Children run about and throw stones in the river, or perhaps even play neolithics and beaker folk (which is the Bronze Age equivalent of cowboys and indians)!

Inside the huts at Legis Tor a number of artefacts have been found including whetstones for edged tools, cooking pots and cooking stones, and hearths for the huts. One of the central larger huts had a complete cooking pot set into the ground in a cooking hole. The pot was broken, presumably through the impact of red-hot cooking stones being dropped into it, but was held together by the earth around it. There is no doubt that Legis Tor was a thriving community for many years, as the effort put into development shows. On the north side of the enclosure, if you look carefully you can see a double V-shaped pattern of stones which forms a vermin trap.

Vermin Traps

These are double V-shaped tracks of stones, meant to draw the undesirable rodent, be it a rat, pole-cat, fox or whatever, into an enclosed and covered tunnel. Upon entering the tunnel, the rodent trips a stick and twine latch which drops two doors on it, one behind and one in front.

And for supper, may I recommend the rat stew or the fox soup?

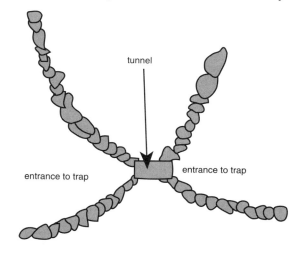

Vermin trap at Legis Tor

Walk 14 – Grimspound and Berry Pound

Distance
4 miles.

Difficulty
Not difficult. The ground on the flanks of Hameldown is steep, but not difficult in any way. Map essential, compass advisory.

Main Features

Berry Pound	*713803*
Blue Jug Stone	*708804*
King Tor	*709815*
Hookney Tor	*698813*
Grimspound	*701809*
Hamel Down Cross	*704801*
Boundary Stones on Hameldown	*70.79.*
Hameldown Beacon	*709789*

Description of Walk
*North of Widecombe, along the little road opposite the church, is Natsworthy Manor, once owned by the Duke of Somerset. Just past the manor on the left, before the road bears right at the southern end of a wood, is a track going off on to the moor (721802). Take the track which follows the East Webburn river at first. Soon the track bears a little left away from the river. Continue to follow the river. Where the ground steepens on the left bank of the river as you go up the little valley, you will find the oval-shaped enclosure of **Berry Pound**. It can be difficult to find in summer and autumn because of the enormous bracken plants that grow here in abundance.*

*Rejoin the river and continue up the valley until you see a boundary stone, where the slope levels off. This is marked **Blue Jug (BS)** on the OS map. If you want to see the one inscribed 'Grey Wethers', continue up the slope in the same direction. They are not difficult to find.*

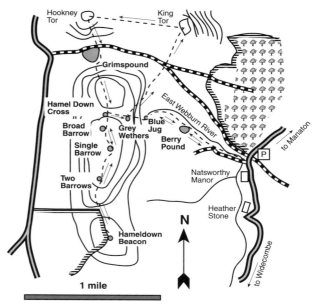

1 mile

To gain a feeling for the environs of Grimspound, it is recommended that you now turn north and walk over to King Tor, passing over the saddle between you and the barrow. There is another boundary stone just up from the saddle.

*From King Tor do not go directly to Grimspound, but make your way over Hookney Down to **Hookney Tor**, where you can view the layout of Grimspound from above it.*

*From here go down the slope to **Grimspound**, which is quite obvious on the opposite slope.*

An alternative route leading from Natsworthy is to take the track which runs to the right of the river, at first along the edge of the wood. This track goes up to the saddle under King Tor.

From Grimspound climb the steep slope of Hameldown Tor behind the pound. At the tor you will find a cairn.

*The walk along the top of Hameldown is well worthwhile. It leads past a number of **boundary stones** with names like **Broad Barrow**, after passing close to Hameldown Cross. Walk right along until you come to **Hameldown Beacon**, which offers superb views over Widecombe and its church.*

In view of the brackeny nature of the ground on the steep east side of Hameldown, it is probably best to retrace your steps until you come to Hameldon Cross again. Then go down the slope to your right, so that you will find the East Webburn on left. Follow the river back down to Natsworthy Manor and your car.

Berry Pound

In the summer it is probably not worth visiting Berry Pound. The bracken, which is the bane of grazing cattle and archaeologists, is as high as a man here and when it is up you can see little of the circular pound. I suppose hunting for the pound could be a good activity for a summer afternoon, though, and there are the remains of a medieval longhouse to the east which take some finding, too. The pound has suffered a bit over the years. It is too near the enclosed field to have escaped being viewed as a convenient source of stone, and the local farmers ploughed it thoroughly some years ago, so that there are practically no hut remains to speak of.

It is unusual because the site is rather steep, and this, too, has caused stone to slip from out of the upper, inner wall, thus further damaging it. Nevertheless, I like it. It has very few visitors, and has a certain atmosphere which the Piccadilly of Grimspound does not possess.

James Hannaford's Dog

If you stand on top of Hameldown Tor above Grimspound and look out to the west you can see Headland Warren House. This used to be an inn, which served the tinners of the mines that lie between here and Warren House Inn. James Hannaford, who lived at Headland Warren, was returning one dark and dismal night from the inn, when he walked too close to one of the old mine shafts. To his horror, his feet fell through and he found himself hanging from some old woodwork half-way down the shaft.

Luckily for him, his dog remained at the top of the shaft, and stayed there through the rainy night. Some time during the next day Hannaford's friends came to look for him, and found the dog still keeping guard. Hannaford was crippled by the exposure he suffered during the night, but he never forgot the debt he owed to his faithful dog.

There is a practical side to this tale, too, namely that you should take care when walking around places such as Headland Warren where there are known to be deep shafts. There are very few such places on Dartmoor, most of the workings being essentially surface ones.

Grimspound

This large enclosure, placed on the north slope of Hameldown, and overlooking the splendid Hookney Tor, has everything. It has about twenty-four early Bronze Age huts dating from around 1400BC. Because of its relatively isolated position the site has remained safe from the theft of stones which has ruined so many other Bronze Age remains around the moor. It is an absolute must to visit, and if you can do so by coming at it from the high ground above it on Hameldown, so much the better, since you can then see not only the impressive layout of the walls themselves, but also the fine position in which the pound has been placed.

Why is it here? Many antiquaries of the last century were of the rather foolish opinion that Grimspound was a defensive position, but anyone who seriously believes this has not played a determined game of soldiers here with their children. The site can be surprised from at least two directions by ten-year-olds with lethal bracken-stalk rifles. The pound is, in fact, sited here because it has an excellent water source available in the form of Grimslake, and has good grazing all round. It is set on relatively level ground, and has a generally open and healthy aspect. Besides that it is clearly a pleasant place to live.

What is it? Grimspound, like the other enclosures on the moor was a place in which cattle were put to keep them together and in which they were kept away from crops as necessary. We do not think that the pounds were places to which the Bronze Age folk retreated to defend themselves, even when, towards the end of the Bronze Age, the incidence of attacks by groups of threatening newcomers increased. More likely is the theory that they would have been good places to keep stock such as lambs when attack from wolves, or indeed foxes, was likely.

Grimspound would have had about eight or so inhabited huts, so that would give it a population of, say, fifty souls. Together with the sheep, goats, cattle and pigs it would have been alive with activity, with smoke rising, children playing and getting into trouble, women preparing food,

two separate walls, with a passageway in between, or one single, enormously thick wall, filled with rubble and stones. In spite of the situation of Grimspound, I rather favour the double-wall view, as if I were forced to defend it against wolves or other predators, let alone man, I would prefer to do it from a double-wall than a single one. An infantry officer of my acquaintance has other views, however. In his opinion, an attacker able to gain the top of the very thick wall would

Grimspound so special. Somehow when the hut doors are thrown down the hut circles look just like that – hut circles. But when, as at Grimspound, the doorways are substantially erect, the whole scene is brought alive, and you can crouch in the doorways and imagine what it must have been like to be part of this thriving and highly successful farming community. Most of the work of the Dartmoor Exploration Committee today lies covered by the ubiquitous mud layer in the huts.

Hut Entrance at Grimspound

or gathering nuts, berries and roots according to the season, and tending the crops. The men would go out hunting to supplement the pot and to keep down the predator population, and would protect the stock from theft or predation on the slopes.

The wall at Grimspound is impressive. Go and take a look at it. You will see that it seems to consist of two separate walls each about 10 feet from the other. According to your point of view these were either

have been in a better position to attack the defenders below him than if he were standing at the same level as them but outside the wall.

The huts here were excavated by the Dartmoor Exploration Committee in the last century, and they did a good job of building one hut in particular up to its original height. They re-established the central bearing stone for the roof support, the hearth and the doorway. But for me it is the door-jambs which make

Very few artefacts have been found in Grimspound – a few cooking pots, shards and some flint bits – but this does not mean that the place was not busy, just that the excavations are incomplete. In due course I am sure that the site will be excavated fully.

Here, too, the actual entrance to the pound has been re-erected. With its paved entrance and walls 6 feet high, the pound must have looked an impressive place to the tinkers who made their way to this upland village in order to sell their tools and repair damaged ones if necessary.

Lastly, we should perhaps ask who the Grim of Grimspound was. There are a number of explanations. Some say that Grim was another name for Grima, or the Devil. Others say that Grim was a Viking who set up his village here. A third theory is that the name drives from Graham or Graeme. Since the Vikings never penetrated the moor on any other occasion we can safely discount the second, and given a choice between the supernatural and the explicable, I'll plump for reality. So, Graeme's Pound it is.

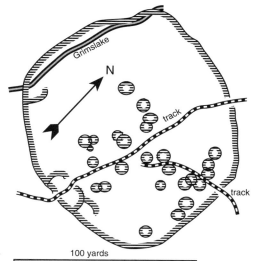

Grimspound

100 yards

Hameldon Beacon

You will have noticed that Hameldown is spelled in many different ways: Hamel Down, Hameldown, Hameldon, Hamilton. Place-names do get spelled in different ways, as many of them originate from a time when they did not need to be written down. Then when the map-makers came along they wrote down what they heard. I like the story about the English map-makers in Wales in the early days of map-making, who pointed to a distant hill and asked a Welsh speaker the name of the hill. He replied in Welsh that he didn't have a

Widecombe Church

clue, so the hill is now called 'Dim gwybod', which means 'I dunno' in Welsh.

Not a lot of people know that the kangaroo got its name because a naturalist hired an aboriginal guide from a part of Australia where there are no kangaroos, so when he saw a kangaroo for the first time he pointed at it and said '*Kangaroo!*' or, in English, 'What the hell is that!' And so the name stuck.

Whatever the spelling, Hameldown Beacon has fantastic views over the in-country, the lower lying land around the high moor. It lies on the line of beacon sites on which fires were lit to broadcast news of significant events during Elizabethan times in particular. News could be passed quite quickly from beacon to beacon, and there was no doubt that a specific message could be carried the length of the country in hours rather than the days it would take a man on horseback. There had to be no doubt as to what the message was, of course. It would have been a great shame to have lit the beacons to tell London that the Armada had arrived when the message started in Plymouth actually announced that the mayor's wife had just given birth to a baby boy!

The view to Widecombe and its splendid church is quite superb. The church is known as 'The Cathedral of the Moor' and its elegant tower commands the view for many miles. The tower is over a hundred feet high and is constructed in a splendid, buttressed, Perpendicular style. Although you cannot see it from here, there is a boss in the church which shows the traditional sign of the tinners, namely three rabbits, to commemorate their building of the church. Some people doubt that they built it, but there is every reason at least to suppose that they provided significant funds towards the building.

Crossing tells the story of a tremendous thunderstorm which took place on 21 October 1638, where huge stones fell from the tower into the church, killing four people and injuring another sixty-two. There are some lines of poetry in the church commemorating the event.

Boundary Stones

The boundary stones which are so entertainingly named in this part of the moor date from the 1850s and were set up or replaced by the Duke of Somerset, who took over the Natsworthy Manor estate at that time. The boundary stones in this area are therefore known as 'duke stones'.

> Here are some of the names on the duke stones:
> Broad Burrow
> Single Burrow
> Two Burrows
> Hamilton Beacon
> Old House
> Grey Wether (not engraved)
> Hameldon Cross (engraved HC DS 1854)
> Blue Jug
> Pit

Near the farm of Heathercombe, under King's Barrow, is another interesting stone with three fishes engraved in it. It was erected by a Mr Pike of Heathercombe. There is also a memorial stone which was erected to commemorate the crew of an RAF aircraft which crashed near here in 1941.

Remains on Hameldown

VAB

Bronze dagger

The barrows on top of Hameldown were, like many prominent remains on the moor, investigated by Victorian antiquaries in the late 19th century. These barrows on Hameldown were excavated by Spence Bate and Rowe in 1872.

They found Single Burrow rather disappointing. It had been cut into some time before and all that was left was a little charcoal, indicating a ritual fire, and a single flint flake. The site at Two Barrows, however, showed much more of interest. Some cremated bones were the first sign. Near the bones they found the handle of a dagger, made of amber with hundreds of gold pins decorating it. Amber was highly valued in the Bronze Age and

formed the basis for trade with the Baltic. The dagger handle dates from the late Bronze Age, about 1500BC, and was lodged in the Plymouth Institution Museum until it was destroyed in 1941 by bombing. Near the handle was found a bronze dagger blade.

The thought that this dagger was the property of the chief of Grimspound is highly attractive. It is easy to imagine the scene up here on the down when the body was interred with ritual fires of wheat and barley, and his personal goods were reverently interred with him by his relations and friends.

Walk 15 – Rider's Rings, Huntingdon Cross and Avon Dam

Distance
Six miles.

Difficulty
Requires care in navigation. Map and compass are essential. The ground can be wet at times. There are, however, a number of features to help you find your way, and the walk is not strenuous. Carry wet-weather clothing.

Main Features

Hunters' Stone	682632
Zeal Tramway	682632
Petre's Pits	658648
Petre's Cross	654654
Huntingdon Cross	665661
Settlement by the Avon	669654
Avon Dam	675653
Rider's Rings	678644

Description of Walk
Leave the car at Shipley Bridge, where there is a large car-park. The place is very popular at summer weekends, as is the whole of the valley of Long-a-traw, which is the river under the Shipley Bridge. Do lock your car and leave valuables out of sight.

From Shipley Bridge car park walk up the obvious track towards the Avon Dam. On your left you will soon see a metalled road leading to the left and signposted 'Avon Filtration Works'. Immediately before the junction is the **Hunters' Stone**. It is an obvious boulder.

Take the road to the filtration works and, after the immediate steep climb, ignore the road to the left to the works and continue along the course of the original **Zeal tramway**. The tramway turns back on itself and winds its way up the slope, leaving Hunter's Stone behind it.

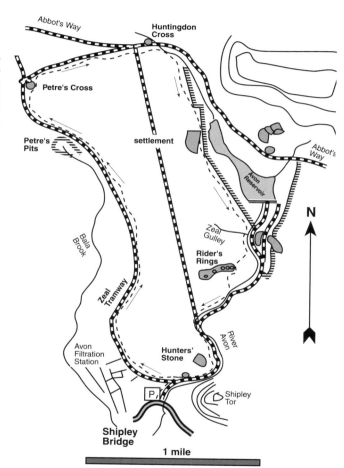

Follow the tramway for a long mile until you have climbed the left flank of Brent Moor. Eventually the tramway peters out. The small river on your left, the Bala Brook, runs down from **Petre's Pits**. Go to the river, and follow it up to the source, where the tinners' working at Petre's Pits will be found.

From Petre's Pits go north until you meet the tramway again. About three-quarters of a mile further on it comes close to the large mound of stone known as Western White Barrow. **Petre's Cross** is set here.

From Western White Barrow walk north-east, keeping the conical

Hunters' Stone

*shape of Red Lake on your left, and aiming for the valley between Western White Barrow and Huntingdon Warren. **Huntingdon Cross** is to be found on the left-hand side of the Avon as you move downstream. Regain the right-hand (south) bank. Head for the hillside slightly above the southern side of the Avon Reservoir to a **settlement**.*

*To find Rider's Rings, you need to continue around on the same level towards the **Avon Dam**, until you reach the little valley of Zeal Gully running west–east. Continue at the same level and you will encounter **Rider's Rings** lying to the top of the hillside where it begins to level off.*

From here, go down the slope until you meet the track in Long-a-traw. Turn right and walk down the busy valley track to the car-park.

Hunters' Stone

On the hillside above the Avon on the left as you go upstream, you will see a huge rock which commemorates the friendship of four hunting men, Treby, Bulteel, Colyton and Carey. The memorial was engraved by Mr CA Mohun-Harris, who lived at Brent Tor House. The names of the first three are easy to find, but the fourth is on top of the rock.

The Avon Dam

The Avon Dam was built in 1954. In spite of having drowned a very interesting valley and, for all I know, a beautiful one, it is not an eyesore, and provides a welcome target for the thousands of walkers who appear at Shipley Bridge on summer weekends. The reservoir is about 1° miles up a good track from the car-park along a beautiful stretch of pools and cascades over granite shelves. It is full of drinking water, so please do not pollute it any way by paddling in it or washing your dogs in it. The dam itself is almost 300 yards long.

In times of drought you can sometimes see the rectangular shape of a medieval farmstead just on the edge of the waters.

Petre's Pits

The pit is just the extensive and steep-sided tin working which lies at the top of Black Brook. It takes its name from the nearby cross. Several tin-workings have interesting names. Many have the word 'lake' in the name, from the water-working necessary to pan the tin. Others have obscure names attached – Dead Lake, Red Lake, Skew Gert, T Gert, Spriddle Lake, Hook Lake – the list goes on. We shall meet all these in the chapter on Tinning & Quarrying, and in preparation for that it is worth your while exploring the workings of Petre's Pits. Here you can see how the tinners have worked their way gradually upstream towards the mother lode, leaving banks of unproductive residue along the sides of the valley.

Shipley Bridge

The river running down from the dam above Shipley Bridge is magical. Even if you are not walking the route described here you can spend a delightful hour or two exploring the river just above the busy car-park. The picture opposite was taken within a hundred yards of the ice-cream van, where the river drops and turns as it falls into a pool. Take care if you go down into the river bed as the rocks are very slippery.

The river drops sharply over the steps formed as the granite wears away at its rectangular joints, thus causing the vertical and horizontal features of the river. Above the car-park the river sweeps over long steps with only low risers, following the natural lines of the rock underneath.

Petre's Cross

The cross on Western White Barrow is known as Petre's Cross. The name is derived from Sir William Petre, who was granted the church estates near by after the dissolution of the monasteries in 1539. Sir William died in 1571, leaving a son, John, who became Lord Peter of Writtle in Essex in 1603. His descendant, the seventh Lord Petre provided the model for Pope's *Rape of the Lock*

by stealing a lock of hair from his beautiful cousin, Arabella Fermor. Petre's Cross was erected as one of the boundary marks of Sir William Petre's new estates.

The cross is not that easy to see unless you know what you are looking for, as it is badly damaged and has been inserted upside-down into the remains of the barrow. The cross

was badly savaged about 1847 by workmen who built themselves a hut on the barrow. They knocked off the arms of the cross and used it as the lintel of a fireplace. The cross has now been recovered and there is about 4 feet of the shaft remaining, some of which is hidden in the cairn. Today you can see the tenon for fitting the cross into its base pointing up at the sky.

Zeal Tramway

Waterfall near Shipley Bridge

This track, which runs from a point near Red Lake to the buildings at Shipley, was used latterly to carry material to the China clay works at Brent Moor. Originally, however, it was built to carry peat from the high moor down to some naphtha works, which were bought out by the Brent Moor china clay company. The naphtha, an aromatic carbon compound, was extracted from the peat and used to create a number of products, the best-known of these being mothballs. The company lasted about three years.

The tramway had granite sleepers with wooden rails which were bolted to them. Horses were used to draw the wagons in the same way as at Holwell Quarry (Walk 32). The tramway was kept in quite good condition until about 1875 when the operations stopped. In its northern part it runs quite near to Western White Barrow and then descends to the large turf ties at Red Lake, where substantial quantities of peat have been extracted by teams of labourers working on the moor in all weathers. There were two sidings, one located about a third of the way along on Zeal Plain and the other at Western White Barrow.

Rider's Rings

High on the slopes of Zeal Plains sits the strange shape of Rider's Rings, a Bronze Age enclosure, in a set with the two pounds on the opposite bank of Long-a-traw. It consists of two parts: a roughly rectangular enclosure to the south, and a later, thinner structure to the north. There are about thirty huts altogether, so it represents a substantial settlement. The whole area around what is now the Avon Reservoir was heavily populated from 1000–600BC.

The thirty huts do not, of course represent thirty families. Many of the huts would have been storage outhouses or used to shelter the stock in winter. It would, however, be reasonable to assume that perhaps ten of the huts were full-scale family homes, giving a population the same as that of Grimspound, around fifty people.

The walls are about 5 feet thick, built in the well-known manner with two drystone outer walls with relatively large stone blocks, infilled with small stones and rubble. It is unfortunate that the area, like Berry Pound, is covered in bracken in the summer months, but it is still worth visiting none the less.

The pound is quite well preserved, being a fair distance from the nearest farming enclosures. Many of the remains have been robbed in the earlier years of the century by opportunists, and only the distant ones have remained untouched.

The hut circles in Rider's Rings are slightly unusual, in that whereas the inside walls of the majority are constructed with large slabs, here, because there is little surface stone slab, the insides are constructed completely of drystone walling. One of the huts exhibits a particularly well-designed fireplace, far more developed than the usual stone slab. It has a slanted fireback to shield the fire from the draught from the doorway.

The main characteristic of Rider's Rings is that the huts are mostly confined to the centre of the enclosures, with the rings, or pens, being arranged around the walls. This is rather unusual, since the Bronze Age pound-builders usually incorporated the huts in the wall. Possibly these huts were built after the pound was constructed. The

location of the original entrance is open to conjecture. One possibility is the gap in the southern border, where the stonework on each side appears to have been finished off neatly. Another is in the north wall of the newer northern enclosure, where there does not seem to be enough material left to fill the existing hole.

With its companion pounds and settlements over on the other side of the valley, Rider's Rings formed part of an extensive Bronze Age farming community. The grazing and watering here would have been good, and there would have been a certain amount of shelter from the prevailing winds. Altogether, it seems that the settlement was quite a good place to live and bring up your children and raise your stock.

Huntingdon Cross

This fine cross stands on the Abbots' Way on the ford over the Avon. The cross was erected about 1550 to define the boundary of the Manor of Brent, part of the estates of Buckland Abbey. After the dissolution of the monasteries in 1539, the estates came into the ownership of Sir Thomas Denys and Sir William Petre, who ordered boundary markers to be set up. This is the same Petre whose name appears in connection with the Pits and the Cross in the earlier part of the walk.

Huntingdon Cross is well formed and substantial. It is about 5 feet high and 2 feet across. It was an important waymark for the monks, whose duties included looking after the vast holy woolly flocks on the moor, as well as the human ones below.

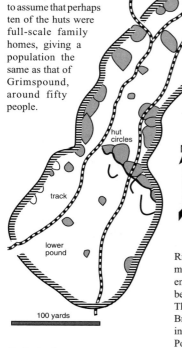

Rider's Rings

Walk 16 – Standon Down and Watern Oke

This walk takes you into a range area.

Check that no firing is planned by ringing the numbers on page 139 or by consulting the national park information centres or post offices.

Do not cross the line of red and white poles if firing is planned.

Distance
About 5 miles.

Difficulty
Map and compass should be carried. No great difficulty in walking over typical northern moorland. Crossing the Tavy can be tricky in wet weather.

Main Features
Standon Hill Settlements **552826**
Tavy Cleave **553832**
Watern Oke Settlements **566834**
Mine Leat **540827**

Description of Walk
From Mary Tavy take the road through Horndon to Higher Willsworthy and then to Lane Head, where you will find a large car-park at the end of the road. Walk back down the road, passing a farm on your left, and you will come to a small road on your left opposite a gate. High in the hedge you will see a signpost indicating the Lich Way. Follow the sign to Baggator via stepping stones. Walk past Higher Willsworthy Farm and through the gates in the obvious track. You will come to the footbridge known as Standon Steps after going slightly downhill and to the left. Cross the long footbridge. At the end of it you will find an old wall running across the track with a gap in it. Go through the gap and turn left, keeping the wall on your left. After a few hundred yards you will come to a gate leading on to the moor. The two enclosures to your left and right form a funnel ahead of you. The **Standon Hill Settlements** can be seen up-slope from here, about half a mile away on the breast of the hill, well above the valley, before the slope increases towards the river. There are some hawthorn trees in a group between you and the settlements.

From here make your way down to **Tavy Cleave** and follow the river upstream until you come to the point where a large stream joins it from the right. This is Western Red Lake. Eastern Red Lake joins it a quarter of a mile further on at the crossing known as Sandy Ford.

Cross the Tavy here on to its north bank. Go downstream now until you are opposite Western Red Lake. You can, of course, try to cross the Tavy at this point rather than walking up to Sandy Ford, if that is possible. The **Watern Oke Settlements** are opposite Western Red Lake 100 yards or so from the river.

From the Watern Oke Settlements continue downstream until you meet a large stream, the Dead Lake, coming down from the north. Follow this up until you can see on the opposite bank a track running away from the Dead Lake and in a south-westerly direction. Cross the stream and make your way to this track.

Staying above the Tavy, follow the track until you approach Ger Tor. Before you get to Ger Tor itself, however, you will pick up the traces of the Ger Tor Settlements.

From Ger Tor continue in a south-westerly direction towards the obvious road end at Lane End. You will cross **Mine Leat** on the way.

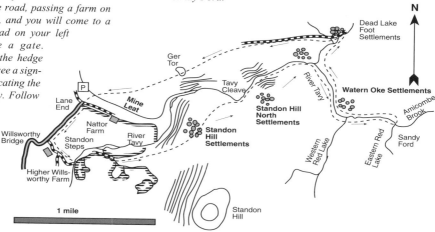

91

Standon Settlements

There are around seventy huts here, showing one of the best examples of an integrated Bronze Age village in Britain. Many of the huts were excavated by the Dartmoor Exploration Committee towards the end of the last century, and these huts can be recognized by their slightly deeper floors, made uneven by the trenching. The only other interference with the original huts has been the rebuilding carried out by shepherds, but these parts can be easily recognized as essentially newer in appearance than the originals.

The settlement sits on the bank of the Tavy. The original entrance which led down to the river where the beasts could be watered and the drinking- and washing-water gathered is shown on the diagram weaving its way between the huts. The huts are all linked with low walls, which would have stood about 3 feet high. Some of them are now hidden under the earth, but you can easily imagine the original network of low walls, separating various paddocks, where animals would have been kept when it was necessary for them to be near the village. These paddocks probably served as gardens, too, so that crops could be cultivated where the munching of Bronze Age sheep could be strictly controlled.

Hut A is clearly a magnificent dwelling for the chief of the village. Bronze Age societies seem to have been half-way between the purely local organization of the late Stone Age and the regional chiefdoms of the Iron Age. This transition was completed about 1400BC in the main part, and these huts at Standon probably represent a period around 1200–1300BC when local chiefdoms were becoming more powerful. Such stability was needed in a region where conflict and strife (brought about by a shortage of usable land as the climate deteriorated), were becoming more common. It is unfortunate that most of the huts, including the chief's hut, were paved, so that there is little remaining of the artefacts of this particular village. In the chief's hut, for example, only a single flint flake from a worked stone tool was found.

In some of the other huts the usual array of cooking stones and potsherds were discovered,

Standon Hill settlements

along with what seem to be the playing pieces of a Bronze Age game. The huts range from about 6 to 25 feet in diameter. As is always the case, not all the huts were used for accommodation, the others being either roughly roofed or not roofed at all, and used for storing crops, sheltering beasts, or for workshop areas out of the weather. Some of the huts show a late Bronze Age development, an internal wall in the hut. This was not to allow people

and beasts to live together (that uncivilized arrangement only came in later), but was to allow a little privacy in the larger huts. It also probably reduced draughts, too!

Look in the huts for hearth stones, for the stones which were placed at the centre of the hut to support a central pillar, and in Hut B for the two door-jambs which are still standing. Very near the doorway of Hut B you can still see the door-lintel which was placed over the two jambs to make the entrance. Going into a Bronze Age hut meant that you had to stoop down. Once inside, however, there was sufficient headroom, because the floor was dug out to about 2 feet to provide a neat wall, to reduce the mud in wet conditions, and to give good insulation against the cold.

The local name for this settlement is Standon Houses, and the tale is that they were abandoned because the Devil used to live on Standon Tor, and he used to make so much noise that the inhabitants had to leave in order to get some peace!

Tavy Cleave

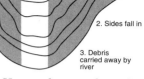

1. River cuts directly down centre

2. Sides fall in

3. Debris carried away by river

How a cleave is formed

The village was abandoned for a more believable reason, of course. Modern archaeological thought says that the adverse change in the weather around 800BC, when the climate became colder and wetter, produced a pressure on farming land, so that the continued existence of marginally productive settlements like Standon became less easy. This was not just because the moor became inhospitable, but also because the rarity of good farming land became a cause of a deterioration in the social order, so that open conflict became more commonplace. This drove people to gather together in more defensible places such as White Tor, where they could protect themselves collectively.

Coffin Wood

You may be wondering why this little wood is known by such a sinister name.

The wood lies on the Lich Way which links the centre of the moor with Lydford. In earlier times there was no opportunity to bury the dead in the villages of the moor, so corpses were carried across a well-marked path, over the streams and rivers at fixed points. One of these crossings was Standon Steps, and the wood near by was a place where the coffin bearers would rest in the shelter of the trees before struggling up the remainder of the route, which went through Willsworthy and Yellowmead and eventually to Lydford. The Lich Way is not named on the OS map here, but the track itself is well marked along the way, although on the higher moor it becomes rather indistinct in places.

The river Tavy flows through a narrow gorge-like area known as Tavy Cleave. If you look at the sides of the Tavy Cleave here you can see that the valley is sharply V-shaped. As the river has worn its way down through natural cleavage lines in the granite, the steep sides of the valley have then collapsed, leaving the vast amounts of debris on the valley sides. This debris is called clitter, or sometimes clatter, and is the outfall from the tors when they have been attacked by erosion, that is to say by physical battering or wearing down, as opposed to corrosion, or chemical wearing. The chemical wearing attacks the feldspar which you can see in the granite, and which appears in the form of crystals. As the feldspar is broken down its disappearance weakens the granite, which forms a gravelly mixture, grey in colour, called growan.

The River Tavy flows over horizontal beds of granite, which causes it to tumble down over rock shelves in a most attractive manner, forming little waterfalls and cascades.

The steep sides which you see on the edges of the cleave are even now in the process of being ground down by the frost and the rain. Eventually the whole cleave will be no more than a rough depression in the Dartmoor landscape, with nothing to mark it as something special at all. You don't need to hurry, however – it will take a few million years to disappear.

Tavy Cleave

Watern Oke

The Ordnance Survey map marks this hill as Watern Oke, but the local people refer to it as Outer Standon. 'Outer' is a typical Dartmoor word meaning 'furthest from home' as opposed to 'homer', which means 'nearer to home'. You can see this in the names for the two Red Lake rivers, which are called Outer Red Lake and Homer Red Lake.

The settlement here is a typical Bronze Age village which I shall describe below. In the area is a mysterious mound, thought by some to have been thrown up by tinners. It could well have been created by them, but the locals consider that it is some kind of fortification, and call it Lord Mayor's Castle.

There are nearly a hundred huts here, all dating from the late Bronze Age. They were thoroughly excavated in 1905 by the Rev Irvine K Anderson of Mary Tavy, who camped out for some weeks. Some very interesting artefacts have been found here, including a slingshot and a single blue glass bead, with a hole bored through it. This was probably an item of jewellery. Apart from that the huts, when last excavated, yielded the usual litter of discarded cooking stones (used to heat water and other liquids in pots which could not be put on a fire) and some stone arrowheads. Even though bronze was available, it was not used exclusively, and stone arrow heads seemed to remain popular right up until the Iron Age.

Some of the huts are paved throughout, to improve the living conditions, and nearly half of them show evidence of hearths, indicating that they were occupied. There are a few slightly larger huts than normal, which were probably for the use of

Bronze Age Stone Game

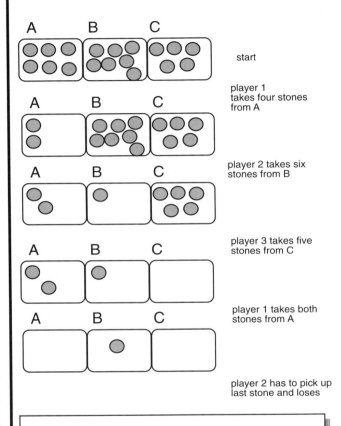

start

player 1
takes four stones
from A

player 2 takes six
stones from B

player 3 takes five
stones from C

player 1 takes both
stones from A

player 2 has to pick up
last stone and loses

Any number of piles and any number of stones can be used to start.
Any number of stones can be taken from any one pile.
The last player to pick up the last stone loses.

the local chief. My favourite hut is the one nearest the river, with its view over the River Tavy.

With over forty huts occupied, there must have been around 150 people in the settlement, which would have made it a pretty large village by

Bronze Age standards. You can easily imagine the hubbub and noise in the area as a hundred people and all their beasts went about their daily business. It looks a pretty good place to live, too, with a source of water nearby, and a good open aspect facing towards the south-west.

Ger Tor

The stone playing pieces found in Standon, and indeed elsewhere on the moor, suggest that Bronze Age farmers used to play their own form of Ludo after a hard day at the ard (Bronze Age plough). This may seem somewhat unlikely, but they could indeed have played games like the pick-up game pictured opposite. Why not try it?

Take a number of stones, say about thirty, and divide them roughly into three piles. It's better if the piles are of different sizes, but it doesn't really matter.

The players take it in turns to remove as many stones as they wish from any one pile on any one go. You must take at least one stone. The loser is the one who takes the last stone.

You can play the Bronze Age stone game with any number of objects (such as pebbles or wood chips) in any number of piles, and with two or more players.

Red Lake

There are two Red Lakes here. One is called Outer or Easter Red Lake and the other is called Homer or Wester Red Lake. They both get their name from the peculiar colour of the water and mud which comes from the iron-bearing ores in the area. The upper reaches of the Outer Red Lake were the subject of extensive peat-workings in earlier times in order to keep the mine and furnaces at Wheal Betsy, to the west, working away. Tinners have worked this area of the moor for many hundreds of years, but because of falls in tin prices, all the working has now stopped.

The Ger Tor settlements appear to have been defensive in nature, sited as they are on the north-east side of this steep tor. They have been excavated but did not show up any particular items of interest, except for some slingshots. Defending such a place would have been relatively easy, the very steep side of Ger Tor meaning that attackers would have had to outflank the defenders. A pile of stones for slingshots would have been a useful stockpile in the rather wobbly times towards the end of the Bronze Age. You may notice some reaves running along the hillside. They look like stone rows, but

they actually served a different purpose as field boundaries.

The view from here back along Tavy Cleave is superb, and well worth the climb up. Notice the Tavy below, and the leat which winds its way along the valley near it. Ger Tor gets its name from the word for a tinners' excavation, a gert.

View from Tavy Cleave back towards Ger Tor

The Mine Leat

As you descend from Ger Tor you will cross a prominent leat. A leat is a contouring channel which brings water from the high moors to farms and other users lower down. Leats are easily recognizable because they are punctilious in following the contours of the ground, are steep-sided and are regular in width, being usually no more than about 4–5 feet wide. They are cunningly sized so that you think you can jump across, but when you actually come to do it, you find one foot slips into the water. This particular leat is taken off the Tavy and was used to supply the mines of Wheal Jewell and, I believe, Wheal Betsy further to the east.

Leave leats alone; they are used for drinking-water for humans as well as for stock, so please do not foul them.

Walk 17 – Kes Tor, Round Pound and Shovel Down

Distance
About 3 miles.

Difficulty
No difficulty. Wear stout footwear as the section between Kes Tor and the Longstone can be wet. Suitable for all the family as the car can be regained quickly from any part of the walk.

Main Features
Round Pound	**663868**
Kes Tor Rock Basin	**666863**
Kes Tor Hut Circles	**667868**
Kes Tor Field Systems	**667865**
Longstone	**660857**
Shovel Down Stone Rows	**660857**
Cow Bridge	**662863**

Description of Walk
Leave your car at Batworthy Corner. Walk back down the road to **Round Pound,** which you will find on the left-hand side of the road.

Having examined Round Pound, put your back to its centre and walk at ninety degrees to the road up the slope. You will come to another less interesting enclosure after 20 yards or so. Continue up the slope to the top of the ridge, and then use the diagram on the opposite page to orientate yourself.

Walk down towards the wood on your left first and visit hut A. You will find Hut B located some 30 yards up the slope toward Kes Tor.

Between Hut B and the enclosure wall you will find the trackway that served the farmstead.

After you have had your fill of hut circles, go directly to the top of **Kes Tor** and find the splendid **rock basin** there. Then identify the **Bronze Age field systems** all around you.

From Kes Tor walk towards the right-hand edge of the large forest on the skyline. You will soon be able to identify the lonely **Longstone** menhir ahead of you and slightly to the left.

From the Longstone there is a clear track back along the **Shovel Down Stone Rows** towards Batworthy Corner.

From the bottom of the rows, make your way back towards the car along the obvious track. **Cow Bridge**, the final object of interest, is near the wall on your left below Batworthy Corner.

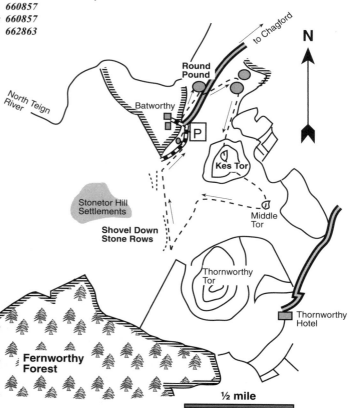

Round Pound

As you walk back down the road from Batworthy you will soon come to an enclosure on the left of the road. It is circular in shape with quite high walls, and sits like a fortification at the side of the modern metalled road. This is Round Pound.

The walls of the enclosure are very substantial, and are built of solid stone, so it is not surprising that the modern road-builders made their way around it rather than through it. The pound has been there for some 3,000 years, with various additions having been made up to about 1000BC by the original users, and then subsequent ones by tinners in more recent times.

These tinners set fires in the compound and in the huts, and used the area as a sheltered space in which they could carry out their smelting. In fact, they did not do a great deal of damage and the pound is largely unchanged from late Bronze Age times.

The pound consists of a large hut in the centre surrounded by a substantial wall and divided into five paddocks. At least three of these paddocks had their own entrance, probably shut by a wooden or wattle gate, with the other two probably having been used as crop-growing gardens or as storage areas. It is most unlikely to have been used originally as a defensive structure in any serious sense. There is also an unroofed stock pen north of the central hut.

A prehistoric field boundary called a reave runs away from the north entrance, and as this underlies the pound itself we can be sure that the field boundaries were set out first and the pound constructed over the

top of them later. This is consistent with the idea that the whole area has been subject to farming activity since neolithic times.

An alternative suggestion for the five paddock walls is that they are the result of a shepherd using the pound as a shelter in the 12th century. Fragments of late pottery have been found against one of the walls. Most likely, however, is that the walls are partly Bronze Age, with perhaps one or two being added in more recent times.

The doorway of Round Pound is as massive as the walls, which are up to 12 feet across. The lintel of the door can still be seen, and would have stood only about 4 feet high.

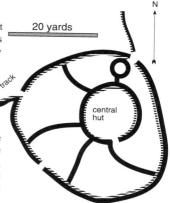

Plan of Round Pound

Quite why a lintel was needed in such a substantial structure as this is difficult to see.

Hut circles near Round Pound

Kes Tor Huts

As you breast the slope above Round Tor as described in the walk, you enter an extended field system with huts and enclosures dating back to the Bronze Age. You can see the present-day fields around you and if you look carefully as you cross the moorland you will detect the raised stone rows of the reaves, or field boundaries, which the Bronze Age inhabitants set up.

These reaves extend for miles across the moor in many areas, but here, although numerous, they are localized. The diagram shows only the main ones you will encounter, in order to allow you to orientate yourself to find the three superb huts in the Bronze Age village. Probably the best way to find the huts is to walk directly towards the existing wall boundary opposite. You will then find traces of a Bronze Age track running across your path, which will lead you to Hut A. This is a very impressive large hut, clearly associated with the field system whose walls (reaves) you see marked on the ground.

Follow the track roughly north-west and you will see on your left-hand side another superb hut, Hut B, which has a complete inner face of huge stones, giving an excellent impression of the inside of a Bronze Age hut. It has a garden or paddock attached to it. Other huts further up-slope, although not so well preserved, are worth visiting as they give a good impression of the density of population in this extraordinary area.

The huts were excavated by Lady Fox in the 1950s, and many artefacts were found in the huts

nearer Round Pound. Finds included quartz gaming pieces, whetstones and hunting materials.

Just sit in one of the high-walled huts and look around at the extent of the investment made by these early farmers in their village. The huts would have been conical structures dominating the scene all around, and the whole field system would have been populated with animals, and farmers looking after the stock. Fires would have been lit in the huts, and children and small animals would have been playing near them. The whole picture lies before you as you walk up towards Kes Tor in order to gain an overall impression of the settlement.

Kes Tor Settlement

The area to the north, north-east and west of Kes Tor shows clear evidence of an occupation by Bronze Age man from his earliest appearance with the Beaker Folk, but we can equally well be sure that the area was attractive to Stone Age man. A quantity of neolithic artefacts has been found within the enclosures of Batworthy, which you see opposite you surrounding the house at the end of the road. By 1889 over 6,000 scrapers, arrowheads and knives had been discovered at Batworthy. Some of these can be traced to a particular kind of stone found at Sidmouth, so we have reason to believe that Stone Age man had a trade route between here and the coast. This is by no means the longest trade route, however, for the great stone axe factory at Langdale in the Lake District exported material all over the country, and for all we know to the Continent as well. Earlier even than the neolithic farmers were the opportunistic mesolithic people, who also took advantage of the game in the area, trapping and gathering as they maintained their largely nomadic lifestyle.

If you stand at the top of Kes Tor and face Batworthy House, you can see around you the clear evidence of a large and well-organized community of Bronze Age

Kes Tor village

farmers. The prehistoric scene is dominated by a pattern of field boundaries which spread from your left to your right. Most of the fields were to your right, with about thirty huts being placed among the distinctive field boundaries and reaves. The settlement is rather more open than others in the moor, and this indicates a more relaxed lifestyle, possibly reflecting the early settlement of the area.

Even though the weather was rather more conducive to an open-air life in 2000BC, there was still a reluctance on the part of the Bronze Age folk to colonize the moor above about 1500 feet. Here at Kes Tor we see a comfortable, well-watered and pastured area, which must have been able to support a considerable community. To your left you can see on Shovel Down the ritual sites of the stone rows which served as a church and meeting place.

In the main part the huts are to the north (to your right) mainly because of the presence there of surface stone to provide building material for the inner retaining walls of the huts and for the upper walls which rose only about 3 feet above ground-level. Many of the huts here show the characteristic paving and inner walling of a Bronze Age hut, together with the hearth, usually placed away from the main entrance. Excavations have uncovered the usual array of domestic articles, hearth stones, cooking stones, cooking holes – used for baking and hot ember roasting – and pounding tools and knives, both made from stone.

As we have noted elsewhere, just because bronze was available did not mean that it was used for every purpose. Bronze was expensive, and actually did not produce as keen a cutting edge as a good flint. For cutting skins or butchery, flint knives

would have been cheaper and more effective. Bronze, on the other hand, did look good against the Bronze Age woven kilt and tunic, done up with a carefully braided and dyed belt. No Bronze Age chieftain would have been without his bronze dagger or sword, ideal for fighting because of its strength and weight. Compared with stone weapons using bronze was like a machine-gun against a pistol.

You can help yourself imagine the area in the Bronze Age by trying to rub out the makings of modern civilization from the scene. Remove Batworthy House and the walls and remove the road. Then add a warmer climate, and many more people busying themselves about in the extensive field system and out hunting for game in the adjoining hills. Then you will be well on your way to seeing the life that would have been spread before you.

Kes Tor Rock Basin

On the top of Kes Tor you will find a superb example of a granite rock basin. Such features have been the subject of much speculation over the centuries; during Victorian times there was a theory that they were the receptacles for the blood of victims of ancient Druidic rites. The more prosaic true explanation is that they are caused by the effects of freezing and thawing on the laminated granite. The moisture in the air is drawn into tiny cracks in the granite. When the moisture freezes, it expands and causes a small piece of granite to fall away. Over the years this will cause an undercutting of the rock into the shape seen today.

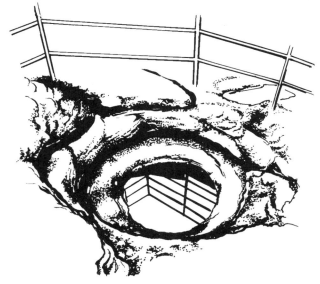

Shovel Down Antiquities

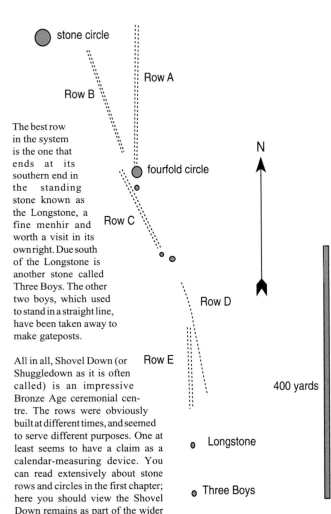

This extensive system of rows and standing stones formed the parish church for the communities at Kes Tor and other neighbouring villages. It is one of the best systems of standing stones on the moor.

As you can see from the diagram, there are really five different features; the group was not intended to form a single whole. You can see that from visiting the site and just looking at the alignments which present themselves from the diagram. You will find that many parts cannot be seen from the others.

The row marked A in the diagram is a double row which has lost a number of its members through robbery. It ends in the most unusual fourfold circle at the south end. This is a Bronze Age circle (as opposed to the Stone Age circles at Scorhill and elsewhere) and formed a structure within a burial mound, only slight traces of which can now be seen. The row was probably composed of matching pairs of stones, gradually increasing in size until they reached a blocking stone – a stone set across the line to end the row. As is often the case there is a barrow in line with the row.

The row marked B is pretty faint. It is 400 yards long, but has been robbed enthusiastically for walling stone.

Row C is more impressive, and consists of pairs of stones about 5 feet apart. It is 200 yards or more in length and still provides an impressive view of Bronze Age ritual monuments.

The row marked D is rather weak and turns to the right as you head to the south.

The best row in the system is the one that ends at its southern end in the standing stone known as the Longstone, a fine menhir and worth a visit in its own right. Due south of the Longstone is another stone called Three Boys. The other two boys, which used to stand in a straight line, have been taken away to make gateposts.

All in all, Shovel Down (or Shuggledown as it is often called) is an impressive Bronze Age ceremonial centre. The rows were obviously built at different times, and seemed to serve different purposes. One at least seems to have a claim as a calendar-measuring device. You can read extensively about stone rows and circles in the first chapter; here you should view the Shovel Down remains as part of the wider reach of the Kes Tor settlements, as they provided a ceremonial service to the families who lived here. They provided a centre for burying the dead, for measuring the seasons, and for meeting to celebrate the turns in the year's path.

The Shovel Down rows

Walk 18 – Foale's Arrishes

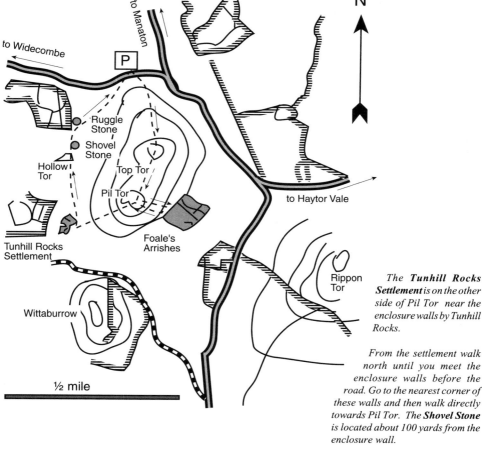

N

to Manaton

to Widecombe

P

Ruggle Stone

Shovel Stone

Hollow Tor

Top Tor

Pil Tor

to Haytor Vale

Tunhill Rocks Settlement

Foale's Arrishes

Rippon Tor

Wittaburrow

½ mile

*The **Tunhill Rocks Settlement** is on the other side of Pil Tor near the enclosure walls by Tunhill Rocks.*

*From the settlement walk north until you meet the enclosure walls before the road. Go to the nearest corner of these walls and then walk directly towards Pil Tor. The **Shovel Stone** is located about 100 yards from the enclosure wall.*

Distance
2 miles.

Difficulties
None at all. Wear sensible footwear. Ideal walk for any family.

Main Features

Foale's Arrishes	738759
Tunhill Rocks Settlement	731757
The Shovel Stone	733763
The Ruggle Stone	732764

Description of Walk
*From Widecombe take the Hay Tor road. Leave the car at the junction on the left after you have climbed the steep hill out of Widecombe. This is Harefoot Cross (**736766**).*

*From the junction walk to Top Tor, and then to Pil Tor, where you will see **Foale's Arrishes** down the slope to the left. From the enclosures walk back up to Pil Tor.*

*To reach the logan or rocking stone called the **Ruggle Stone**, walk directly west down the slope, to the enclosure walls and then turn along the wall. You will soon see it. It is situated about 600 yards from the Shovel Stone.*

To return to your car head up the slope and to the left. You will soon see the road; follow it uphill to the car-park.

Foale's Arrishes

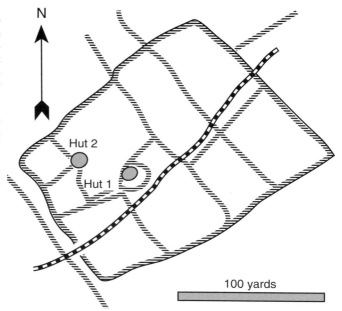

The word 'arrish' in west country dialect refers to a cornfield. Here the field used to belong to the inn-keeper who lived near by. The last owner of the pub, now long gone, was a man called Foale. So that's how the feature got its name.

Foale's Arrishes is a very late Bronze Age settlement of about eight huts, some of which show several interesting characteristics. It is a confusing site to visit because firstly, there is a lot of bracken around it in the summer months, and secondly, there have been many different colonizations of the site.

We can assume that shortly after the main influx of the Beaker culture, the site was picked out for its farming potential. We do not know for certain, however, what early Bronze Age settlement took place, because the excellent huts you can see there today are built on those original sites. There are eight huts, around the two in the diagram. One of the huts has a most unusual entrance porch which seems to have served no real purpose at all in the way of a porch, since it does not come across the doorway in order to shelter it from the wind. This arrangement is unique to Dartmoor, and was possibly a tool-shed or a kitchen.

The huts are quite large, over 10 feet in diameter, and show all the characteristics of late Bronze Age huts. They are circular, dug down into the ground (although you will not notice this because of the influx of soil), and have the usual fittings of a hearth opposite the doorway and a cooking hole near a wall. The walls were about 3 feet high on the outside and were quite thick, of the order of 5–6 feet. The roof was set upon the wall so that the water from

Foale's Arrishes

it drained into the core of the wall. The roof was conical and was supported in the centre by a single stout tree length, set on a flat stone in the middle of the hut. One of the huts in Foale's Arrishes appears to have had a bench seat in it, with flat stones set upon a framework of wooden stakes. Most huts of the period had a dais on which people could sit, or possibly sleep, in some comfort away from the rather damp floor.

The usual remains have been found at Foale's Arrishes. Cooking stones and flint arrowheads made right up until the end of the Bronze Age were very prevalent and were found on the site when it was excavated in 1896. Although we cannot see it on the site today, some interesting marked pottery has been found which has a decoration of a different

pattern from the usual chevron markings or twisted cord impressions which were used to relieve the monotony of the household crockery. This pottery was marked with crescent impressions from human nails. Now you may not think that this is a particularly significant innovation, but you must understand that archaeologists set great store by how people mark their pottery, and characterize whole civilizations by names such as 'The Black Pottery with Reddy Brown Splodges Folk' and 'The People Who Had Pottery Shaped a Bit Like The Hittites But More Rounded'. The archaeologists don't for a minute think, though, that the people actually thought about themselves in those terms. They had more sensible methods of characterizing themselves, like 'The People Who Live over That Big

Tunhill Rocks Settlement

Range of Mountains Who do Those Very Nice Fruit Pastry Things with Nuts in'. There is one big failure, of course, in this second approach. Fruit pastries with nuts in tend not to last for 4,000 years, not in my house anyway. Pottery, on the other hand, does hang around a bit even after it has been discarded. The pottery found in Foale's Arrishes is therefore important because it indicates a changing culture at the end of Bronze Age.

We can see at Foale's Arrishes, then, one of the last vestiges of pre-Iron Age settlement. The group of huts is very similar in layout to the other enclosures which you may already have visited, but it is smaller and more developed in its individual dwellings. Overlaying the site you can see the remains of medieval walls and enclosures, cutting across the lines of the Bronze Age reaves or field boundaries.

On the east side of Tunhill Rocks, which are roughly west of Foale's Arrishes, you will find some remains, marked on the OS map as a homestead. It is unusual in that there are two different shapes of hut here. One is circular and the other is rectangular. The latter rectangular type of hut is not completely unknown, but it is most unusual.

When the excavators dug the round hut they found a large cooking pot which was set into the ground and used to heat liquids such as soup or water. The problem with Bronze Age pots was that they could not be put directly on to the fire. The pottery was porous, and so water in the clay formed steam when it was heated directly, blowing the pot apart and depositing the nourishing stew into the embers. The answer was simple: a cooking stone was used. This was heated in the fire and then carefully dropped into the liquid in

the pot. Naturally, the pots sometimes broke from the impact of red-hot pebbles striking their base, but this did not matter because the pieces of thick pot were held together by the surrounding earth.

The rectangular hut is located near the rocks themselves. The excavators considered that it may be an outhouse or kitchen. Similar pieces of pottery were found in both huts, so it is suspected that they were occupied at the same time.

All around the homestead you can just see the remains of the boundaries of a field system which was used into medieval times. You can see a sort of gateway at one point which served as an entrance to the field system. Like most of these remains, the patterns are more clearly visible in winter time, but with care and imagination you can make them out during most of the year.

The Ruggle Stone

The Ruggle Stone lies about 800 yards west of Hollow Tor. It is an example of a logan stone which can be set rocking with little effort as long as the force is applied rhythmically. Unfortunately, although the Ruggle Stone is one of the best known logan stones it has lost the ability to rock over the past hundred years. The diagram shows why.

There are various stories about these stones, which are supposed to have magical properties. Druids are said to have used them in their ceremonies. The Ruggle Stone itself had to be 'opened' with the key to Widecombe church before it would rock.

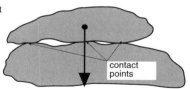

Top stone does not rock because it is supported at more than one point.

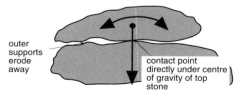

outer supports erode away

contact point directly under centre of gravity of top stone

The outer supports erode away and some stones are left with a single support under their centre of gravity. It can then be rocked.

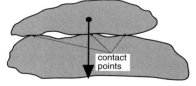

Erosion causes the stone to be balanced on two points again. It is no longer a logan stone.

Walk 19 – Walkham Valley and White Tor Fort

This walk takes you into a range area.

Check that no firing is planned by ringing the numbers on page 139 or by consulting the national park information centres or post offices.

Do not cross the line of red and white poles if firing is planned.

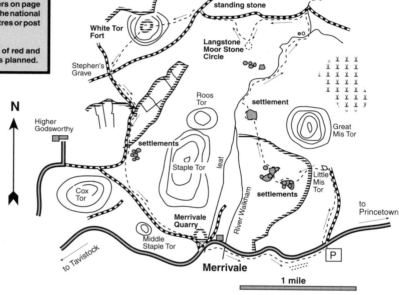

N

Distance
8 miles.

Difficulty
A classic Dartmoor walk. A map and compass are essential. You will be a fair way from the road and your car, so carry wet weather gear.

Main Features

Walkham Valley Settlements	556763
North Walkham Valley Settlements	555773
Dead Lake Settlement	565782
Langstone Moor Circle	556782
Langstone	550788
White Tor Fort	542787
Great Staple Tor	543760
Merrivale Quarry	546753

Description of Walk

Leave the car at the Four Winds car-park (**561749**) between Two Bridges and Merrivale. This is prime territory for car thieves, so secure your vehicle. Walk up the track opposite until you reach Little Mis Tor, the square-shaped mass of rock on the left of the path. From here walk downhill directly towards Great Staple Tor opposite, past a red and white range pole. You will soon come across a large drystone wall. Turn right along the wall and you will see a stile over the wall about 100 yards up the slope. Before you cross the stile, have a look at the map on a post near it which will allow you to get your bearings. Having crossed the stile, continue downhill directly towards the Merrivale Quarry. You will reach the **Walkham Valley Settlements** after passing an area of clitter on your left. You should be able to see the enclosure walls quite clearly from the slope above.

To reach the upper settlement walk towards some trees to the north. Do not go any nearer the river. This second settlement is about 200–300 yards away from the first Walkham Valley settlement.

From the settlements walk up the valley of the Walkham, keeping the river on your left. You will pass through a gate in a drystone wall, and then eventually you will see that

Grimstone and Sortridge Leat

the Walkham goes into a narrow cleft after a marshy spot (560779). Keep the river on your left. After the little cleft the river bends to the right. Cross here wherever you can (there are some stepping-stones). Follow the river around for 200 yards or so and you will see Dead Lake running into the Walkham from the north. Dead Lake is a definite stream enclosed in tinners' gullies. The little **Dead Lake Settlement** *is on its left as you look up the stream, located on a small plateau near the bottom of the ravine.*

Turn downstream on the Walkham and follow it back to the upper end of the ravine through which you have just walked. Here you will see a shallow gully going away from the river. Climb up the slope and you will find yourself on the lower reaches of Langstone Moor. There is another small homestead here on the breast of the moor before it flattens out on to the top. This is the **North Walkham Settlement**.

From this settlement walk up the slope away from the river and you will sight the **Langstone Moor Stone Circle** *on the flattish top.*

Alternatively, walk directly up the Dead Lake until you reach the track which crosses it near its source. Turn left here and follow the track, keeping an eye open for the Langstone Moor Stone Circle on your left about a quarter of a mile away.

From the Langstone Moor Stone Circle walk towards the prominent fort on White Tor. You should see the **Langstone** *at the path junction before you climb up to White Tor. Just across the junction you will find the stone row.*

As you descend towards the settlements, look out across the valley and you will see a remarkable line on the side of the hill which appears to climb up from right to left. This is an optical illusion. It is, in fact, an old watercourse which falls gently the other way, carrying its water down towards the south.

A leat is a steep-banked man-made watercourse which is used to carry water over long distances, on Dartmoor in particular. The leats can be used for many purposes. Many were built during the period of tin-mining on the moor to turn water-wheels which drove hammers to pound the ore before smelting. Many are used today for watering farm animals. In the days before organized water provision, most houses on the moor had a small leat running through them for the provision of domestic water.

The use of water on Dartmoor is a sensitive issue. In order to regulate the use of water by one farmer so that his neighbour's beasts are not left short, a bullseye stone or a small weir can be inserted into the narrow canal to allow a fixed flow of water to be drawn off. You can imagine that this could easily be blocked by

a neighbour who resented the amount of water being abstracted in dry weather. Similarly, the other neighbour could raise the level of the leat by the careful placement of a few rocks or turfs, with similar results. You can see one of these bullseye stones on this particular leat further downstream from here near the Windy Post reached by following Walk 11.

The Grimstone and Sortridge leat starts on the Walkham and was originally used for the purposes of tinners further downstream. It still runs and is used by farmers to water the many farm animals that graze downstream of here.

Without the leats the water would be confined to the lower slopes of the hills, whereas with a carefully designed leat the water can be brought quite high up as it contours its way gently downstream. There is considerable skill in setting the course of a leat. Do not pollute leats as many of them continue to be used for drinking water.

You will be able to get a closer look at the leat right at the end of the walk when you cross it to get back to the main road.

From the path junction make your way to the top of **White Tor**. *As you climb be aware of the fortifications made by the ditches on the slopes. From the top walk south to the track and turn right. Follow this track to the junction marked 'Stephen's Grave'. Here you will find a track running down to the left, which makes its way back towards Merrivale; after a mile it bends towards Higher Godsworthy. Leave the track here and make your way*

directly towards the top of **Great Staple Tor**. *From Great Staple Tor, walk directly towards Middle Staple Tor. About half-way between the two tors you will meet the track running down towards* **Merrivale Quarry**. *Take it to the main road.*

To return to your car, follow the main road to the left up the hill to the Four Winds car-park. Take care with animals as you walk along this busy road.

Walkham Settlements

There are over a hundred Bronze Age huts in this and its associated settlements. It has all the advantages that a Bronze Age settler would want: water near by, abundant building materials, adequate pasture and a reasonably sheltered position from north-west winds. It certainly appears to have been popular around 1200BC.

The diagram shows you the general layout. A combination of huts and enclosure walls makes up a group of huts which, because of their isolation and the savage clitter around them, have escaped the ravages of the farmers. Many hut groups have been utterly ruined by the quite reasonable desire of local farmers to build walls. The local stone was used undressed by both modern farmers and Bronze Age ones, so it is often very difficult to distinguish between moorstone lying on the surface and ancient construction material.

The best and largest hut to visit is marked on the diagram, and it lies outside the enclosure. It appears to have been the hut of the village leader since it is at least 4 feet bigger than any other. It is the first that you will see as you come down the slope towards the settlement, in all probability. Take some time to look around this hut, because it is beautifully delineated, and stands about 2 feet proud of the turf. You can see very clearly how it was made with two walls, one within the other. The roof fitted over this and rain-water ran down between the two walls. Notice how close the enclosures are to the hut. You can imagine the scene quite easily as you sit in the hut and look at the site of the fire, the dais and the central post hole, now marked by a slight lump in the middle of the hut.

One or two of the other huts are worth seeking out because they have door-frames still standing; two of them also have internal walls.

Try sitting in one of the huts and imagining the roof over your head. The smells of the cooking (and of your family!) waft through the hut, and outside you can hear the mooing of a cow as it makes its way into your vegetable patch.

The settlement upstream of this is interesting, too, as it has a number of huts with their door-jambs still standing and you can see a bury, or pillow mound, near one of the huts. This was a rabbit farm built by the tinners to give their main source of meat a nice dry home.

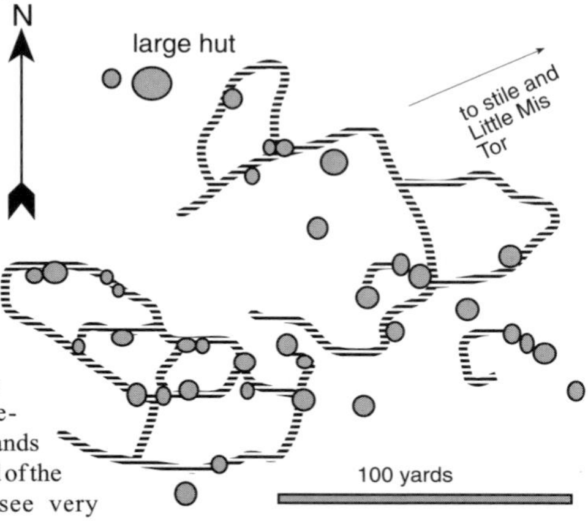

Reaves

As the intensity of farming increased in the Bronze Age and populations became larger, it became necessary to mark out the ownership of land. At first this was done by wooden fences and ditches. Later, more substantial walls of stone were constructed, and these later structures are known as reaves. They can extend for many miles across the moor and are characteristic of the prehistoric settlements on Dartmoor. On the side of White Tor you can see (depending on the light) the marks of these reaves, which form an extensive pattern of fields, each controlled or owned by an individual farmer or his family.

To archaeologists these fields can give important information about the make-up of society and the ownership of land, and can help to estimate the population of the area. Where there were a lot of families, the system of reaves was most extensive, and you can see here that White Tor must have been a veritable Piccadilly Circus in late Bronze Age times. Many of the diagrams and maps in this book were drawn up after flights over Dartmoor in winter, when these reaves are very visible – particularly in photographs. The reaves spread in great networks of rectilinear marks in the short lighter-coloured grass of winter, indicating the extended lines of influence of the Bronze Age farmers.

The area around Kes Tor is a particularly fine area for these markings, and you can see them simply by standing on the top of the tor and looking out to the north and east. Indeed, they are so clear that you can see the right-angled junctions of different farmers' fields. You can then examine their construction at closer quarters.

N

large hut

to stile and
Little Mis
Tor

100 yards

Dead Lake Settlement

The little settlement at the foot of the Walkham Dead Lake is not the most exciting on the moor, but it is a lovely setting, high up on the Walkham, and it has some unusual features. There are fourteen huts in the immediate area, which formed a small community. You can really only see three or four today because of vandalism and the ravages of time. The ability of the little community to expand was, as you can see, limited by the very steep hillside at the back, which confines it to the narrow bank of the river. The site is quite a good one, with neighbours quite near just downstream and decent grazing on Langstone Moor and further upstream. The early sun on the south facing slope would also have ensured an early lambing from the sheep which were grazed here. Notice how the opposite, north-facing bank of the Walkham has no settlement, even though it is sheltered from the predominant south-westerly winds.

The huts have been altered a little during their 3,000-year lives. One of them has been divided into three and another has been made smaller by fitting another wall inside it.

It must have been quite lonely up here on the moor, with only your beasts to keep you company. Even in the Bronze Age when the weather was decidedly warmer, the winters here would have been forbidding at times, and you would have been cut off from your neighbours for long periods in some winters. The huts here have no enclosure associated with them. Probably the natural

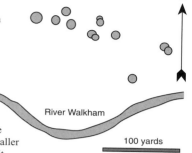

River Walkham

100 yards

Dead Lake Huts

layout of the slope served as a sort of containment for the animals. The Bronze Age enclosures which we see around the moor were used for keeping the stock near the huts in times of trouble, and for creating crop fields near habitation that could be kept free of grazing sheep and cows, and that were easy to till.

Langstone Moor Stone Circle

This circle, originally some 60 feet in diameter, was built before the arrival of the Beaker Folk in the early Bronze Age, who brought with them the use of bronze to the late Stone Age people. The structure consisted of sixteen stones in a circle on the side of Langstone Moor. There is some thought that it could have been one of the comparatively rare D-shaped circles.

In the late 19th century the circle was restored by the Dartmoor Exploration Committee, who could see the pits in the turf where the stones had originally been placed. The group re-erected the stones, which must have formed a very fine sight.

Today, however, the stones are not so fine. During World War II this priceless monument was used for target practice by the military, so that only three stones from the whole circle now remain in situ.

You can read much more about these early ritual centres in the first chapter. They were used as ceremonial centres by the people who inhabited the area before the Bronze Age folk.

There was no sudden disappearance of these Stone Age people, and we can imagine that the circles were used extensively by both peoples until they became unfashionable around 1500BC.

Langstone Row

The largest stone of the Langstone Row is called the Langstone, and gives its name to the whole moor. It is the chief stone of a rather good stone row which spreads northwards from it, and which contains twenty-six stones. On a winter's evening the wind whistles dramatically around this row, and I would not like to be one of the cows that seem to use it for shelter from the driving hail of December.

Only a dozen stones remain standing and they are not very high. The row has suffered from the same fate as the Langstone Circle, namely of being used as target practice during World War II.

White Tor Fort

This steep-sided fortification dominates this part of the moor from every angle, silhouetting itself against the skyline in a dramatic manner. It is the site of an important centre of power, and indeed of trade. From the flint flakes which have been found there, the hut in the centre of the diagram has been found to be the site of a stone arrowhead and axe factory. A huge concentric pattern of ditches, now somewhat eroded, surrounds a relatively small settlement, kept safe from intrusion by the steep walls and the ditches.

White Tor looks like an Iron Age fort, guarding the approaches to the lands to the east, but it isn't. Or at least it doesn't appear to be. It certainly does have the appearance of the steep-walled and ditched structures which we are familiar with from Maiden Castle in Dorset to the Iron Age forts in the north of Dartmoor, such as Raven's Tor, Cranbrook and Prestonbury (visited in Walk 29). But one piece of simple archaeology tells us that the huts, which are definitely Bronze Age from their structure, layout and remains, were built after the fort itself fell into disuse.

First of all, identify huts A and B on the diagram and then make your way to them. Have a good look around. You should be able to identify the ditches of the fort and the walls of the huts. Ask yourself which has been broken into to make the other. I think you will agree that it is clearly the case that the ditches were destroyed in the making of the

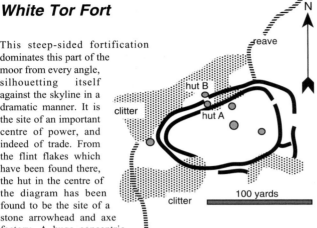

Plan of White Tor fort

huts. Hence the huts were built second, and the fort cannot be Iron Age. Congratulations, you can now call yourself an archaeologist!

This general area has been inhabited for many thousands of years. In the nearby valley, mesolithic stone tools and weapons have been found, and late Stone Age material has been found here too.

Apart from its splendid setting there is nothing extraordinary about White Tor. The inhabitants would have felt very safe up here, but they would have had a long climb to tend the beasts and to fetch water. There was little need in the Bronze Age to protect one's property since it was not until 1200BC or so that the pressure on land became so great that there was substantial intertribal warfare. In the Iron Age, of course, the rise of local chiefs and the smaller amount of valuable land and material per person led to a greater degree of conflict, and hence to a closer grouping of huts and settlements and the rise in popularity of the hill fort.

Merrivale Quarry

The last time I walked through Merrivale Quarry I was privileged to see at the side of the track cut stone that had been sliced by an enormous grinding saw into thin sheets a few inches thick. In them you could see the grains of crystal in the granite, forced up millions of years ago into the roof of sedimentary rocks above, and then cooled to form the magnificent diamond-studded sheets that glistened in the rain. Soon I saw more sheets, this time of the original sedimentary rock, formed million of years ago before the granite intrusion appeared. The sandy brown stone shone dully in the evening light, and the strange waves of subtle colour changes showed the patterns of the sand from which the rock was formed. The presence of these waves in the sand, frozen under the weight of subsequent layers of tide-borne sand, brought alive a sea-bed set in aspic all that time ago. It is easy to forget that Dartmoor is as old as time itself. In some respects little has changed. The animals live and die, the seasons come and go and gradually the climate changes – even today. Eventually all that we see will be ground down to a flat plain, and hidden in the rocks that form will be the footprints which you left in the mud today.

You can read more about the quarry in Walk 30, along with other quarries in the area such as Foggintor and King Tor. The quarries provided a lot of the stone for building the Princetown Railway which curves its way around the tors to the south of here. In fact, the promontory of large stones which you see as you leave the quarry was intended to be part of a link with that railway, to avoid having to take the quarry stone out by road.

Roos Tor Settlement

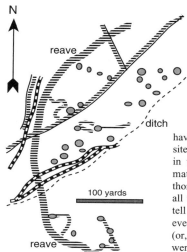

The Roos Tor huts

As you come out of the modern enclosures on your way to Staple Tor you will pass the very large settlement of Roos Tor. There are over seventy huts here, none of which has been excavated. This may not immediately seem to be an advantage to you, but the damage done by well-meaning diggers, even those as well organized as the Dartmoor Exploration Committee, who operated in the late 19th century, can be considerable. There is a great debate going on today as to whether we have the right to excavate major sites since those who have excavated in the past have often destroyed material. You cannot dig a site thoroughly twice, since you destroy all the layers in the ground which tell so much about the timing of events, and the time that artefacts (or, to use a technical term, things) were discarded or lost.

The boundary reave here is particularly thick and large, and where the tracks shown in the diagram pass through it is quite well preserved. It appears to have been a boundary marker to ensure that the people from the settlement opposite, on Cox Tor, knew their place.

The huts below the ditch which runs through the site are the best preserved.

Shillapark Farm

On your way down from Staple Tor you can see the upland farm of Shillapark. It is interesting to contrast the style of farming here with that of the Bronze Age and Iron Age farmers whose settlements you have just visited.

Both farmers are subject to the weather of the moor, Both have beasts to look after in all weathers and both have to keep warm and dry. Each also makes an enclosure of his land. At Shillapark this is primarily to keep the beasts in when necessary, but it also serves, as did the Bronze Age enclosures, to keep the animals from the crops. Both farmers have cows and sheep. The Bronze Age sheep were interbred with the goats (known as ovi-caprids), whereas the Shillapark stock is genetically sound and bred deliberately to produce a hardy stock. The Bronze Age farmers tended to use sheep and goat milk almost exclusively, as the cattle of the day were rather wild and did not give good, regular supplies of milk.

And, of course, the Bronze Age farms received no financial aid from the European Union!

Staple Tor

Staple Tor is one of the finest tors on the moor, and its remarkable towers and spires form a marvellous seat from which to survey one of the best views. Many people have seen animals and people in the rocks, and you could well spend a half hour doing the same.

The towers from which the tors get their name (from *twr*, the Celtic for tower), are formed by a combination of wind and frost getting into the cracks in the granite, thereby forming rectangular jointing systems. These are further eroded by water getting into the cracks. When the frost comes in the winter, the water expands, producing huge pressures which split off pieces of the granite. Staple Tor is one of the best examples of the final effect of thousands of years of wearing down by this process.

The spires of Staple Tor

109

Geography

& Geology

T he prospect of Dartmoor from the point of view of the writer of a textbook on physical geography is a promising one. Here we can see the effects of millions of years of geological change, as rocks rose, crumpled, were driven back into the Earth's mantle, and rose again as huge bubbles of granite. In the great tors of the north moor, huge grey behemoths lumbering slowly over the landscape, we can see the effects of the upwelling of granite underneath a thick cap of sedimentary rocks, laid down when south-west England lay under a shallow tropical sea some 500 million years ago. As the granite rose it cooled and cracked into the square, jointed structures we see today. It is difficult to visualize the huge mountains which were created over the granite boss as the Variscan mountain folding took place some 280 million years ago. The resultant mountains, at least as high as the present Alps, were formed during a period in the history of Devon which, in geological terms, was violent, nasty and brutish.

Other processes are not so violent. We shall trace the life of a river as it makes its way down from the peaty uplands, rushing down over ancient sea-cliffs to meander over what used to be a beach, but is now a soggy upland with brown, limpid pools and cattle paddling in its shallows. We can see the effect of rocks on the formation of waterfalls, and look at the formation of meanders. We can see the effect of a river as it runs through ground of differing hardness, and lastly we can enjoy the sheer beauty of Dartmoor rivers as they plunge off the moor and into the wooded valleys of the lower in-country.

We must not forget the peat. This great, green, wet desert in both south and north moors makes Dartmoor what it is. It provides a haven for wildlife and a reservoir of water for both man and beast.

If you wish you can view the walks in this chapter as just that; walks which you can enjoy without studying the supporting text in any great detail. I have aimed in this chapter, however, to give you something interesting to think about as you plod along over the high moor on what are some of the longer walks in the book. Geographical features tend to be picturesque in themselves, so the enjoyment of the walks should not be harmed by the more technical descriptions. For me, knowing how a waterfall grows adds to its beauty rather than detracts from it, but I fully understand those people who simply want to walk and enjoy the scenery rather than arguing about how it came to be there. But if I can interest you at all in the way in which the rivers run and the tors stand, I will be satisfied.

Rock Types

There are only three types of rocks and they are classified according to their origins.

The easiest to understand are the igneous rocks. These are rocks that come directly from the hot material underneath the crust of the Earth. The material is under great pressure in the Earth's mantle, and when a path opens to release that pressure, the hot rock becomes molten, and can be pushed towards the surface. Sometimes the rock is spurted out directly to form what are known as extrusive rocks. An example of such extrusion would be an erupting volcano. When this happens, cooling is extremely quick at the surface and rocks which we know as lava and basalt are formed. When the molten rock cools more slowly and under pressure, normally when it works its way gradually upwards into other rocks, it forms intrusive rocks, such as granite. As the rock cools more slowly crystals of minerals can form, and it is this slower cooling which gives certain types of granite their almost pearly appearance. It is during this cooling process that the beds of minerals and metals are formed which eventually produce lodes of ore such as those of the tin, iron and other minerals which are mined on Dartmoor.

The second type of rocks are formed by the accumulation of layer upon layer of material under water; these are known as sedimentary rocks. In any body of water, mud and debris fall to the bottom, and after millions of years the pressure from the layers on top can cause the layers first laid down to change form, to harden and to become rock. Normally these rocks are rather soft, but some limestones which have been pressured for millions of years can be very hard. Some sedimentary rocks are quite soft,– chalk, for example, which has a very high percentage of shells in its original composition. Other basic construction materials for sedimentary rocks are coral reefs, sands and muds. These sedimentary rocks can contain large numbers of fossils, which are hardened shells of animals trapped in the layers. If you can get a sight of these rocks after they have been sliced cleanly by a stone-cutter's saw – for example at Merrivale Quarry – you will be able to see the remarkable way in which sandstones retain the original wave markings of the beaches from which they were made.

The last type is called metamorphic rock. These rocks are formed when molten rock is brought into contact with existing rock. The added heat of the intrusion then alters the nature of the original rocks. This process is very significant in the Dartmoor area, because when the granite batholith rose underneath the existing sedimentary rocks, a ring of changed, metamorphic rock was created. This is known as the metamorphic aureole, and its effects can be seen today in the geological map of Dartmoor (see left).

Boundary of National Park

Granite

Metamorphic Rocks

Geological Eras

The diagram on the next page shows the names which geologists use to describe different periods of time in the Earth's history.

The Earth began life around 4,600 million years ago, and the period from today back to that time is shown on the left. Geologists divide that enormous period of time into seven eras, from the oldest, the Archaean, to the youngest, the Cenozoic. The period up until 570 million years ago is known as the Precambrian age. Before that time it is very difficult to date rocks accurately, but after that time sea animals began to appear, and the rocks can be dated relatively accurately. Therefore, before the Precambrian age the geologists know very little about the detailed history of the rocks, although (before any geologists take offence) they do know a lot about the general history.

In the diagram, the time from now until the end of the Precambrian age has been expanded, and is shown on the right-hand column. Here you can see the smaller subdivisions, known to geologists as periods, such as the Permian period, when Britain was in a tropical desert climate, and the Jurassic, when dinosaurs walked around the country.

Do remember the time-scale. The Precambrian age covers 80 per cent of the whole life of the Earth. Dartmoor rose out of the Earth's mantle only(!) about 300 million years ago, less than 10 per cent of the age of the Earth. Man appeared at about 1 per cent of the age of the Earth.

Much of the surface of Dartmoor was produced over the past 200 million years, when the granite core was exposed by weathering.

Geography & Geology

The Geological Calendar

The vast majority of the Earth's life is unknown to us because we cannot date accurately rocks that formed before the beginning of the Cambrian period when marine animals began to appear.

The time after this is shown on the right, with the key events in the formation of Dartmoor shown at the side.

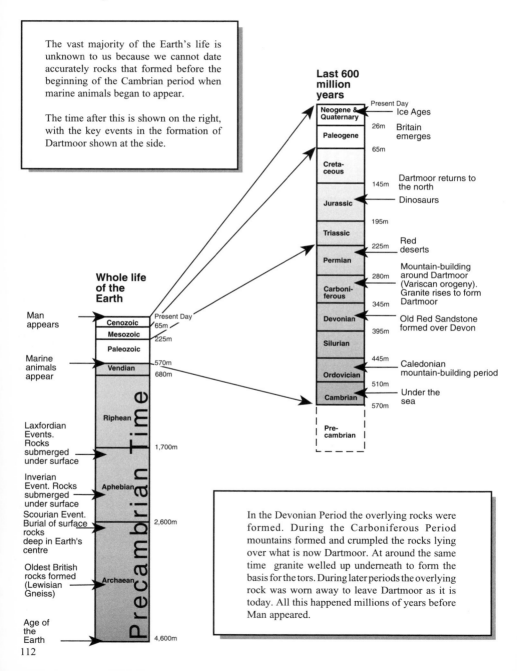

In the Devonian Period the overlying rocks were formed. During the Carboniferous Period mountains formed and crumpled the rocks lying over what is now Dartmoor. At around the same time granite welled up underneath to form the basis for the tors. During later periods the overlying rock was worn away to leave Dartmoor as it is today. All this happened millions of years before Man appeared.

The Origins of Britain and Dartmoor

In the Beginning – Precambrian Time

Precambrian rocks in Britain

Precambrian rocks at the surface today

In the very far north of Scotland and on the fringes of north-west Ireland and Wales lie the oldest surface rocks in Britain. They were laid down some 3,000 million years ago by a chain of volcanoes. The rocks then spent some 2,000 million years buried deep within the earth, being remelted, folded and deformed, until they reappeared as Lewisian Gneiss, a grey, crystalline metamorphic rock which forms the base of the extraordinary terrain north of Ullapool in Scotland, where weird, isolated mountains sit on a plain of lochs and low hillocks in a theatre of

time called Inverpollaidh. Only here can you appreciate the amazing extent by which the mountains of Britain have been eroded by millions of years of weathering to produce the hills and mountains of today.

Until the appearance of fossils in rocks formed about 600 million years ago, geologists have only rough dates by which to fix the major Earth-building events in an understandable time-scale. The earliest identifiable event in the British structure is known as the Scourian event, which, using isotope

dating can be fixed at about 2,700 million years ago. What happened to the original volcanic rocks at the time of the Scourian Event was dramatic to say the least. They were suddenly folded deep within the Earth's crust and placed under enormous pressure and heat. This changed the structure of the rocks fundamentally, so that their form altered and they became recrystallized. Further events, known as the Inverian Event, and the Laxfordian Events further messed up the volcanic rock until, about 1,000 million years ago it was raised back to the surface and the process of building a sedimentary overlayer commenced.

So far we have covered about 80 per cent of the life of the Earth. We cannot know in anything but the most superficial detail what happened during this period. Anything that occurred near the surface has been irretrievably lost in the jumble of subsequent 'events'.

Under the Sea – the Cambrian Period

Around 570 million years ago the mangled Precambrian rocks found themselves back on the Earth's surface, covered by a shallow sea which stretched over the centre of Britain. For about 50 million years these seas dropped mud and silt over the Precambrian bedrock, forming huge layers of sedimentary rocks. We can still see these today in the layered mountains of Torridon in Scotland, and in north Wales. This process of deposition went on in what is known as the Ordovician period to form the sedimentary rocks of the Lake District and the mountains of mid-Wales.

Geography & Geology

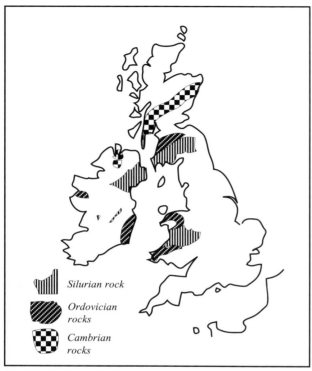

Cambrian rocks at the surface today

Silurian rock

Ordovician rocks

Cambrian rocks

of north Wales and the Scottish Highlands, known as the Caledonian Orogeny, which is just a ten-dollar word meaning Scottish mountain-building period.

Red Sand and Coal – the Devonian Period

So about 400 million years ago Britain found itself near the equator, forming part of a huge continent which contained Europe and America. A large tropical sea extended to the south, with its coastline stretching from the Bristol Channel towards London, more or less along the line of the present M4 motorway. From the continent to the north, which consisted of ruddy coloured rocks, flowed rivers which deposited their silt and mud over the shallow sea-bed near the coastlines. These sediments eventually hardened to produce the Old Red

During this period Britain was divided into two. What is now Northern Ireland and Scotland were on one side of a narrow pre-Atlantic Ocean, and the rest of the islands were attached to a northern Europe oceanic plate. What is perhaps more striking is that because of movements of the poles, both halves lay in warmer waters near the position of the Equator today. It is in this period that the reefs of the Silurian period were active, producing valuable fossil remains. These allow geologists to date rocks of this period relatively accurately, and to compare the ages of rocks across the world.

Towards the end of this period, there was a strong folding of the mountains

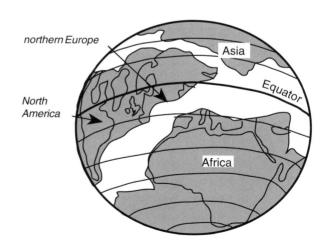

During the Devonian Dartmoor was near the Equator

114

Devonian rock

Carboniferous rock

Carboniferous and Devonian rocks at the surface today

are now seen as the extensive coal seams of Britain.

The Permian Desert and the Formation of Dartmoor

Some 280 million years ago the huge deposits of Devonian sedimentary rock which have just been described were rocked and buckled by a very active mountain-building phase known as the Variscan Orogeny. The word orogeny simply means mountain-building. Here it took the form of a wholesale movement of the plates to the south of Britain in a northerly direction. The result of this was that the layers of sedimentary rock overrode one another, forming huge, overlapping folds and leaves of rock. The layers buckled against one another, and against the great mass of rock still present after the Caledonian mountain building to the North. At this time the surface of Britain was part of a large red desert, called the Permian Desert. We can tell the shape of this folding by examining the way in which the remains of the layers lie today. We can tell that the folding was extreme, with two separate systems of folds appearing over Devon. The added extra in the extreme south-west of Britain was the slow rising of the granite batholith.

Under the weakened folds, lying over a thin oceanic crust only 2–3 miles thick, the molten rock of the Earth's mantle began to rise upward. This occurred partly because light surface rocks had been pushed down into it as the Variscan folds were created, forming 'bubbles' of light rock, but also because a pathway for the release of pressure appeared as the crust weakened. The result was

Sandstone. Thick muds, which were subsequently reheated to form shales and slates, were deposited in south Devon and the east side of Cornwall, and in west Cornwall the steep slopes of the northern landmass gave off slumps of material which formed rocks known as turbidites.

This is the first appearance of Dartmoor as a recognizable entity, in the sense that the sedimentary rocks which were formed at this time feature significantly in the subsequent formation of the country which we see today. The rocks themselves are mostly gone, having been eroded away over the millennia,

but these sedimentary rocks formed the mould for the rising granite which today forms the visible rock of most of Dartmoor.

During the succeeding millennia, the Caledonian Mountains to the north were gradually eroded away, the result being that great swamps were produced, edged by shallow seas. In these enormous swamps grew vast quantities of plants, which died and then dropped into the mud to produce very rich deposits of vegetable material, this being high in carbon. These deposits, subsequently pressurized by layers of rock that formed on top of them,

115

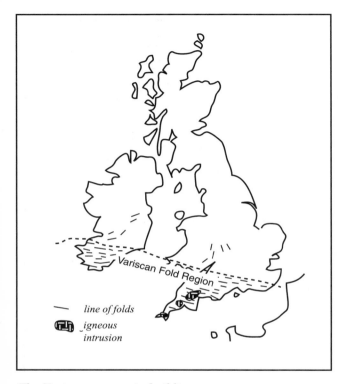

The Variscan mountain-building process

the slow upwelling of a gigantic dome of molten rock, which gradually cooled to form granite. This granite batholith, as it is called, stretched from the Scilly Isles eastwards to Dartmoor. It pushed its way up wherever the weaknesses appeared, and as the two folding systems already mentioned met over Dartmoor, here the crust was weakest, and here the granite came up highest.

Where the batholith came into direct contact with sedimentary rocks, either above it or to its side, it changed them by baking them into rather different rocks. Mud was changed into shales and slate; limestone was changed into marble. This was the origin of the ring of altered sedimentary rocks around Dartmoor called the metamorphic aureole.

Gradually the granite cooled and the mountain building stopped, and everything settled back into relative stability. So Dartmoor at this time lay on the edge of a continent near

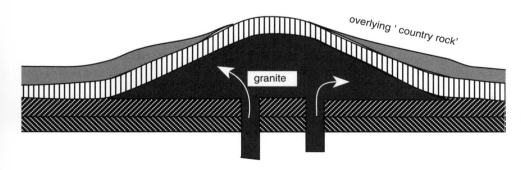

As the Variscan mountain-building processes formed folds and weaknesses, the granite welled up from below, pushing up the overlying sedimentary rocks and forming the granite batholith beneath them

the Equator, hidden deep beneath the sedimentary rocks of the Devonian period, which had been folded over one on the other by the Variscan orogeny.

Return to the North – the Jurassic and Cretaceous Periods

By the start of the Jurassic Period, when dinosaurs roamed freely round the Earth, Britain had moved back towards the north and the Earth began to subside in the south of Britain as tensions in the crust relaxed. Dartmoor, with its overlying covering of Devonian rocks, still lay under the shallow seas of the south-west.

Some 60 million years ago the land rose to the north-west and Dartmoor appeared above the surface of the sea. It was covered now by an additional layer of chalky rock but the slow process of erosion began to expose the granite batholith and the metamorphic rocks around it.

Britain Emerges – Neogene and Quaternary Periods

It was 25 million years ago that Britain began to emerge from the shallow seas around it. The Atlantic Ocean had been widening for a very long time, and by this stage the edge of the European plate had become warped and stretched. Britain rose while the North Sea area dropped, giving the land much the shape that it has today. During the previous 50 to 70 million years the sedimentary rocks overlying the granite structure of Dartmoor had been eroded and weathered as water ate away at the structure of the rocks and moved the softer sedimentary rock downstream into the shallow seas. The

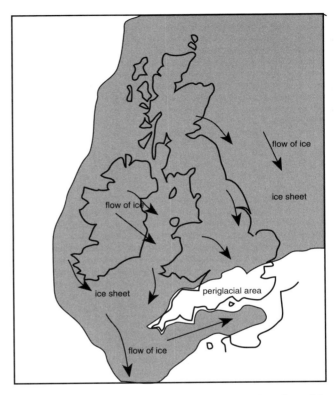

Dartmoor was not covered by the ice sheets, but the cold climate affected the land

scene was set for the dramatic effect of the Ice Age glaciers.

It must be remembered that the great glaciers which grew and retreated half a dozen times over this period never actually reached Dartmoor. The area exhibits no glacial features similar to those of the Snowdon region, say, or the Lake District. This does not mean that the Ice Age was unimportant, however, because the climate had indeed altered fundamentally. The warm-weather processes that had worn down the

sedimentary overlayer in the main part were strengthened by the weathering processes which take place in very cold climates today, processes known as periglaciation.

Periglaciation means on the edge of glaciation and refers to such things as freeze-thaw shattering of rocks, and the slumping of soils as the top layers of frozen soils thaw, allowing the top layer to skid downhill on the frozen sub-soil. The effect of both these and of the warm-weather processes, was to eat into the granite and

117

weather away the overlying rocks to expose the tors. This is explained in more detail on page 119.

We must also remember that the melting of the ice during the Ice Age period produced dramatic changes in the sea-level, with a rise as the ice melted in the interglacial periods between the cold spells, and a dropping as the ice caps increased in size and entrapped water. This caused rivers to cut their paths in different ways and led to the formation of raised beaches, noticeable by the striking horizontal surfaces formed as the waves carved planes in the rocks. These changes had important

effects in the flow of the rivers of Dartmoor. They now flow over these old sea levels, which form nick points at which there are sudden increases in the gradient of the river as it leaves the old beach level.

Yesterday, Today and Tomorrow

By 5,000 years ago the dramatic climatic changes of the Ice Ages had more or less finished, and the climate had settled down into a rather warmer version of today. There were still variations, of course, as there are today, but the last 5,000–6,000 years have been relatively stable.

So, that's the story of the origins of Dartmoor. It began 4,600 million years ago when the Earth's surface was formed. Layer upon layer of sedimentary rocks were deposited under tropical seas, and these rocks were then crumpled and deformed by the shifting plates which form the Earth's crust. Some 280 million years ago the Variscan mountain building then crumpled the last layer to be put down, and the hot, pressurized rocks of the Earth's mantle rose up under the new mountains. The resultant great granite dome was exposed when the layers of soft rock above it were worn away by rivers and weather.

Granite

The most commonly found igneous rock anywhere on the Earth's surface is granite. On Dartmoor the granite is highly visible and constitutes almost all of the underlying rock. On the edges of the moor you will find metamorphosed rocks and some sedimentary rock, but the majority is granite.

Granite comes from the upper layers of the earth's mantle, which is the layer of highly pressurized material below the crust of the Earth on which we walk. Some 20 miles below our feet is a fiercely hot sphere of rock under so much pressure that it remains in a semi-solid state. When the pressure is released, however, the upper edges of the mantle become fluid and work their way upwards until they appear at the earth's crust as either basalt or granite. Both originate from the upper parts of the mantle, but differ in their chemical make-up and structure. Geologists are not exactly

sure how the two different rocks are separated, but two theories are discussed. The first assumes that the difference arises because as

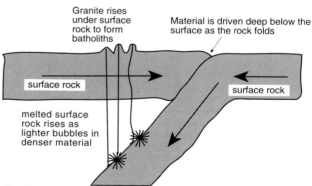

crystallization of the molten rock takes place, the mixture of the rock changes locally, so that the region around a crystal will be of one composition, and the remaining

region will be short of those elements which went to make up the crystal. The two rocks could therefore become differentiated.

The second, and perhaps the easier theory to understand explains that as the crust under a continental land mass becomes thinner, magma, the molten rock from the mantle,

Surface rocks are driven down during mountain-building to rise as granite

intrudes into the continental crust and heats the bottom layers to melting point. Similarly, pieces of the bottom of the continental 'island', that floats on the mantle, become dislodged, are drawn into the mantle and are melted, particularly during mountain-building episodes. Now this rock from the continental island is less dense than the material of the magma, and so it floats upwards, working its way back into the continental material. As it has not had time to become mixed into the material of the mantle, it retains its original make-up. It is what we know today as granite.

Granite contains large numbers of small crystals. These are called feldspar, and make up the shiny appearance of the granite when it is freshly broken. After a while in the open air the granite becomes dull, but if you go to one of the quarries, you can see freshly worked pieces of granite which sparkle and shine in the sunlight. These feldspar crystals sit in a matrix of other material. As the granite is attacked by chemical and other processes, it breaks down into a material known as kaolinite, from which we obtain kaolin, or china clay, and into a residue of gritty, crystalline material, grey in colour, which we see piled into great banks as waste products of the china clay industry. On the high moor this breaking down of granite produces the calm, or growan, which underlies the turf and peat, and which can be seen in paths where the subsoil has been exposed.

In its formation, under the thick layers of sedimentary rock, the granite cooled rather slowly, being pushed from underneath at the same time by the enormous pressures of the Earth's mantle. As the top cooled and set it became brittle, cracking both horizontally and vertically to form the fault lines which we can see today. Some types of granite, particularly on the tors, may look as though they are sedimentary rocks. They are not; the cracking was formed as the granite was pushed from underneath. The joints allowed weathering to take place producing the characteristic shapes of the tors.

On Dartmoor, because granite is found literally lying around, it has been used as gateposts and door frames for at least 3,000 years. Quarrying has now taken over, and Walk 30 will show you the extent to which the granite has provided a lucrative industry for the area for many years. Granite's shiny surface and uniform strength makes it a very attractive building material. Its only disadvantage is its density and the difficulty of working its surface.

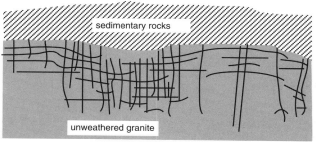

Granite forms under sedimentary rocks. The fractures in granite are lines of weakness where weathering can occur

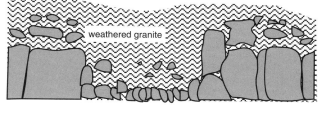

Eventually the weathered rock is carried away and the core rocks are left behind to form the towers and blocks of the main tor.

Tor formation

Tors

The tors are Dartmoor. If there is one aspect of the great wilderness in the south-west that sets it apart from other moorland areas of Britain, it is these forbidding castles of dark granite, rising like the prows of ancient ships from the green sea of the high moor. The name itself is ancient, coming as it does from the Celtic *twr*, meaning a tower. It sounds as if the word has been borrowed from English, but this is not the case. It has a common ancestor with the Italian *torre* and the French *tour*.

The tors themselves were there well before the Celts gave them their name. Their origins lie deep beneath the original sedimentary rocks laid down over the south-west of Britain many millions of years ago. As you have already seen, because of the movements of the great plates of crust which form the surface of the Earth, a great upwelling of molten rock, called *magma*, occurred. This raised the layers of sedimentary rock, but not sufficiently to burst through. The result was a great dome of molten rock, which cooled fairly slowly under its umbrella of sedimentary rock, eventually forming the granite which we see today. We can see the outcroppings of this granite dome in the Scilly Isles, in Dartmoor, in Exmoor, in Bodmin Moor, and a few other places in the far south-west of Britain.

It is important to retain the time-scale of this process; the granite took many thousands of years to raise itself up into a dome. The top layer cooled as it came into contact with the sedimentary roof, and as that cooled granite was itself pushed slowly upwards, it cracked vertically and horizontally to form the characteristic jointing we see today.

This process is illustrated in the diagram on page 116. Eventually the flow from below stopped. The granite cooled, and set into the shape you can see in the diagram. Much of the granite was heavily jointed and broken up by the crushing from below.

There are two theories as to what happened next. The first is that the soft sedimentary rocks overlying the granite were eroded away over a very long time to expose the granite corestones. These were then attacked by water, which infiltrated the joints and froze during the nights and the winters, producing enormous pressures which cracked away parts of the rock. This process was made easy by the existence of the vertical and horizontal fault lines in the granite. Today, a few million years later, we are left with the bare skeleton of the tor, where only the relatively uncracked corestones of the original upwelling remain.

The other theory relies not on the freeze-thaw cycle, but on the corrosion that takes place when water infiltrates the granite, causing chemical reactions which break down the rock into its separate elements. This produces china clay and a residue, grey in colour, of all the crystalline material. If you dig down into the peat on Dartmoor you will find this grey underlayer, called growan by geologists and calm by the locals. Vast quantities of this growan mixture were then trapped under the overlying sedimentary rocks and in between the solid corestones of the granite. When the sedimentary rocks were then worn away by weathering, the extremely soft growan mixture was washed away from between the joints to produce the recognizable and

characteristic shape of the tors which we see today.

In either case, we now have a tower of granite surrounded by a cone of rubbish from the material between the joints. Even though the granite corestone is substantial, it still has cracks and joints in it. The process of freeze-thawing continued to wear it down still further, but in larger lumps since the joints in the remaining granite are further apart. Such lumps fall off and form the piles of rock known as clitter, which surround every tor.

There is one puzzle about the clitter, however. Normally, lumps of rock which fall off mountains do not transport themselves magically a mile or so away down a very gentle slope towards the valley, and yet the piles of clitter surrounding, for example Fur Tor, are much further away than one would reasonably expect. The answer to the puzzle is that the clitter has transported itself away from the tor by two means. First, rock falling on a snowfield will skid further on a more gentle angle than without the snow. Second, when the ground became frozen the Ice Age, a process known as gelifluction took place. This allowed the rocks to flow downhill very easily, so that even small slopes could transport rocks over large distances. Gelifluction occurs when the whole of the soil down to the bedrock becomes frozen. When the top layer melts, all the water is released and has nowhere to go since the underlying layer, still frozen, is completely impervious. A layer of thin frozen mud then lies on top of a sloping, slippery layer of muddy ice. The surface can then slip wholesale down even a very shallow slope.

Peat and Bogs

When you walk over the great upland moors of Britain you are frequently traversing what the geographers refer to as blanket bog. This is very extensive on Dartmoor and covers two separate areas: the northern morass and the southern bog. Both are formed by the accumulation of plant remains in conditions of poor growth. In both areas the nutrients in the growan, the decayed remnants of the granite, is at a low level, so that the ground becomes acidic, and able to support only a limited variety of plants. Because of the acidity of the ground, the plant material does not decay in the way in which we are used to in the lowland areas, and so it builds up until it forms layers which can be many tens of yards thick. One of the best places to see this accumulation is on Cut Hill near Fur Tor, but on the southern moor you can see areas where a track has worn through the peat to give a clear cross-section through it.

This cross-section will show you a deep layer of dark-coloured peat containing stems of heathers and indistinguishable plant remains. This layer will frequently be sodden with water. On top of it lies, in summer at least, a drier layer of lighter coloured peat, and on top of that a living layer of meagre plants.

The peat provides the basis for the flow of the rivers on Dartmoor. It acts as a huge sump from which the water is drawn gradually, rather than just rushing immediately downhill as it would if it fell on a bare rock surface.

The peat can take many thousands of years to form as the plant material drops down and decays. At present it looks as though the great peat

Peat hags

masses are declining, and we do not quite know why. You can see the evidence for this in what are known as the peat hags – islands of peat which appear as the body of the peat shrinks. Again, Cut Hill is an excellent place to see these strange mesas of soggy peat on Dartmoor.

The peat, because it has only partly decayed, provides a good fuel, and the right to cut peat on the moor, known as turbary, is guarded jealously by the moormen. The peat is cut with a strangely shaped right-angled cutter. This is driven down to form long rectangular 'bricks' of peat which are then piled up on the

side of the cutting. These are left to dry and, when convenient, are transported back in the middle of the summer to dry out thoroughly. You see more of this procedure on the hills of Scotland, but it can be seen in places on Dartmoor today. The peat burns well, producing a fragrant smoke. It is usually supplemented with coal where available. In Walk 15 you can visit the site of the Zeal Tramway, which was built to transport peat from the moor to a naphtha factor near Shipley Bridge. The organic components of the peat can be used for many derivatives, just like those of coal.

In the valleys you will find a particularly noxious type of bog called the valley bog. This bog is particularly unpleasant and lies in valley bottoms where the drainage is poor. Wet, soggy mosses, particularly the type known as sphagnum, collect here along with a thin liquid mud. This forms a deep muddy pool with a bright green topping to it; if you step on the moss you will go in up to your middle. There is a good story about a man walking along a valley bottom in the north moor who sees a top hat lying in the ground. He gives it a good kick for devilment, and a voice calls out, 'Oi! Stop kicking my 'at!' The walker looks down to see a man's head just sticking out of a valley bog. He asks the unfortunate man what he is doing there, to which the head replies, 'Sitting on my 'oss!' So the moral is, don't step in any bright green patches in the valley bottoms.

Geography & Geology

Rivers

All the rivers on Dartmoor start their lives on the upland peaty plateau as insignificant puddles and ponds in the thick brown peat. All over the map in the central areas, north and south, you will see confident statements by the Ordnance Survey such as East Dart Head, Erme Head and Teign Head. In some cases you can indeed identify fairly accurately the point at which the river starts its life, but in many cases the river begins as an oozing tentative suggestion towards the sea rather than the definitive and confident start of, say, a glacier-borne river.

The peat on Dartmoor holds millions of litres of water, most of which will pass through your boots at one time or another. It is a characteristic of the peat that it can hold these vast quantities of water for great periods of time, with the result that the flow of the rivers in the high moor is rarely very much stronger at one time than another. The effect of this is that the rivers rarely build up a head of steam. Riverbank erosion is a function of the velocity of the river, so at first the river valleys are shallow meanders in the peat. Only later do they gain enough energy to cut straight valleys.

Gradually, rivulets join together and form more strenuous streams, in turn amalgamating to form the upper reaches of the river. Because the upland plateau is so flat, this adolescent stream can often flow for some time at a fairly easy angle. The East Dart, for example, which you will visit on Walk 20, drops quite quickly from the top plateau to a height of around 1600 feet, above Kit Rocks. There it establishes itself as a single flow, but still without the headlong rush towards the sea which we might expect.

On Dartmoor there is another characteristic of the profile of a river which is common to all the rivers, and which originates in the rise and fall of the ice sheets during the Ice Age. As the ice caps grew and entrapped water, the amount of water in the seas fell, and so the effective sealevel dropped. Conversely, as the ice sheets melted the sealevel rose as the water was released. The crust rose and fell also because of the mass of ice weighing down on it, but the alteration of the height of the land because of this took a great deal longer than the release of water into the sea due to the melting. All this presented the river with three or four old sealevels, one at about 1200 feet above sea-level, one at about 800 feet and one at about 400 feet. As you follow any Dartmoor river down off the high plateau you can see these old sea beaches as distinctive levellings of the river. The North Teign is an excellent example, as it runs off the old beach level by Teign-e-ver clapper into the next rush down to the lower level. The same effect can be seen in the East Dart. As the river reaches these old levels, it tends to widen out and can form a soggy, waterlogged, meandering area, such as the plain of the North Teign below Watern Tor and as far as Scorhill Tor.

Once the river has formed into a substantial channel it tends to create rectangular cross-sections with vertical banks, as the growan in which it now flows tends to stand up to erosion at the sides rather well. You may notice that as the river cuts through less substantial ground it spreads out as the banks fall in, but as it cuts into the rotten granite of the upland plain it produces dark-brown well-contained channels, with deep, clear pools.

At the bends in the river's course you will see where the speed of the river on the outside of the bend has cut away the banks, and where, on the slower-moving inside, material has been deposited. Look on the inside of the bends and you will see sand bars of light material. The erosion of the outside and the deposition on the inside combine to cause meanders, which, in soft ground, wander about. You can see this effect better in rivers which flow into estuarial plains, but the effect on the high moors is noticeable none the less.

Dartmoor rivers tend to flood. You can see the effects of this on most of the rivers, particularly where they are confined – for example in Tavy Cleave. Here you can see debris left lying around after the river has dropped and slowed down, thus reducing its capacity to carry heavy material such as boulders and trees. Huge boulders can be left lying around as if in some giant's playpen. Where the channel is artificially enlarged by floods, the river can make a number of routes through the debris deposited in times of greater carrying capacity, forming parallel routes called braided channels. You can see the large banks running along the length of the river in places, dividing one channel from another. Another spectacular effect of flood and heavy rain is rotational landslip, where large sections of a steep bank can slump downward. Often the tracks of sheep can cause a fracture line along which the slope breaks, and the waterlogged soil collapses downwards. Look high up on the sides of river valleys for this effect.

Soon we come to the influence of man. Tinners searching for ore

Waterfall on the East Dart

would often bank the sides of rivers and narrow them in order to increase the speed of flow of the water. The higher the speed of flow, the further the lighter ores would be carried. This allowed the tinners to separate out the heavy rock from the lighter ore more easily.

As the rivers drop from the high plateau you will often find beautiful waterfalls. The greater speed of the river cuts down until it reaches the underlying granite. The granite has strong horizontal and vertical joints and is also rather hard and resistant to erosion where it is unjointed. The result is that the river falls over a sharp edge. In time, the river will

create a pool at the bottom of the fall, where, perhaps, the strata are softer, or more faulted. The river will also eat back into the face of the fall, creating the sublime formations which we can see at the East Dart (pictured above), at Lydford Gorge (White Lady Waterfall – *see* page 154) and, again, above Shipley Bridge.

Where the river is flowing fast, look in the banks and on the exposed bed for potholes. These are formed as small stones and rocks are caught in an eddy grinding away at the sides so as to produce a cauldron-shaped hole in what appears to be solid rock. There are good examples of

potholes in the river that flows through the beautiful Lydford Gorge in particular.

Soon the river drops down into the in-country, below the high moor. By this time it will have grown substantially, and will cut its way down through even quite hard rocks to form a steep-sided valley. Typical of this type of formation is the Dart Valley below Dartmeet, where the river swings around in a steep-sided valley covered in trees. The particularly steep-sided formation of Tavy Cleave is interesting and photogenic. It has been formed as the Tavy has cut down through soft rock as the ground rose beneath it.

Walk 20 – West & East Dart Rivers, Sandy Hole Pass

Distance
About 14 miles to the East Dart Head, but if you go just as far as Kit Rocks, about 10 miles.

Difficulties
A long but relatively straightforward walk until you reach Kit Rocks. Thereafter, although you are following the rapidly dwindling river, it is possible to become disorientated. A compass must therefore be carried, together with a map. This is a long walk, so full waterproof clothing and suitable food must be carried. The top section between the West Dart and East Dart can be extremely wet after rain, but it is not dangerous. Take notice of the range restrictions.

Main Features
Brown's House	**615798**
West Dart	**612798**
Kit Rocks	**614827**
East Dart Head (optional)	**607856**
Sandy Hole Pass	**612815**
East Dart Waterfall	**627811**
Sheepfold	**645808**
Beehive Hut	**639814**
Postbridge Clapper	**647788**

Description of Walk
Leave your car at the Postbridge Information Centre car-park. Please be sure to leave the parking fee when you leave, and secure your car thoroughly against thieves.

*Take the path at the Two Bridges end of the car-park which leads up the Dart. After a short distance a signpost indicates a path off to the left which leads off towards Archerton (**636792**). Take this over a very wet meadow. Eventually the path leads on to a metalled track at which you turn right. At this point the map is wrong, since the path has been changed. Before the house turn right*

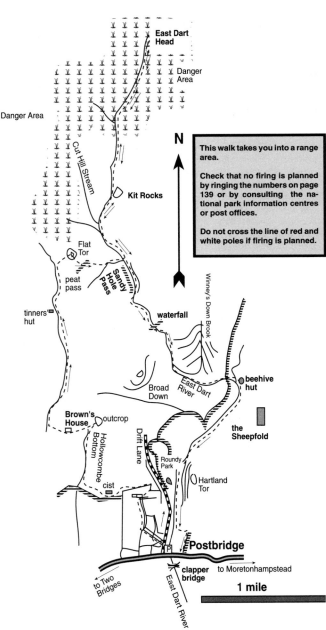

N

This walk takes you into a range area.

Check that no firing is planned by ringing the numbers on page 139 or by consulting the national park information centres or post offices.

Do not cross the line of red and white poles if firing is planned.

124

at a signpost and follow the path on to the end, where another path leads you out onto the moor.

Turn left here and follow the wall. At the point where it turns sharp left, cross over to the wall opposite where you will see a gate. Continue to follow this second wall in roughly the same direction.

You will soon cross a stream. The wall then extends downslope towards Hollowcombe Bottom (614794), which is the depression between you and Higher White Tor and Lower White Tor opposite. About a hundred yards after the stream you will notice a cist about ten yards away from the wall.

Continue to follow the wall until it drops more quickly towards Hollowcombe Bottom. Turn right and follow the general line of the stream up into the bottom. Keep up from the stream on the edge of the bank to avoid the swampy bits which lie near it.

Follow the line of the stream until you reach the stile at the top of the steep defile. Here turn right and walk to the outcrop up the slope. From the outcrop make directly for Rough Tor opposite; you should be able to see the ruins of **Brown's House** on the same line. If it has been very wet take a line more to the right to avoid a very swampy bit in the middle. Even so, walk directly towards Rough Tor after your detour. Brown's House is slightly to your right.

From Brown's House continue to walk towards Rough Tor. Before you reach the **West Dart**, turn right and follow the line of the river, again staying this side of it to avoid the swampy areas after wet weather. After some time you will see a red and white range pole, which marks the edge of the military firing area. You should now be able to see a range notice board on your side of the West Dart. Between the two you will see the ruins of a tinners' hut (**608807**).

From the tinners' hut walk upstream. The river becomes indistinct, but it swings to the left. You will see another range pole on the river bank further up. At this point you should see a low outcrop slightly to your right, which has on it a red and white pole and a range notice board (the latter is side on). This is Flat Tor. Make your way up the slope to this (**608816**).

From the outcrop you will see, to the south-east, a pool in the peat. Walk towards this and after a hundred yards you should see, to your right, a small granite marker post (**612814**). This marks the end of a peat pass shown on the map. Turn left and follow the ill-defined track down towards the Dart Valley, which you can see in the direction of Fernworthy Forest, the latter peeking above the hills to the east. You should meet another peat-pass marker, and then a neat clapper bridge. Walk downhill and you will enter some tin-workings. Keep going downhill and you will reach the East Dart Valley at Broad Marsh (**615818**).

Decide here if you wish to visit the impressively squidgy **East Dart Head**. If you do, turn left and follow the river up past **Kit Rocks** until it disappears into the peat. This detour is longer than you think.

If you can do without the visit to East Dart Head, turn right here, at Broad Marsh and follow the river down to **Sandy Hole Pass**. To get the best view of the pass you will have to drop down after Broad Marsh more or less to the bank of the river.

Stay on the west side of the river. Below Sandy Hole Pass the river is slow and meandering. After this level section it suddenly drops over a **waterfall**. You can cross here even when the river is in full spate.

Pick up the path on the east side of the river below the waterfall. It will lead you high above the river as it drops down below the waterfall. You will pass by a section of old leat for a while, and then cut across a stream called Whinney's Down Brook. You can see the **Sheepfold** on the same bank further down the river. Cross Whinney's Down Brook.

You will soon notice an island in the river, the latter then swinging abruptly to the right. Notice the wide flood plain on the meander. Make your way down to the next stream and turn left. After 50 yards or so you will see a ruined **beehive hut**.

From the beehive hut continue over the bank on the same side of the East Dart and follow the river until you reach a gate into a small wood near Roundy Park. After the next gate you will see a signpost off to the left, avoiding a swampy area and some private land. Turn left here. Do not be tempted to carry on; it is simply a waste of effort as you will have to turn left to join the legal path anyway. Follow the footpath to the road, turning right at the appropriate point, and you will reach the main road at the **Postbridge Clapper**. Turn right here and walk back along the road to the Information Centre car-park.

Drift Lane

This walled road joining Postbridge to the slopes of Broad Down is one of the ancient tracks of Dartmoor. It allows moormen access to the high moor from the Postbridge area, and cattle were driven up it in the spring to allow them to benefit from the good grazing on the upper slopes. At the end of the summer the animals were rounded up and brought back down to the comparative shelter of the lower fields.

Drift Lane links up with the Lich Way, which was used to transport corpses from the eastern side of the moor to Lydney, where they could be given a decent burial. The most obvious section of the Lich Way in this part of the moor is the one which leads past Powder Mills Farm to the west of here.

Bradden Lake

Bradden is almost certainly a corruption of Broad Down, on which this old tin-working area sits. The natural flow of the stream down towards the Dart has provided a source for the ore, at which the tin-miners dug away until they reached the 'mother lode'. Sometimes there was no attainable mother lode because the source of the tin in the bed of the river was hidden underground. It was only in relatively modern times that the techniques of burrowing safely underground using a sloping tunnel or adit were used.

The word lake here does not refer to a broad expanse of water, but to the river workings themselves. These produced the power for the pounding machinery by which the ore was broken up for smelting.

Roundy Park

When the Bronze Age people settled Dartmoor around 4,000 years ago they built huts at first, and then, when they needed to protect their animals from wandering, and from human and animal predators, they built walls to provide an enclosure. Roundy Park is one of these Bronze Age enclosures. You can read more about the way of life of these people in the previous chapter. Generally, these enclosures were about 4 feet high and made of substantial stone. Usually you can find other remains of the people who built and used them if you look carefully. Here, for example, is a large kistvaen, or cist, which is a Bronze Age grave. A hole was lined with stone slabs and the body placed in it in a crouching position. The grave at Roundy Park has been restored, which is not the blessing it seems since the restorers, probably in late-Victorian times, were kind enough to make it rather bigger than the original. Most cists are a deal smaller than this, just large enough to contain a small adult in a foetal position.

Nevertheless, the enclosure or pound at Roundy Park is a good example. If you stand in it looking over the valley you can easily imagine the scene when the Dart Valley was peopled extensively by Bronze Age folk, the smoke from their huts drifting gently upwards over the dark green background of the valley opposite.

Up the slope towards Broad Down itself lie the enclosures of Broadun and Broadun Ring, the former being the largest on Dartmoor. You have a long walk if you are going to get to East Dart Head, however, so I recommend that you pay only a brief visit to Roundy Park and its kistvaen before moving on.

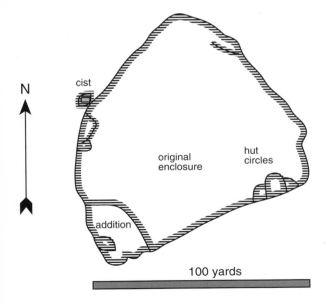

Roundy Park

Powder Mills Leat

The leat which you cross near Bradden Lake at the top of Drift Lane is Powder Mills Leat, which provided water for the workings at Powder Mills. At one time gunpowder was made here, and, like any other factory, the mills required water. The leat is taken off the Dart further up the valley and contours around until it can fall gently to the Powder Mills Farm. Gunpowder-making has stopped here now, but the farm contains a pottery which still takes water from the leat.

Dartmoor is networked with these very efficient water channels, which require a certain amount of native cunning to route across the moor. It is important that the gradient of the leat is just right. Too little and the water will flow sluggishly; too much and the banks will be worn away at the bends.

The Sheepfold

Under Stannon Tor on the opposite side of the valley from Broad Down lies one of the most magnificent buildings on Dartmoor, the Sheepfold. It was built, so Crossing says, by a Scot who wished to shelter a flock of Scottish sheep. Since the Sheepfold covers the best part of an acre, it must have been an impressive flock indeed. The walls of the Sheepfold are very thick and come up to the shoulder. They are built, as one might expect, from moorstone, the local name for the surface stone covering the moor. Every few yards or so the wall is strengthened by a huge granite slab. The entrance to the Sheepfold is on the up-slope side, and at the lower end you can find the remains of a hut of sorts, clearly for the use of the shepherd. The Sheepfold has been used on occasions for sheltering cattle and for counting ponies.

Dart Waterfall

Under Broad Down on the East Dart lies a wonderful waterfall. Here the water slips and rushes over cascades and terraces until it reaches a dramatic drop over three or four larger walls. In no case is the drop very large; any waterfall in the country could beat it for scale, and force of torrent, but the beauty and isolation of the scene makes up for all that. What appears to have happened here is that the water has met a harder layer of rock where the river had previously cut away a flat platform. When the sea-level dropped, the river gained more energy by virtue of its now greater altitude and so it began to cut back into the layer of granite.

The granite, as you will know from the introduction to this chapter, tends to form a layered rock structure, which the river smashes over as it drops down. As you look at the waterfall you can see that the fault line of the granite lies at an angle to the flow, so that the natural breakage lines have caused the river to form a wall at an angle to the flow line of the river.

Eventually the river will cut its way back, gradually eroding the waterfall wall so that it progresses upstream. But you don't need to rush in case it has all worn away by the time you get there; the erosion process will take millions of years to wear it all away. In the meantime, of course, the sea-level may fall again and another waterfall will start to be formed somewhere else.

I thoroughly recommend that you walk out to see this waterfall. Its natural beauty and form as it drops and turns over the granite shelves make it one of the most attractive features on this part of Dartmoor.

The process of waterfall formation

Sandy Hole Pass

One of my favourite places on a hot summer's day is Sandy Hole. Unfortunately, in Dartmoor terms, it gets quite busy. You can see as many as half a dozen people during the course of a summer's day, and this massive influx of humanity can spoil this interesting and picturesque place.

If you approach Sandy Hole from lower down the Dart you come across an area upstream from the big waterfalls under Broad Down where there are extensive tin-workings. Here the valley spreads out and forms a rather marshy area. There are paths on both sides. At the top of this marshy area the valley narrows rapidly and enters a narrow cleft or gorge. The name Sandy Hole comes, not surprisingly, from the amount of sand which is present in the stream bed. In its natural state the river would have been constricted and speeded up because of the constraining natural walls, but the tinners have further narrowed the stream passage to speed up the flow even more so as to provide more usable energy from the river. The faster a river flows the more energy it has available to move material and, as you can read in the Tinning & Quarrying chapter, the tin-miners needed to move a great deal of ore and waste around in order to separate the former from the latter. They therefore banked up the sides and narrowed the channel. The effect of this is to make the river rush madly along a narrow stone lined channel towards a cascade over large rocks at the lower end.

The upper end of the Pass is rather disappointing, as the river only gradually spreads out into the upper flood plain above the tin-workers' walling. Here, however, you can

Sandy Hole Pass is an artificially banked section of the River Dart

see the way in which the tinners worked their way back up the valley of the subsidiary streams in their search for ore. By observing the pattern of ore deposits in the bed of the stream, the tinners became very clever at detecting where the stream

cut into the main ore lode, in order that they could dig along its path to win the ore. Surprisingly perhaps, because of the flow of water, the ore found in the stream bed was more pure than that won directly from the main lode.

Peat Pass

On the OS map you will find marked about half a dozen peat passes. These are wide pathways cut down through the peat layers until the solid subsoil is reached. In many cases the passes are 20 feet wide, with the depth of the peat equalling that. In the bottom of the peat passes you can see the underlying growan or calm which is the residue of the weathered granite. It provides a free-draining and substantial surface for horses to walk on. Originally the peat passes were constructed to allow hunters on horseback to traverse the boggiest parts of the moor. They were constructed by a Victorian called Phillpotts and are today referred to as Phillpotts' Peat Passes. At the top and bottom of most of them you will find a memorial stone about 2 feet or so in height, on which the relatives of Phillpotts have fixed a metal plaque commemorating his endeavours.

Peat pass marker

Kit Rocks

Kit Rocks (also known as Kit Tor) is one of the boundaries of the ancient forest that is defined by the Perambulation of the Forest, a ceremony akin to beating the bounds. The boundary here runs up from the West Dart and left towards Teign Head higher up on the moor. Kit Rocks is one of the few granite extrusions on this part of the moor, and stands out strikingly from the rolling peaty wetlands around.

Kit Steps, a convenient crossing place, can be found lower down the river. Unfortunately who Kit was I cannot establish nor whether he was the same Kit who placed a boundary stone in the south moor, near the Pupers Rocks.

Kit Rocks is an excellent place to eat lunch, watch the upland birds and admire the desolate scenery of this upper part of the moor. It also worth knowing where it is because in bad weather it is a marvellous place to aim for as a final fix before heading off into the high moor or back down to Postbridge.

If you search in the cracks you may find some letterboxes. If you do, please return them securely to their hiding places after writing your name in the book provided.

Statt's House

This is a tinner's or peat-cutter's hut perched on the top of Winney's Down. The hut makes a good objective for a walk in the northern moor, as it lies on the edge of the real wilderness, but is also easy to reach. An old fireplace can be seen in one end of the hut. Although the walls are fairly low now, they would not have been that much higher when it had the turf roof in place to protect the occupants.

Just below the summit of Winney's Down is the top marker of one of the Phillpotts' Peat Passes, with its distinctive granite marker and its memorial plate.

Geography & Geology

East Dart Head

After your long plod up the valley of the Dart you will be looking to see the little spring from which this beautiful river rises. You probably envisage weeping willows all around and golden flags bobbing their colourful heads in the slight breeze that ripples the surface of the chattering adolescent stream.

Forget it. East Dart Head is undistinguished. The river rises from the edge of a peaty area in the north moor with no redeeming features whatsoever. There is a pool of sorts in wet weather, but the river almost draws itself out of the wet ground, and as you follow it upstream towards its source, you suddenly lose it. When this happens you are at East Dart Head.

There are a number of heads of rivers in the immediate area, but it would not be wise to go seeking them as the area north of here is well known for its boggy areas. These are called feather beds, for their habit of providing the final resting place of careless walkers.

As you will have seen on your walk up, the Dart rises rapidly in size and quite quickly becomes a rather attractive upland stream, with stretches of deep-brown pools interspersed with more rapid and shallower runs over the granite bottom. Notice the steep sides of the peaty channels.

It is quite easy to lose a few hours up here looking for the small fish in the peaty runs of the young river. The dragonflies and nymphs that proliferate in summer certainly make the long walk worth while.

Beehive Hut

The circular remains of the pointed hut which you will see as you make your way back towards Postbridge is a good example of a beehive hut, technically known as a corbelled hut because of the method of roof construction. These rather strange-looking huts were built by the tinners who needed somewhere to hide both their tools and also quite often their ingots of tin while they were away.

A hut was built in a domed form, and covered with turfs and soil. When the turf took root the hut was almost indistinguishable from a natural mound in the earth, particularly when so much disruption was already visible from the rounded shapes of the waste piles left by the tinners themselves.

Local tales have it that these caches were the hiding places for smugglers, who brought illegal spirits up from Cornwall and Dorset to sell to the tinners, but then any hole in the ground seems to have that story attached to it! There was undoubtedly a good trade in smuggled brandy from the south coast, but there is no particular reason why the smugglers should have hidden their stuff half-way up the Dart.

Beehive hut

Valley Bog

One of the most important geographical features of Dartmoor, and of this area in particular, is the valley bog. Unlike the blanket bogs of the upper slopes, these are caused in the main part by the slowing down of the rivers as they reach the flatter parts of their courses. These are frequently the old beach levels caused as the rivers cut flat areas when they reached the various sealevels as the sea rose and fell in the Pleistocene Ice Age. A well-defined raised beach lies at about 1200 feet above the present sea level. As the flow of the river slackens off, the particles which it has carried down from its more energetic upper reaches are dropped to form a bed of peaty soil that is waterlogged and attractive to plants. These plants then colonize the watery soil, their roots consolidating it to a degree.

The effect of this is to create an important habitat for plants, but it also provides certain difficulties for the walker. Where the underlying ground is hollowed, the water can collect to form a particularly soggy region where sphagnum moss grows. This forms an attractive carpet of green over the pit of liquid mud.

This is all very well until you step on it, when it gives way and deposits you into a foul-smelling muddy mess. Very few such bogs are really dangerous, but it is best to be careful since if you are tired or unlucky, or both, you could end up not being able to extricate yourself.

There are stories about ponies being caught in these feather-beds, as they are known, and it is certain that the corpses of one or two ponies have been found. As mentioned above, though, the pits are not all that dangerous, as they give immediate warning that your footing is uncertain by a wholesale trembling and shivering. At this point retrace your footsteps very carefully, and work your way round the sticky green mess. If you don't you will be sorry.

Sphagnum moss, the main plant constituent of the valley bogs, was used during World War I as a component of field dressings. Its extraordinary water retaining properties made it, when sterilized,

Sphagnum moss

ideal for staunching the flow of blood from wounds.

Another common type of valley bog is caused when water flows down a hillside and meets a rather impervious feature at the bottom of the slope. As a result of this you will often find a strip of valley bogs at the foot of steep valley sides, often making walking difficult. In these circumstances it is often better to climb up the slope in order to avoid the sticky mess at the bottom.

Below: the formation of a valley bog

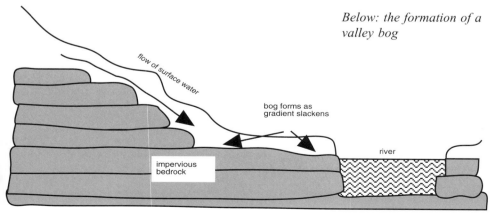

flow of surface water

bog forms as
gradient slackens

river

impervious
bedrock

Walk 21 – Watern Tor and Cranmere Pool

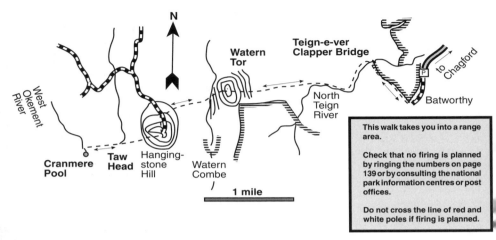

This walk takes you into a range area.

Check that no firing is planned by ringing the numbers on page 139 or by consulting the national park information centres or post offices.

Do not cross the line of red and white poles if firing is planned.

Distance
13 miles.

Difficulties
This is a walk over some of the most desolate country in England. You need full waterproofs, a map and compass, and appropriate food supplies, not just for eating on the way but for emergency use. The weather can change quickly, and the Dartmoor mists can be extremely confusing. The latter part of the walk over the peat will be wet and difficult, so stout boots should be worn.

Main Features

Teign Valley	**64.86.**
Clapper Bridge	**655870**
Watern Tor and the Thirlstone	**629869**
Taw Head	**609859**
Cranmere Pool	**603868**

Description of Walk
Leave the car at Batworthy Corner west of Chagford. Make sure that you have secured your vehicle and placed anything valuable in the boot. This is prime hunting country for car thieves.

Walk up the track away from the road, and turn right at the corner of the enclosure wall, following it eventually to the Teign. Cross the Teign over the **Teign-e-ver Clapper Bridge**, and turn left. Follow the river upstream. After about half a mile the Teign turns right through a right-angle. Continue to follow the river, which separates into a number of streams here. After another half a mile you will come to some tin-workings, and the river reverts to its original direction by sweeping sharply to the left. At this point you should leave the river and begin to climb in an easterly direction towards prominent Watern Tor on the skyline. There is a rough bridle path for part of the way.

On reaching **Watern Tor** explore the top, with its three separate outcrops. The **Thirlstone** is the outcrop furthest to the north.

The best route from here is to aim at Hangingstone Hill. There is a military road which approaches Hangingstone from the north, so you should drop down into the deep cleft of Watern Combe to the east. Climb the other side and aim directly west, meeting the road about a mile from Watern Tor. Turn left on to the road and climb up until the top of Hangingstone is reached. There is an army observation post and a cairn at the top.

From Hangingstone Hill continue in a westerly direction until you reach **Taw Head**. This is not easy to identify, but when you find yourself at the top of a peaty valley with a marshy bog at the head of it, you will have arrived.

From Taw Head again continue in a westerly direction until you eventually come across the depression which contains **Cranmere Pool**. The West Okement runs away from the pool to the north-west, so you can aim off slightly to the north by going directly west, rather than attempting to hit the pool nose on. The letterbox is in the middle of the depression in the peat.

You return to your car the same way but with wetter feet!

Clapper Bridges

When you follow the old routes on the moor you will frequently come across these slabs of stone, often substantial, laid across rivers and streams. As is always the case on Dartmoor, the antiquity of these clapper bridges is overestimated. They were built in historic times rather than being the product of the Bronze or Iron Age, although it must have been the most natural thing in the world to throw a large, flat stone over a stream to avoid getting wet feet. In fact, most were built after 1400, and there is a record of one being built as late as 1835.

The stone used is the granite which lies all over the moor, known as moorstone. Because it tends to break in layers the rock forms the slabs which are so convenient. Imagine the labour involved in transporting the slabs to build the larger bridges, such as the one you cross on this walk over the Teign. The bridge is called Teign-e-ver Clapper and it crosses the river where it narrows, some 3 feet above the surface of the fast-moving water. It is fairly safe from flood here, and the bridge provides a much better way of crossing the river than the ford

upstream. The nearby Wallabrook also has a fine clapper.

Both of these bridges are single span, the simplest type of clapper. If you go to Postbridge you can see a superb example of a multiple-span bridge, standing way above the river on pillars of local granite. The River Dart here can rise very quickly and contains a great deal of flood water after rain, as the water runs off the saturated peat mass above. The height of the pillars was therefore important. The bridge at Dartmeet uses the same principle.

Clapper Bridge at Dartmeet

Watern Tor and the Thirlstone

This tor is one of my favourites. It stands in the northern moor a long way from civilization, like a huge ship at sea. From the northern end you can see forever over the great valley between Dartmoor and Exmoor, and the plain of mid-Devon stretches out before you. Directly north of you is Hound Tor, and to the left is the aptly named Steeperton Tor. The valley to the west, on your left, is a splendid steep-sided trench cut in the rock by the Wallabrook.

The rocks to the northern end of Watern Tor are collectively called the Thirlstone. *Thirl* is an Anglo-Saxon word meaning hole. (Nostril derives from *nose thirl*.) The feature gets its name from the appearance that it presents from certain angles when the erodeded rock, formed into plates by the effect of frost and acidic water on the fault lines in the granite, appears to have a hole in it. You can see this from certain angles from both sides, and it makes a good photographic subject.

The Thirlstone was one of the bond marks of the Perambulation of 1240 which defined the boundary of the Royal Forest of Dartmoor.

The Thirlstone

Thirlstone and the Perambulation

In 1215 King John granted a charter of the Forest of Dartmoor, having earlier disafforested all the rest of Devon except for Exmoor. The term forest did not mean a wooded area; rather it was an area of reserved hunting for the nobles, in this instance the king. Within the bounds of the forest certain rights were given to the inhabitants, and certain duties expected. For example, the foresters were allowed to collect fallen wood, pasture their cattle and cut peat. They were not, however, allowed to hunt the game.

In 1224 another charter, by Henry III, disafforested large portions of England. As a result it became necessary to identify clearly the boundaries of those forests which remained. In 1240 the first definition of these boundaries for the Forest of Dartmoor was made.

This first tour or perambulation (walking around) of the boundary of the forest was made by twelve knights, whose job was to identify the 'bond marks' which defined the borders.

It would be a very lengthy task to define all the bond marks of the forest, but in the area of this walk the boundary runs from Cosdon Hill to Little Hound Tor and then to Thirlstone on Watern Tor, leaving it to go to off to the west.

If you stand on Watern Tor, then, near the Thirlstone at the north end, you are standing in the footsteps of those twelve medieval knights who first defined the Forest of Dartmoor's boundaries in the Perambulation of 1240.

Peat and Blanket Bogs

The uplands of Dartmoor are mainly covered in a marshy vegetation which, in contrast to the wet swamps of the valleys, is called blanket bog or hill bog. There are no trees and little vegetation of the type which we find in the valleys. This is because of the high winds, the wet climate and the acidity of the peat-based soil.

However, while this is a rather hostile climate for the plants of the lower valleys, it provides a niche for the survival of plants which would be crowded out by the more rampant flowering species. Mosses, liverworts and lichens thrive here at the expense of bluebells and willow. The low profiles of these plants allow them to survive the high winds of winter.

VAB

The insect-catching sundew

These plants are in many cases relics from earlier climates, left there, for example, when the ice sheets to the north retreated, allowing the periglacial region on their edges to

VAB

Peat hag

warm. We can see these plants, such as crowberry, cranberry and the clubmosses, today further north in Europe in the tundra of Scandinavia and also further to the east. We can find the pollen from these plants in the peat which was laid down in prehistoric times, and so we can be sure that our interpretation of the origin of these types is correct. Pollen spores are very distinctive and certain idiosyncratic archaeologists make a living from identifying and interpreting them.

Certain plants in this wet morass on the high hills are extremely rare. The bog orchis, for example, grows deep in the sphagnum moss, and has only been seen twice in the last century.

In the summer you can catch sight of snipe and grouse, and the whole of the blanket bog of the moor is inhabited by pipits and skylarks. One of the greatest pleasures at this time is to lie in a (dry!) spot and look up at the skylarks singing far above against the brilliant blue sky. One of the least pleasures, of course, is to lie in a wet patch of the blanket bog in winter, having skidded off a peat

hag into a wet pool, and to lie there on one's back watching the rain pour down in unrelenting sheets. But you can't have everything, even on Dartmoor.

The peat of the blanket bog is shrinking, although no one knows quite why. You can tell this is so because of the way in which the peat hags (the steep-sided hillocks of peat) give the impression of a broken crust. There are very few places today where peat is actually forming.

All in all, the hill bog is an unattractive place unless you are prepared to make a study of the plants, the insects, the birds, the lichens and mosses, the foxes and badgers which occasionally traverse it...

Actually it's quite fascinating.

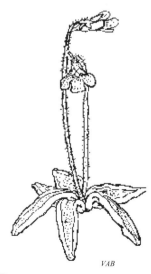

VAB

Butterwort

135

Cranmere Pool

This is the most unlikely Mecca for walkers you will ever see. It is a low, damp area, often containing a certain amount of sludgy, peaty mud surrounded by banks of unremitting peat, its brown walls producing an almost claustrophobic atmosphere. Admittedly, in high summer the calls of the upland birds provide a backdrop to the desolation of this unusual focal point, as the oppressive dampness of the high summer upland bears down upon you. But why did it become such a focus?

In Victorian times there was a vogue for long journeys into the wilderness in various parts of the British Isles, and for a long time Chagford became a centre for such expeditions, with Victorian matrons being transported over the peat hags on donkeys. For some reason the pool at Cranmere became known as the centre of the moor, because it was inaccessible and because it was known to be near the source of the Taw, the Dart, the Okement, the Tavy and the Teign rivers; in fact most of the rivers of Dartmoor.

Rather later a fashion arose for leaving postcards on the moor in prominent spots. Fur Tor, for example, was one of the first. When you got to the relevant spot you looked for a container and signed a visitors' book that was placed there. If you wished you could leave a postcard, which the next visitor was obliged to take and post. The longer it took for your postcard to reach its destination, the more remote was your objective, therefore, and the more kudos you gained. One of these sites was at Cranmere. A stone receptacle was built there by a James Perrott, one of the Dartmoor guides from Chagford, firstly so that Victorian adventurers could leave their visiting cards there, and later for postcards. It provided a permanent home for the visitors' book. It is still there today, and you can sign your name and take a copy of the rubber stamp which has been placed there. Put one on the back of your map to commemorate your walk, because it will have taken you a fair amount of effort to negotiate the desert of peat hags which surround the pool. Please leave the stamp and book for other walkers to record their blisters!

Cranmere Pool letterbox stamp

The name Cranmere means the crow pool, and although there is only a vestige of a pool there today, there must have been one at some time. There are a number of local stories associated with the pool regarding Binjie Gear, a black spirit which haunts this part of the desolate northern moor, and who is said to be trapped there until he empties Cranmere Pool with a sieve. He must be winning because the last time I went to Cranmere there was only a vestige of water among the black sludgy mud in the bottom of the hollow.

Imagine the scene at Cranmere late in the last century when dozens of Victorians dressed completely inappropriately in long dresses and thick tweed suits, encumbered with the necessaries for what they saw as a major expedition into one of the wildernesses of Britain, all arrived on donkeys and ponies. Imagine also their surprise at seeing the great Cranmere Pool, which they had laboured all day to reach, reduced to a sludgy mess in the peat banks. How disappointing it must have been!

Ravens are often seen above the blanket bog

Letterboxing

In the beginning the Victorians set up particular spots on the moor (notably Cranmere Pool) to leave their visiting cards in order to prove to their friends that they had completed the perilous journey to the dreaded centre of the moor. Soon people started leaving postcards there, stamped and addressed, so that the next visitor would take them back to civilization to post them on to you. Naturally, if the letters took a long time to reach you it was because you had been to a spot which was rarely visited, and so the perilous nature of your journey was enhanced.

Gradually, the number of these boxes increased. They began to appear at prominent tors such as Fur Tor and Crow Tor. All these places are quite difficult to reach, and it was quite something to collect a souvenir of them. People began to leave a rubber stamp and inkpad at these sites, so that you could sign the visitors' book and take an impression of the stamp that you found there.

The number of sites began to increase. Statt's House had one, and Duck's Pool in the south moor had one (there is a memorial to William Crossing, the great Dartmoor guide and writer there). Soon most of the tors had one.

There are thousands of established sites on the moor, and many more temporary ones. Some are well established 'boxes' with substantial books, others are plastic boxes put out on the moor by enthusiasts who then take them in to collect the stamps which visitors themselves have put in (it has become the fashion to have your own rubber stamp to imprint the visitors' book).

Some of the stamps are very attractive and each has some connection with the moor, although the link can be somewhat tenuous. The whole scheme is administered by an organization known as the 'Dartmoor 100 Club', which takes its name from the entry conditions. If you want to become a member and obtain the right to a copy of the register of boxes, with details of where the letterboxes are hidden, you have to provide evidence that without the catalogue of clues you have collected a hundred stamp impressions. This is to ensure that you are a bona fide lover of Dartmoor and not some selfish thief.

It can take quite a time to collect a hundred stamps, and I'm not going to give you any clues other than the half-dozen above, but if you visit one of the pubs in Princetown which has a connection with the Prince of Wales and ask behind the bar, you will be given a visitors' book in which you can write your name. If you are lucky you will find some clues in the book left by previous visitors, which should get you on your way. Most of the clues require a compass. Many of the other pubs on the moor have 'a stamp' and if you ask for it you will be given a box, sometimes with a number of commemorative rubber stamps. Each counts towards your hundred.

The real pleasure of letterboxing doesn't lie in sitting in the pubs, of course, but in scouring the upper slopes of Great Mis Tor or Staple Tor in the rain looking in holes in the rock and in the clitter for obscure plastic boxes containing a soggy notebook and a wet stamp. And that's your last clue!

Letterbox stamp from Cosdon Hill

137

Walk 22 – East Mill Tor, Yes Tor, High Willhays

Distance
About 6 miles.

Difficulties
You are in the highest parts of the moor on this walk, even though you are mostly walking on the military roads in the area. Do not underestimate the changeability of the weather, and be prepared with waterproofs and warm clothing. Take enough food to allow for emergencies. A map and compass are necessary, because the military roads can be confusing. You need to follow the range precautions on this walk (see box below).

Main Features

Yes Tor	**581902**
High Willhays	**580895**
Dinger Tor	**586881**
East Mill Tor	**599897**

Description of Walk
*Take the road from Okehampton past Okehampton Army Camp. The road continues past the camp and swings left, over a ford and past Moorgate Cottage. Continue along the rough military road, taking first a right fork and later a left fork until you reach a sign forbidding you to drive any further. This is New Bridge (596904), marked on the map. Park your car here. Near the New Bridge no entry sign is a track to the left (if you are facing Okehampton). Follow it up slope until it meets another military road. Turn back on yourself to the right and follow this higher road until you reach the road coming down from Yes Tor, about 400 yards further on. Turn left up-slope on this road and climb up until you reach the saddle at the ridge joining Yes Tor and High Willhays. Turn right on the ridge and make for the flag-pole at the top of the outcrop. This is **Yes Tor**.*

*From Yes Tor walk along the broad ridge in a southerly direction until you reach the scattered outcrops of **High Willhays**.*

*From High Willhays walk in a south-easterly direction until you reach the military road. Turn right on the road and walk up to **Dinger Tor**, unmistakable with its Army buildings and observation posts.*

*From Dinger Tor follow the road back, until you see a turning on the right after about half a mile. Take this road on the right, and follow it for about three-quarters of a mile until you come to a cross-roads. Turn left here towards Okehampton, and make your way back to New Bridge and the car. **East Mill Tor** is on your right.*

> **This walk takes you into a range area.**
>
> **Check that no firing is planned by ringing the numbers on page 139 or by consulting the National Park Information Centres or Post Offices.**
>
> **Do not cross the line of red and white poles if firing is planned.**

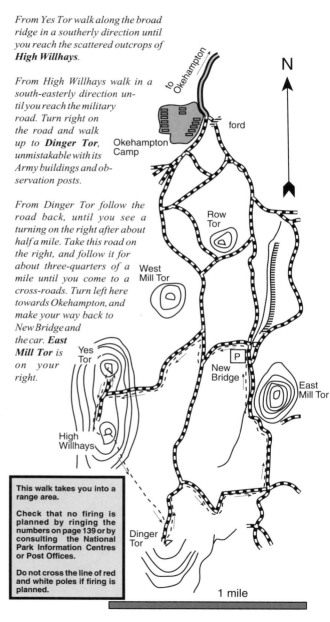

Yes Tor

The top of Yes Tor is home to a huge flag-pole and a couple of huts from where Army exercises are run. On a wet winter's day the shelter is very welcome. A typical exercise would involve one group of soldiers working their way up the slope from the road to the east, while a defending group, dug into shelters in the clitter, attempt to stop it. Both sides use large, relatively harmless fireworks called thunderflashes to represent grenades, and the general effect, with blank rounds and dummy grenades going off, is quite realistic.

The terrain, too, is typical of the upland terrain which British troops are particularly skilled at fighting over, and the hours and days spent training on Dartmoor played a major role in the fitness and skill exhibited by the Royal Marines in the Falklands. You can find many places on the flanks of Yes Tor towards the road where the soldiers have dug in during exercises, but do not touch any material you see there, even spent cartridges.

The name Yes Tor is uncertain in origin. Some people think that it is a corruption of 'highest tor' since the rocky flanks of the tor do give it the definite appearance of being higher than the surrounding land, and High Willhays in particular. It could also come from 'east tor'.

When the summer flush of walkers has gone, you are left with a desolate place high above the green desert-like desolation of the north moor. Around you ravens turn and tumble, calling out their guttural good days to one another. Buzzards lope past on their mysterious daily rounds, and the occasional merlin or sparrowhawk flashes by in pursuit of its prey.

The Army on Dartmoor

If you have walked on the north moor you will not have missed seeing the red and white range poles and the forbidding notices which mark the edges of the areas used by the Army. These mark two main areas in which the military are allowed to engage in live firing. To remove any doubt or uncertainty, when I say live firing, I am referring to high-explosive and rifle rounds being fired at will in the range. You therefore need to know the rules.

Firing takes place quite often throughout the year, and the only way in which you can tell for sure that it is safe at any particular time to go beyond the line of posts is by looking for red flags on the surrounding tors. You will not be left in any doubt as to whether you should proceed. If you do see a large red flag on the relevant tor, then do not cross the line of posts under any circumstances.

You can find out if the ranges will be used on any particular day by ringing one of four telephone numbers (see box). You will hear a recorded message which explains clearly when firing will take place. Alternatively you can go to the post office in any village and get information there.

If, having checked that no firing is taking place, you enter the range area, you will be perfectly safe and you should not be put off by the fact that you are in a live range. Do not, however, pick up anything from the ground and don't go digging.

Generally speaking, the ranges are not used much during August and at weekends, but this is not a reliable means of checking that they are walkable.

Telephone Numbers to ring for Range Information:

Torquay
(01803) 294592
Exeter
(01392) 70164
Plymouth
(01752) 701924
Okehampton
(01837) 52939

Non-Firing Periods

The ranges are not used on the following days:

Saturdays, Sundays and public holidays
The month of August
The week beginning and including the first Sunday in November
20th December to 3rd January inclusive

Okehampton and Merrivale are not used near Easter.

If by 9am from April to September and 10am from October to March the red flags are not flying, then firing will not take place that day. This allows access to the ranges if a last minute cancellation is ordered.

Map Showing the Range Areas

What does the Army do on the ranges? Well, that's an official secret, but apart from training in the use of weapons in conditions which are close to actual combat, the services carry out escape and evasion exercises, where one group of people attempt to clear an area while another group are trying to capture them. You often see small groups of soldiers engaged in patrol drills, where they practise deploying a platoon under fire. The slopes of Yes Tor are particularly useful for practising attacking and defending rocky, steep mountain sides.

One of the great advantages of Dartmoor from the point of view of the Army is that the terrain is very difficult, the weather is often bad and the ground is flat (and therefore tricky to defend) in many places. All this together means that soldiers can train near to barracks in an environment where the safety limitations are not onerous, and the weather and ground conditions are fairly realistic.

Surprisingly, many environmentalists (as opposed to pacifists and walkers' groups) support the use of the moor by the military. While damage is caused, the mere fact that the use by the services excludes many walkers means that there is a degree of protection for the wildlife. The situation is akin to that of the motorway verges which are often very secluded and safe areas for wildlife. They are fine as long as you don't notice the shells in the first case and the lorries in the second!

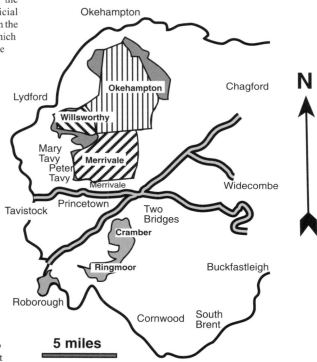

This map is indicative only. Consult the official map for accurate range information.

Okehampton, Merrivale and Willsworthy Ranges are all used for live firings

Jointing

On all the large pieces of granite which you see on this walk, in the most massive of Dartmoor scenery, you will notice that the rock is noticeably jointed both vertically and horizontally. At first it may occur to you that it is a sedimentary rock, laid down under the sea by falling layers of sea shells and mud. Normally such sedimentary rocks reflect the changing rates of deposition, so that, rather like the rings in a tree trunk, they have layers. Granite joints, however, form quite differently.

The granite, as you can read in the introduction to this chapter, welled up from the centre of the Earth many millions of years ago. It forced its way into spaces created as the rocks above it were pushed up by pressure from underneath. This process was not smooth, however, and the granite cooled slightly from time to time. As it cooled it shrank, and as it was then pushed up by a further rising of the molten rock underneath, it tended to crack. These cracks were formed

Clitter

Clitter (or clatter) is the remains of granite which has fallen down from the core of a tor over the years as it is destroyed by the combined action of water, chemicals and frost. The word is related to the well-known clutter which gathers in corners of your home.

Stand near a tor and draw a mental line from the lowest edge of a clitter field to the top of the tor. How did the clitter get so far downslope, when the angle of descent is so small?

an ice sheet. The ground, frozen to depths of tens of yards, would thaw only in the very top layers in the summers. The rocks could then skid down a shallow slope, since they were carried on a thin layer of squidgy mud that overlay a veritable ice rink.

Other reasons for the fact that the clitter lies so far from the original tor is because the walls of the tor stood further out while it was being decayed. A good example of this is

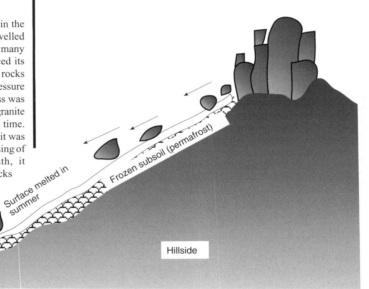

Surface melted in summer

Frozen subsoil (permafrost)

Hillside

Clitter skids down semi-frozen slope during ice age

horizontally as the cooler rock separated from the new, hotter rock, and vertically in the same way as the top of a loaf of bread when it rises in the oven.

The joints were then accentuated as acidic water and frost forced their way into and eroded them.

After all, normally a large piece of rock weighing some 10 tons doesn't throw itself off a tor and land such a long way away. It appears that the rocks of clitter fields were transported so far down a shallow slope by skidding down the half-frozen ground when the area of Britain north of Dartmoor was covered in

any cleave, particularly the one in which the Tavy flows.

Be particularly careful when walking over clitter. One false step and you could experience the agony of a broken ankle and the danger of not being able to get back to your car before nightfall.

High Willhays

You might expect there to be a massive tor on the top of High Willhays, the highest point on Dartmoor, but if you do so you will be disappointed. There is only a low outcrop of rock.

The view, however, makes up for this. The prominent hill behind you, on the same height (actually 10 feet lower) is Yes Tor, which for many years was thought to be the highest tor on the moor. All the moormen knew it wasn't, of course, and it came as no surprise that when the Ordnance Survey measured its height accurately Yes Tor was relegated to being only the second highest spot on Dartmoor. There is no other higher point than High Willhays in England until you get to Ingleborough in Yorkshire. Wales, however, which has proper mountains, rather spoils things by getting in between.

Looking directly towards Dinger Tor you can see a pool of water glinting in the sun (or occasionally glinting in the pouring rain). This is Redaven Pool, sometimes known as Dinger Pool, or Pixies' Pool. Beyond that you can see Hangingstone Hill to the left, and, to the right of Dinger Tor and further away, Cut Hill and the distinguished top of Fur Tor. The whole of the area between you and these tors is a morass of upland bog, a peat desert full of life and movement, but on a scale which you will find difficult to access. As you walk over the land, it seems

devoid of life until you stop, sit and wait for the animal and insect life to make itself known to you.

The name High Willhays is almost certainly a corruption of the Welsh *gwylfa,* which means a watching spot. A number of hills in Wales have the same name, including Yr Wylfa or Snowdon. As the Welsh language and the Cornish come from the same roots, the words are often

VAB

Look for rowan trees in the little valleys on this walk

very similar. There is in Cornwall a hill called Brown Willy, which is further evidence of a Welsh/Cornish derivation, since brown, here, is probably corruption of *bryn,* meaning a hill.

Stop a while here and wait for the birdlife to start appearing. The antics of the ravens when are particularly worth waiting for.

Dinger Tor

This isolated tor has been, in some people's minds, spoiled by the presence of an Army observation post or 'OP'. Like someone wearing a tasteless tie, I would prefer to be behind it looking out rather than looking at it, but each to his own taste. The post has superb views over the northern part of Dartmoor. It is also a good place to sit down and read the explanations elsewhere in this chapter on the formation of peat and the way in which the rivers of Dartmoor leave the high ground, often forming cleaves, or narrow steep-sided valleys which they wear down into the edges of the moor.

The wildlife up here is also fabulous. You will see buzzards and other raptors frequently, including the occasional merlin, and in summer the air is alive with the sound of skylarks and pipits going about their aerial business. The 'cronk cronk' of ravens is a frequent sound, and if you see large black birds tumbling and turning in the air, they are certain to be these. If you lie quietly on the top of the old Army buildings you can often see voles and others small rodents, as well as the foxes which traffic their way back and forth all over the moor, generally in the darker hours.

The Army buildings here form an observation post, number 20, in fact, from which the range flags can be flown, and from where the activities of the exercising soldiers and, more importantly the ordinary citizens on the outside, can be observed. The OP is built from an old cottage which used to occupy the site.

Walk 23 – Tavy Cleave and Fur Tor

Distance
8 miles.

Difficulties
This walk passes through the military ranges, so you must take the relevant range precautions. You will also be going deep into the heart of the north moor, so take adequate waterproof clothing and food. You should carry extra warm clothing and enough food to keep you going in an emergency. You will need a map and compass, plus stout walking boots. The ground can be very wet in places.

Main Features
Mine Leat	540826
Tavy Cleave	553831
Dead Lake Foot	
Settlements	562840
Sandy Ford	572834
Fur Tor	586832

This walk takes you into a range area.

Check that no firing is planned by ringing the numbers on page 139 or by consulting the national park information centres or post offices.

Do not cross the line of red and white poles if firing is planned.

Description of Walk
Take the road from Horndon toward Willsworthy. Go over Willsworthy Bridge and through Higher Willsworthy until you reach the open moor at Lane Head (536824), just past Lane End. Lock your car, and walk directly away from the road upslope until you come across the **Mine Leat**. Look along the leat. In places it looks as if it is running uphill. Turn right along the leat and follow it until it enters **Tavy Cleave**, the gorge through which the Tavy runs under Ger Tor.

Continue upstream along the Tavy through the cleave, until you reach a large tributary on the left. This is **Dead Lake**, and the settlements can be found near the junction of the Dead Lake and the Tavy.

Cross the Dead Lake and continue up the Tavy until you come to a pronounced Y in the river at **Sandy Ford**. Cross to the ground between the two streams ahead of you, to the east of Sandy Ford.

From here **Fur Tor** is a huge rock pile seen easily on the skyline. Make your way up to the top. To return, make your way back down to Sandy Ford, and then retrace your steps to Dead Lake.

From the point where Dead Lake joins the Tavy, turn up Dead Lake and after 200 yards or so turn at right angles to the tributary and walk up the stream on the left. This will take you to a track which picks its way to the south-west under Hare Tor and between it and the Tavy. The track peters out after about a half-mile, at which point you should continue in the same direction until you can make out Ger Tor, on the north side of Tavy Cleave.

From Ger Tor make your way back to the car-park to the south-west, crossing the leat on the way.

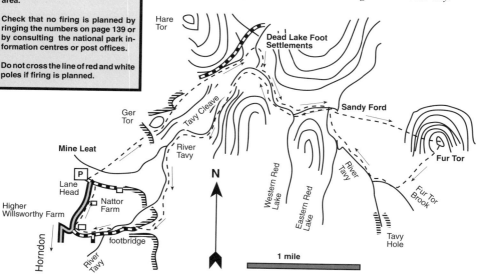

143

Dead Lake Foot Settlement

There is an excellent example of a Bronze Age settlement at the lower end of Dead Lake. If you look carefully in the bracken of summer you can make out the foundations of about sixteen huts, some of them used for accommodation, others for storage purposes or for the sheltering of animals.

You may care to ponder on the sophistication of the placement of the villages. One of the considerations was the warming effect of the sun in the morning or evening, and you find very few on the north-facing slopes of valleys. Ovicaprids (sheep, goats and hybrids) were pastured on northern slopes on occasion, however, because the lambing time of these animals is very dependent upon the length of day, and this can be controlled by choosing where you pasture them.

If you have a fragile flock which nevertheless gives good meat or milk, then you pasture it on a north-facing slope so the animals lamb later when the weather is more clement.

Geologically speaking, Dead Lake Foot is interesting because of the tin-mining remains here. The tinners worked their way upstream, cutting back into the tin lodes after they had exhausted the stream-bed tin which originally indicated the presence of tin further upstream. Dead Lake (a name which occurs frequently) refers to an unproductive lode.

You will have noticed that Walk 19 also visits a Dead Lake Settlement on the river Walkham. The tinners

N

track

Rattle Brook

100 yards

Dead Lake settlement

put a great deal of effort into developing an area, as you can see here, and to find no ore after all that work meant considerable disappointment to them, and in some cases their ruin.

Tavy Hole

Near the top of the profile of the River Tavy is an enclosed area known as Tavy Hole. Don't expect any spectacular drop into the earth as you do in Yorkshire or the Mendips; this is merely a confined place, but a very pleasant one all the same.

To the south-west is an area known as Horsey Park, which is not indicated on the map, but which marks a traditional turf-cutting place for the foresters. It is well known for being a rich source of whinberries, or whorts or hurts as they are called in the area, from which good money could be made in summer.

Tavy Hole is a good place to sit and contemplate the course of the rivers

Amicombe to your right and the little River Tavy on which you sit as they meander their way across this upland plateau.

In particular, you can imagine yourself looking out over a coastal scene, because at one point in Dartmoor's history the sea-level was at the tip of Tavy Cleave itself. When the sea-level dropped, the Tavy was given new energy to cut its way down into the rock thereby forming the cleave.

Tavy Hole

Fur Tor

Most walkers on the moor have a soft spot for Fur Tor. It lies in a most inaccessible place, and anyone you meet here will have had sufficient commitment to walk for a number of hours to reach it. That includes you, and you should congratulate yourself on reaching what used to be one of the most inaccessible places in England. It was here that one of the first letterboxes was set up, where you could leave a postcard for the next visitor to post for you. There is still one here on the side of the main stack.

Fur Tor, or Vurre Tor, is probably the most spectacular example of a granite tor. You can see from the general arrangement of the tor that it consists of a granite top with towers (from whence the word tor came via the Celtic *twr*, a tower), supported by a huge mass of rock hidden by grass and large lumps of broken granite known as clitter. You can see at Fur Tor the way the granite has pushed up into a dome shape and then been worn away to produce the much-eroded structure you see today. Like most tors Fur Tor has a number of towers or stacks, and these are the remains of a much larger granite boss which would have stretched up many times the height of the present structure. Above it would have lain the sedimentary superstructure, and when that cracked and was eroded, acidic water, ice and wind were allowed to work at the original granite.

Gradually the granite boss was eroded, and as it decayed over many thousands of years great lumps of rock fell off, separating along natural fault lines produced in the formation of the granite, until the sides of the tor were covered in a cone of granite

The top of Fur Tor

pieces of various sizes. Where these were most dense they remain to produce the fields of broken rock known as clitter. Elsewhere they were broken down to produce soils and eventually, in some cases, the china clay and growan which appears as a grey gravelly material under your boots.

There are at least three rock basins on the tor. These are formed as water and ice worked their way in between the crystals in the granite and formed natural pools.

As you sit on any of the great towers of Fur Tor you have a view of some the best wilderness in Europe. You can see the great grey-green desert of the northern morass all around you. Ravens and buzzards are common, as are pipits and skylarks, and on the busiest day you can find a place where you could be the last human being, or the first, on Earth.

145

Aircraft on the Moor

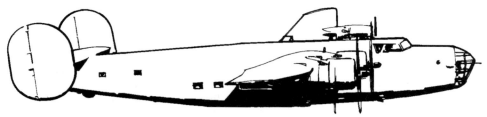

Liberator bomber

On the opposite side of the Tavy from Black Tor lie the remains of a Liberator bomber which came down in the area during its return from a training flight. You can see the remains from that side of the Tavy although they are obscured by clitter and vegetation. There were a number of crashes during World War II, mostly because of the inaccuracy of altimeters and through tiredness of the crews. The sudden rise of the land as you came upon the upper slopes of the moor was a most unwelcome surprise.

Ger Tor

This is a fine spot on which to appreciate the perspective from the point of view of the Bronze Age settlers who established their little village on the top of the slope. This is an obvious place for a settlement because of the easily defensible nature of the ground. From the top you can see down to the present road-end, and this presents an ideal view of strangers arriving to threaten your cattle down on the relatively good pasture below. There would most likely have been a good supply of wood in the valley to your left.

The main reason for coming to Ger Tor from the point of view of the geography is that it allows you to look along the length of the Tavy Cleave. You can see the extent of the slope and the way in which the clitter from the slopes of the valley has been thrown sideways from the slope. This is possible for three reasons. First, some of the clitter will have been formed when the valley first started to be eroded, so it gradually worked its way downwards. Second, the large lumps

Ger Tor and Tavy Cleave

of rock which were shed during the erosion of the steep-sided valley by the river were allowed to trundle downhill gradually because they were thrown on to a slope of snow. Third, the effects of periglaciation in the area were considerable, particularly with regard to the thawing of a thin top layer of soil in the summers of the Ice Age. This allowed a very slippery upper layer of mud to form over a veritable icerink of a subsoil. Big chunks of clitter would then have careered down relatively shallow slopes towards where the river runs today.

Walk 24 – Great Mis Tor

This walk takes you into a range area.

Check that no firing is planned by ringing the numbers on page 139 or by consulting the national park information centres or post offices.

Do not cross the line of red and white poles if firing is planned.

Distance
About 3 miles.

Difficulties
Although this walk takes you up to one of the highest tors, it is not difficult since it follows tracks almost all the way. You must be aware, however, that it lies within the firing ranges of the north moor, and so you should take the appropriate range precautions.

Take warm clothing and water-proofs with you and make sure that you have enough food to keep you going. A map and compass are not essential, but are a useful safety measure since the area is prone to mist, from which Mis(t) Tor gets its name. More people get lost on Great Mis Tor than any other, mostly because it is easily accessible.

Main Features

Little Mis Tor	564764
Great Mis Tor	562769
Mis Tor Pan	562769
Rundlestone	574749
Fice's Well	576758

Description of Walk
From the Four Winds car-park on the Princetown–Tavistock road (**561749**), in between Rundlestone and Merrivale, walk up the graded track opposite. You will soon arrive at **Little Mis Tor**, a cube-shaped mass of rock that lies on the left of the track.

From Little Mis Tor continue up the track towards the mass of **Great Mis Tor**. Soon the track peters out, but you should continue up the slope to the mass of rocks. The granite mass of Great Mis Tor is divided into a number of outcrops. You will find the rock basin called **Mis Tor Pan** on the highest outcrop, towards the north end.

Having had your fill of the views into the great northern morass to the north, go back to the south end of the outcrops and walk directly towards the television mast on North Hessary Tor. You will soon pick up a straight track which leads directly to the little hamlet of **Rundlestone**. Look for the prominent boundary stone near the junction lay-by. Follow this down to the main road, then turn left and walk down the road until you see the signposted footpath on the left leading through the prison grounds north to **Fice's Well**. Return to the main road and turn right heading through Rundlestone eventually to reach the Four Winds car-park

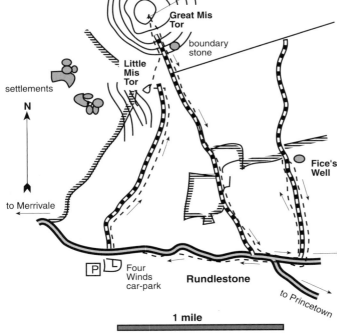

147

Little Mis Tor

The cubical rock mass of Little Mis Tor, or, as it is sometimes called, Wain Tor, is a striking feature of the scene from the road at Four Winds and remains a remarkably shaped rock even as you approach it. The track which you follow is an access road for the military to the observation point at the top of Great Mis Tor, and you can usually see the tracks left by vehicles as they run off the track above Little Mis Tor to offload troops making the short walk to the top.

If you stop and rest at Little Mis Tor, go round to the side away from the road and look into the valley of the Walkham. This valley (which you can visit in Walk 19), has been inhabited for thousands of years. It shows very visible evidence of major Bronze Age settlements, which spread up the valley towards the north.

Equally, the tinners who came to Dartmoor thousands of years later found the Walkham Valley an attractive and profitable place to work, and some of the best-preserved tinners' buildings are to be found there.

As you inspect Little Mis Tor, you might find the odd letterbox in which you can leave your name and address. Take a copy of the stamp you will find in the box, and then return it safely to the same place where you found it. You don't get any detailed directions; you'll just have to look down all the nooks and crannies until you find it.

Great Mis Tor

This high place, towering above the great marsh to its north, is one of the boundary points of the north moor. As you stand among its fantastical rock towers and look out to the north, you have the impression of a Wild West frontier town. Behind you is the comforting track which leads straightforwardly back to your car at

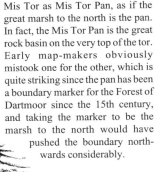

Mis Tor Pan

Four Winds, but ahead of you lies miles of rough walking and wet wilderness among the upland bogs and the huge tors of the north moor.

Great Mis Tor gets its name from the mists which always seem to strike it whenever a weather front comes in. The moormen look to it as the harbinger of rain. It is invariably the first top to be covered in cloud when there is a change in the weather. For this reason, although it is so accessible from the road, don't be tempted to treat it casually. I have been up on the top on half a dozen occasions in thick mist, looking with interest at my compass, to be approached by a group of stiletto-heeled walkers carrying a good book and little else, and wanting to know the way back.

The map here has got it wrong, by the way. It marks the area north of

Mis Tor as Mis Tor Pan, as if the great marsh to the north is the pan. In fact, the Mis Tor Pan is the great rock basin on the very top of the tor. Early map-makers obviously mistook one for the other, which is quite striking since the pan has been a boundary marker for the Forest of Dartmoor since the 15th century, and taking the marker to be the marsh to the north would have pushed the boundary northwards considerably.

The top of Great Mis Tor is a delight for kids and adults alike. The towering pinnacles of rock look tremendously off-putting, but they are all easy to climb, from the back if not the front. The views over to the Staple Tors and northwards into the wilderness are also impressive, particularly on a day of neither unbroken sunshine nor persistent rain.

Note the jointing in the main blocks of granite. Here the huge granite mass shows very strongly the incipient cracks left when it rose upwards under its crust of sedimentary rocks, pausing and cooling, and then regaining its momentum upwards under the tremendous pressure from below. Look carefully at the detail of the rock, and you will see the mica crystals which were formed as the granite finally cooled, the minerals migrating through the just molten rock and collecting in pockets.

To the south-east you will see a prominent standing stone, one of a set of six which marks the boundary between the Forest of Dartmoor and the parish of Walkhampton.

148

Great Mis Tor Pan

I could attract your interest by telling you that the great basin cut in the rock at the very top of Great Mis Tor was made by Druids in ancient times in order to provide a suitable receptacle for the blood which poured from their human victims during the grisly ceremonies that were held here before the Romans invaded. This was certainly what the majority of people believed until the geologists offered a different explanation.

Granite, as we know, has a structure which is layered like puff pastry. When a layer of rock is exposed to the weather, it tends, on Dartmoor of all places, to get wet. The water is drawn into the slightest crack. When the water freezes it expands and, if the rock is flat and suitably cracked, the crack will be widened and small mineral crystals will fall away from its sides. Sometimes this merely

Great Mis Tor

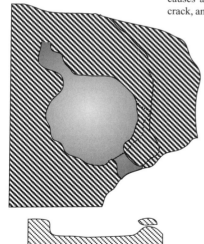

3 feet

Detail of Mis Tor Pan

causes a general widening of the crack, and you can see the effect of this all round you on Great Mis Tor. If, however, the general configuration of the rock is flat, the freeze-thaw process will tend to undercut the edges of the little pool.

After thousands of years, and particularly during the heavy period of freeze-thaw which took place on the edges of the great ice sheets 40,000 years ago, this process of undercutting can take place rather quickly. The result is the remarkable basin that you see in front of you at the very top of the tor.

You can see that the undercutting has been so severe that the basin is pierced on the southern side. This led to further speculation about the esoteric nature of basins such as this.

There are a number of spectacular basins on Dartmoor, but Mis Tor Pan is the best known. It is about 3 feet wide and 6 inches in depth, deepening gradually each year. The rate of growth has decreased dramatically since the end of the last Ice Age because of the reduced intensity of the freeze-thaw process.

The basin has a history which goes back to the late 13th century, and was first called Mistor Pan in 1690. The oldest stories tell of the Devil riding the moors with his evil hounds, and returning to Great Mis Tor to fry his breakfast in the Devil's Frying Pan.

149

Dartmoor Prison and Thomas Tyrwhitt

For some of this walk you will be within the grounds of Dartmoor Prison. The path up to Fice's Well goes through the outer fields of the prison farm, and you will often see bands of workers from the prison in this area. The prison houses long-term prisoners of all types, but only those coming to the end of their sentences and who are trusted not to take advantage are allowed to serve on the prison farm. This is considered very much a privilege not just because it allows access to the open air, but because it offers a skill to inmates about to restart their lives outside.

Thomas Tyrwhitt was the creator of Princetown prison, and indeed the town itself. He set himself up in the area by taking advantage of his friendship with the then Prince of Wales (hence the name of the town) in 1785 at a splendid house called Tor Royal. His declared aim was to improve the lands on Dartmoor by building drainage systems and by importing fertilizer. Sadly, his grand scheme was not feasible, in spite of his being made Warden of the Stannaries, an official post which allowed him virtually complete freedom of action on Dartmoor. He died a bankrupt and broken man.

One of the spin-offs of his great scheme was to build a prison at Princetown to house the prisoners from the Napoleonic Wars. When the Napoleonic Wars finished the prison was shut down, but in the 19th century it was reopened for the housing of civil prisoners. It has remained in use until the present day.

The Rundlestone

Rundlestone is now the name of the small collection of houses a short way from Princetown. It takes its name from a marker stone of the same name which was destroyed around 1882. The stone stood prominently on a hill near the present village. At this point the boundary of the forest ran up from Rundlestone to the top of Great Mis Tor through six large boundary stones. The lowest of these, the Rundlestone, was included in 1702.

The area around here has a number of stones which mark the boundary of the lands of Dartmoor Prison, which stands just north of Princetown. You can tell them by the letters 'DCP' cut into the sides; this stands for Directors of Convict Prisons.

The little village of Rundlestone has an eerie story associated with it. There was a schoolmaster, a competent artist, who taught at the prison. One winter's day he went to Tavistock and became caught in a worsening blizzard some miles from his home in Princetown. He called at a cottage in Moorshop to the west of here, and was advised not to continue, but he did so, wanting to get back to his family. The enclosure wall in Rundlestone marks his final resting place, where he was caught in a swirling Dartmoor blizzard only yards from safety.

The eerie part of the story is that the last work which the amateur artist completed some days before setting off was of a man dying in a snow-storm.

Fice's Well

There are two wells with the name Fitz or Fice's Well. Both have a story of a thirsty nobleman associated with them, the wells being dedicated and walled as a result of his returning from a hunting expedition and finding a source of clear drinkable water to hand. This particular one of the pair commemorates the experience of a John Fice who, with his wife, was led by pixies over the moor while out hunting. They were entrapped for some days by the mischievous fairies. On finding and drinking this water they found themselves free from the fairies' spell. We do know that the well was made in 1568, by someone with the initials JF, so there is some evidence for part of the story at least.

Many of the Celtic rituals involved the dedication of springs and pools to the deities who they believed lived underground. A spring like Fice's Well would have been viewed as an entrance to the underground world of the gods. Other important features of Celtic ritual were the dressing of trees with strips of coloured cloth, and the 'cult of the severed head'. This latter cult used stone models of detached heads, not particularly gruesome in their style, but nevertheless rather offputting to the modern eye. The echoes of the practice of dressing trees can be seen today in a number of local traditions, and at least one authority sees a link with the yellow ribbons tied around trees in the United States for remembrance.

The local people say that Fice's Well gives warm water in winter and cold water in summer, which, although romantic, does reflect the fact that the water, originating from far underground tends to adopt a constant temperature of +3°C.

Walk 25 – Lydford Gorge

Distance
2 miles.

Difficulties
Apart from the occasional slippery rock, there is no danger in this walk whatsoever. The paths are steep and hard work, particularly in hot, sticky weather. Dogs on leads only.

Main Features
Lydford Castle	**509848**
Lydford Gorge	**505843**
White Lady Waterfall	**503832**
Devil's Cauldron	**508845**

Description of Walk
Lydford Gorge is one of Devon's greatest tourist attractions, and is signposted from the centre of Lydford town. Follow the signs to the car-park and pay your money. The gorge is owned by the National Trust, and the money goes towards maintaining it and the other properties owned by the Trust throughout England and Wales.

From the upper car-park take the longer route on the upper side of the valley. You will gradually work your way along at quite a high level until you are at the top of the slope down which the **White Lady Waterfall** descends. The well-waymarked path takes you back along the valley floor, past a number of interesting detailed geological features described in the geological guide to the gorge. The path

eventually leads you to the **Devil's Cauldron**, a spectacular water-worn pot-hole, enclosed by rock walls, into which the river throws itself. The path meanders over and around the river valley, and at one point goes through a rock wall after crossing the gorge on a narrow bridge.

You will eventually reach the car-park, having done a loop above and along the valley. The information

shop sells a map and guide which is worth buying.

After visiting the gorge, go back into Lydford town to see the impressive **Lydford Castle**, a prison in which many men were detained after crossing the tinners. The building has been partly restored and you can go into the prison and walk around, even on the upper floors, and see the places where the unfortunates passed their days.

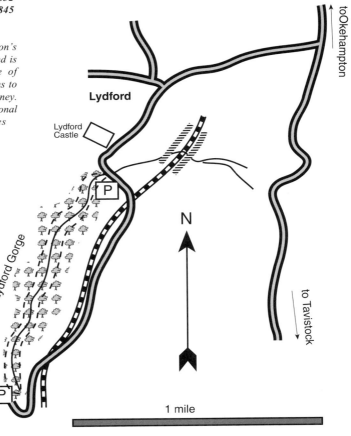

151

Lydford Law

As you come into Lydford you will see the stone mass of Lydford Castle, which was the repository for offenders who transgressed the stannary laws and those of the forest. The severity of the forest laws was legendary and the place came to have a reputation for summary punishment:

I oft have heard of Lydford Law,
How in the morn they hang and
*   draw,*
And sit in judgement after.

In fact, the reputation for arbitrary justice is unfounded, although the penalties for transgressing the forest laws, along with other laws at the time, were indeed very serious. The misconception regarding punishment before trial was due to the timing of the different layers of the justice system. The lowest court was called the Court of Attachments, and was held every forty days. The job of the verderers, the members of the Court of Attachment, was to make presentation to the Court of Swainmote. The latter, being comprised of freemen of the forest, was not subject to being overruled by its superior court, namely The Court of Justice Seat, which was held only once every three years. Hence, even though the superior court had to underwrite the sentence it could not overrule it. So, the offenders could be punished in theory, before the legal process was over.

Lydford Castle was described during Henry VIII's time as 'one of the most annoius (i.e. irritating) contagious and detestable places within this realm'. Its reputation was partly built upon the severity of the forest laws, which sought to protect the interests of the verderers of the forest who held special privileges of pasturing beasts and of gathering

In the bottom of Lydford Gorge

stone and wood, and who protected it ruthlessly. Judge Jeffreys, the notorious 'Hanging Judge', sat at times at Lydford and did nothing to weaken its reputation.

Stannary law refers to the special provisions made for the tin industry on the moor in the 12th and 13th centuries. The first recorded document on the subject of stannary law was by Sir George Harrison in 1198. Tin was only allowed to be taken to one of three towns on the edge of the moor, Tavistock, Chagford, and Ashburton. Later Plympton was made a stannary town to replace Tavistock, which later still reclaimed

its position. Lydford was never a stannary town, but as the centre for justice and punishment, is often included mistakenly.

If you visit the castle, you can still see the deep pit under the ground in which Richard Strode was imprisoned for crossing the tinners. He was the MP for Plympton who sought to stop them silting up the harbour with the spoil from their workings. It is a measure of the power of the tinners through their contribution to the Royal Purse and their rights under Edward I's charter that they could arraign and try Strode, imprisoning him under what is now Lydford Castle.

Lydford Town

The present-day aspect of Lydford is of a rather disorganized village dominated by the castle and by the National Trust site at Lydford Gorge, but it was not always like that. During medieval times the town was a thriving fortified borough which had a mint (no wonder it was fortified!). The coins were made from local silver and in the Castle Inn is an example of a silver penny struck during the reign of Aethelred. The town was a borough by the time of the Domesday Book, late in the 11th century. The Lich Way ended here, where burial ceremonies were carried out for places as far away as Widecombe.

As you can read on page 152, Lydford Castle was actually the correction centre for offenders against the severe forest and stannary Laws, and had a reputation worse than many Mediterranean tourist hotels as far as service, standards of accommodation and food are concerned.

In the pleasant churchyard of St Petrock, on the right-hand side of the church door, you can find the famous epitaph of George Routleigh, a watchmaker – *see* right.

The most famous inhabitants of Lydford were the Gubbins family. They were a godless, savage tribe who lived by plunder in the 17th century. Thomas Fuller, who visited the area in 1644 wrote 'They live in cots (rather holes than houses) like swine, having all in common, multiplied without marriage into many hundreds ... they live by stealing the sheep on the moor; and in vain it is for any to search their houses, being a work ... above the power of any constable. Such [is] their fleetness, they will outrun many horses... '

Here lies in horizontal position
The outside case of
George Routleigh, Watchmaker
Whose abilities in that line were an honour
To his profession.
Integrity was the mainspring
And prudence the regulator
Of all the actions of his life.
Humane generous and liberal
His hand had never stopped
Till he had relieved distress.
So nicely regulated were all his motions
That he never went wrong
Except when set going
By people
Who did not know his key.
Even then he was easily
Set right again.
He had the art of disposing his time
So well
That his hours glided away
In one continual round
Of pleasure and delight
Till an unlucky minute put a period to
His existence.
He departed this life
Nov. 14 1802
Aged 57
Wound up
In hopes of being taken in hand
By his Maker
And of being thoroughly cleaned, repaired
And set agoing
In the world to come.

The gravestone of George Routleigh in St Petrock's church, Lydford

Geography & Geology

Lydford Gorge

Geologically speaking, Lydford Gorge is the result of a river cutting down into hard rock which has been lifted underneath, so increasing the erosive power of the river. As a river proceeds along its path it loses energy. If the ground underneath it is raised, however, either by the rocks rising or by the sea-level falling, the river achieves a greater ability to transport material, and so cuts its way down more quickly. If, in addition, it finds itself cutting down through hard rocks, the sides become very steep. This is because the normal processes of collapse which we would expect to see in softer rocks do not come into play.

The result is a stunning example of a steep-sided gorge with great granite sides and bubbling, swarming pools and torrents. This is an absolute must for anyone who is interested in the geography and geology of Dartmoor.

The River Lyd starts its life high up on Dartmoor just the other side of the watershed of the West Okement, which makes a roughly similar gorge to the north-west of Lydford. The Lyd, however, flows gently away to the south-west until it reaches a band of particularly hard rock in Lydford. On the way it flows over a number of nickpoints caused by the changes in sealevel during the Ice Ages. Here jumps in the river's profile indicate that the ground level has risen under it, thereby increasing its energy and causing a step in its otherwise smooth passage towards the sea. When the river enters the gorge, however, it is constrained in the band of rock and falls over a spectacular waterfall and chute called the White Lady. This is where you begin your walk along the valley bottom, having followed a clear path

The White Lady waterfall in Lydford Gorge

from the upper car-park along the top of the gorge. All is clearly laid out for you by the National Trust, which has control of the area.

Stop at the bottom of the waterfall and remember the way in which a waterfall is formed. The weight of water and the abrasive qualities of the material it carries gradually wear away a pool at the bottom, which you can see clearly, and equally gradually wear the rock wall back. So, the waterfall is moving incredibly slowly back into the rock.

The foot of the gorge is a absolute delight, with many ferns and other water-loving plants clinging to the rocks. At one point you go through

the living rock, looking down on some spectacular pot-holes, that formed as the water, carrying ground rocky material, scoured out a pot-shaped cavity in the bedrock.

The plant life of Lydford Gorge is of considerable interest. Because of the high humidity and ubiquitous surface water mosses and ferns populate the rock walls freely. These plants have colonized areas where the more usual species find it difficult to grow, thus gaining themselves an ecological foothold where they have fewer competitors. Look for the harts tongue fern on the rock walls. It has leaves like a thick green leather belt. Away from the rock walls you will find many woodland species such as wood sorrel (a white-flowered plant with clover-shaped leaves), violets, primrose and bluebell.

In the gorge you will frequently catch sight of the dipper, a white-breasted bird which flits from rock to rock along the tumbling river. It is remarkable in that it hunts for insects underwater, using the downward pressure of the water on its wings to keep it on the bed of the river. You will frequently see the common pied wagtail and the slightly rarer grey wagtail (so called because it is largely yellow), which forage along the stream bed.

Towards the end of the walk, as you climb up the side of the gorge at the other end from the White Lady, you can go along a short platform with handrails to a thunderous hole in the rock that is open to the sky, down which many tons of water thunder to form a boiling vat of spray. This is the Devil's Cauldron. The notice says that this detour is not for the fainthearted, but I would thoroughly recommend it.

House

& Home

During Bronze Age times there were many thousands of dwellings on Dartmoor. We looked at the way of life of those people, who lived about 3,000 years ago, in the Ancient Farms & People chapter, but in this chapter we discover the buildings people built later, from around the 10th century until Victorian times. In particular we visit the medieval village of Houndtor where excavators have left us a marvellous layout on the moor of a medieval farm, farmyard and field system. Here the remains of a typical multi-family farmstead are laid out on the moor as if it had just been left. You can sit down in the farmyard and imagine your stock and yourself as part of the medieval farming scene. The original walls have been exposed by the excavators, and these show the paths and the layout of the buildings in a most accessible way.

Many medieval buildings are still inhabited today, and we will have the opportunity to look at how these developed from being combined cowsheds and sleeping accommodation to become the traditional Dartmoor house of today. On the edge of Dartmoor you can see the distinguished typical Dartmoor house which evolved directly from these primitive medieval dwellings.

Every region has its distinctive style of building, arising primarily from the available materials. On Dartmoor we find the extensive use of local granite, characteristically in what is known as broad and narrow work, where thin slabs of granite are used to face walls. The use of the local stone provides most attractive architectural features, and we shall visit a number of older houses where the features are particularly good. We can also see some of the distinctive features of Dartmoor life, such as potato caves and ash houses.

Later buildings, notably from the 17th century, are particularly fine, with splendid round arches, also made from stone. These provide the basis for a number of fine Dartmoor villages in the in-country, as the region just below the high moor is known. These 17th-century cottages are hardly known outside the area but are well worth visiting.

The splendid house of Castle Drogo, built by Lutyens, provides the focus of the last walk, where we can see the contrast between this and the hovels used by the moormen of earlier centuries. Looking as it does over what many people consider is one of the best views in Devon, this great square house, carefully constructed in dressed granite, is a fabulous example of imaginative early 20th-century architecture and planning.

The Development of the Dartmoor House

The Dartmoor house stemmed in the first instance from a tradition of mixed stone and wooden buildings which goes right back to the Bronze Age at least, if not earlier. In the late Bronze Age and early Iron Age, before the invasion of the lowlands by the Romans, farmers dwelt in groups on the moor. Their small collections of houses had probably a collective yard and garden, which we see today in the rounded enclosures known as pounds.

Iron Age huts and hamlets, known as *oppida,* are not well represented on Dartmoor, although the fort of White Tor (visited in Walk 19) contains some limited remains of living accommodation. The Roman invasion, which interrupted the high civilization of the British and European Celtic Iron Age, hardly touched Dartmoor as we know it today. The invading armies passed north and south of the moor, but the changing climate and living conditions had meant that the majority of the population by AD50 lived away from the moor proper.

Soon the Romans left, bequeathing the Celtic population their roads, laws, civil structures and living habits. Life was not easy for the next few hundred years, however, and

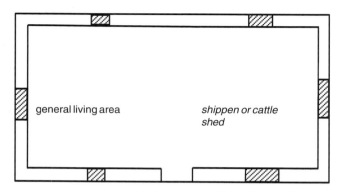

Fig. 1 People and stock live together

the effect of the barbarian invasions was even felt here on the fringes of what used to be the Roman Empire. Trade slowed, unrest made the economy of Europe difficult and Angles, Jutes, Saxons and others arrived on Britain's shores and pushed back the Celtic farmers.

By about AD500 the south-west of Britain had moved noticeably towards what we would recognize today as an early medieval farming lifestyle. We begin to see the monasteries exerting their cultivating influence in the south, and we also begin to see the establishment of medieval hamlets and farmsteads in the region.

A step backward had been taken, however, in terms of living conditions. Whereas in the Iron Age there was a separation between the people and the livestock, medieval practice was to build one longhouse and live together with the animals. It has been said by one medieval historian that by the end of the winter you stepped up a foot to enter these early farmhouses, and when the manure from the animals was cleared out in the spring, you stepped down 2 feet to enter! There was one great advantage, however, in that you kept warm, since the heat generated by the rotting manure and by the beasts themselves made an effctive central-heating system which supplemented the open-hearth fire.

You can see the layout of this sort of simple shelter in Fig. 1. The left-hand side is primarily for the people while the right is for the cattle and any sheep that needed shelter.

Soon the builders developed a partition, firstly in wood, and later in stone to divide the cattle area, or shippen as it was known, from the kitchen and dairy. This provided easy access to the stock without

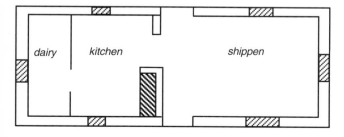

Fig. 2 Partition built between beasts and people

having to go outside, but gave an element of separation from the beasts themselves, although the stench of manure would still have been impressive to the refined modern nose. In Fig. 2 you can see how the hearth has been extended to form part of the partition, and another wall has been built to give people access to the kitchen and to the shippen. At first the partition would have been wooden, but the provision of a stone partition later allowed its eventual extension upwards to provide a first floor. At this early stage in the development of the Dartmoor longhouse, however, we are looking at a single-storey dwelling.

We can see other examples of this type of hut in the west of Ireland and Scotland today. Known as the *tigh dubh*, or black house, they represent a very practical solution to low-cost housing and the exigencies of upland weather. If you are prepared to live cheek by muzzle with the animals, the turf roof and low walls give you a very practical dwelling at no cost. The walls are of drystone walling, picked up from the moorland clitter, and the inside is dug down to provide a clean earth floor, somewhat damp but certainly draught-proof.

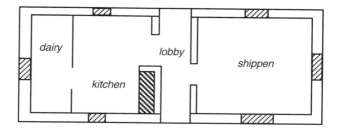

Fig. 3 *Lobby separates people and stock*

The next enhancement is the complete separation of man from animals by the building of another partition. Initially in wood and later in stone, this provided a lobby between the shippen and the kitchen. This must have been a major improvement, because the animals could now be driven in by one door away from the internal kitchen door, and then right into the cowshed. The manure was removed from the back door in due course. With the building of a stone partition in this fashion, the way was open for first-floor building, and we begin to see rooms constructed above the shippen and the kitchen/parlour.

All the time here we are making out that each house developed in the same way. This is, of course, not

true. Some built outhouses (known on Dartmoor as 'outshots') to replace the dairy, for example, while others had a different door arrangement.

Even the Bronze Age people had porches to protect them from the cold winds, and it was not long before the provision of a porch with seats on both sides, made entirely of stone, was the star attraction at the AD900 Ideal Home Exhibition. Everyone had to have one and we can imagine the porch being a very attractive sitting-out area in the summer, after the milking was done and the hay turned. A typical arrangement of this can be seen in Fig. 4.

The last desirable addition to the Dartmoor longhouse continues the wish to keep the cattle completely separate from the people. This is easily achieved by knocking through the shippen wall to provide a self-contained cattle shed, so that there need be no contact with the cattle at all. The door in the lobby wall was very useful, however, since it allowed access to the shippen in all weathers without actually going out in to the wind and rain.

This style of house has been a practical form of farm building for a thousand years. I can remember

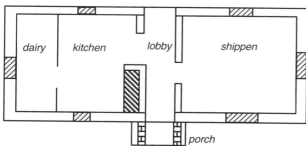

Fig. 4 *A porch is added*

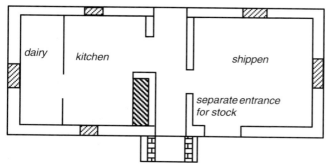

Fig. 5 Stock area has a separate entrance

myself living in one in the farming country of south Wales (not very far away), the only difference being that the door between the shippen and the farmhouse was blocked up, but you could still hear the occasional cow mooing late at night. It was a very clean and practical way to live, too, since, as soon as you separate the cattle coming and going from the people, you can achieve a level of cleanliness which the early medieval folk of, say, AD400 would hardly have dreamed of or desired.

Conditions in the houses would not have been exactly pleasant to our standards. Everyone was thrown together with little privacy, but we must remember that the vast majority of the human race even today lives in such conditions. The close contact with other human beings presented an opportunity for conversation, story-telling and music, which was taken with both hands by our forefathers. We should not become too romantic, though; conditions were hard, the work long, and the weather unforgiving. Winters were generally harder in the Middle Ages. There would have been little time left for enjoyment except perhaps in the autumn. The houses were dark with few windows and with shutters rather than glazing, so activity more or less stopped when it became dark. Equipment and furniture within the houses were robust, with stout wooden furniture providing the basics. Clothes and other things were kept in heavy wooden chests, usually with a hasp and padlock or other lock. This indicates both that there was a need to lock things away, and that it was necessary to move gear around in order to create space. We find all sorts of remains in the buildings, from weapons to spurs, snares and other pieces of riding and hunting equipment.

Broad and Narrow Work

One of the most distinctive features of Dartmoor buildings is the technique known as broad and narrow work. In this, flagstones are placed so that they present the appearance of a massive stone to the front, but when seen from the sides are actually narrow. The effect is achieved by constructing the corners carefully, as you can see from the diagram. The inside of the wall is filled with any old rubble, and although the wall is not as strong as it seems it is efficient in its use of stone, although the labour involved in dressing it must have been substantial. If you see such work you are certainly looking at a medieval building.

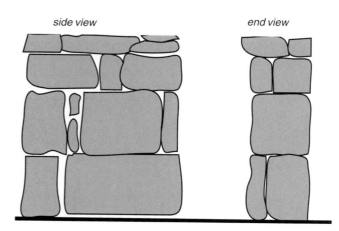

Broad and narrow work

Later Dartmoor Houses

In the parts of Dartmoor which had access to the more fertile and better sheltered land under the high moor, a number of very interesting and distinguished houses can be seen, dating mostly from the early 17th century.

Like the earlier designs we have been looking at, these are substantial and practical dwellings, but they have a degree of finish which is not always visible in the earlier houses. For example, a very distinctive feature of these 17th-century houses is the round arch which can be seen on many of those houses in the Chagford area we visit. On the other, eastern side of the moor, the four-centred arch was more common. Traditionally, you would expect to see a cheese press and a cider press associated with these houses, and indeed many of them do have fine examples of these. Of necessity, however, these are not usually in view from the road.

Many of these more modern houses have very fine outhouses attached to them or associated with them. In many cases the pig sties are built to a standard uncommon today for estate houses. Granite was cheap and the builders were well accustomed to its use, so the pigs got to live in veritable palaces.

The houses often had two other rather unusual 'buildings' associated with them, namely the ashhouse, and the potato cave. The former was a round house, with a chute at the front and a doorway at the back. Every night the ashes would be taken from the fireplace and placed in this little house, which, being made entirely of stone, would not burn down. The effects of a fire in an isolated farmhouse on Dartmoor would have been terrible, and the placing of the ashes in these strange-looking houses was a wise precaution.

The potato cave, on first encountering it, looks a peculiar device. It is usually a deep cave driven back into the growan, or rotted granite. It has a granite door-jamb and lintel, and a wooden door. The potatoes could be stored away from frost and light, and yet could remain easily accessible when needed. These caves were substantially built and lasted many hundreds of years, the usual cause of their destruction being the roots of trees which eventually broke in through the roof.

The water supply in these houses was often troublesome because it was brought down from the higher moors by a small open leat, usually shared among a number of neighbouring houses. The amount of water which could be taken was often controlled by a stone with a hole in it, placed across the leat. The judicious damming of the leat to raise the water level near your particular holed stone would improve your water supply, but would also bring the wrath of your neighbour down on your head. There are a few examples of pot water leats on Dartmoor, but none in the walks in this chapter; you can, however, see one at Ditsworthy Warren House in Walk 6.

Grimstone & Sortridge Leat

Medieval Farming

The farmsteads we visit in this chapter are more than groups of houses brought together randomly by the accidents of settlement. They represent the livelihoods and wishes of individuals who needed a reason before they would incur the friction of living cheek by jowl with others. So, why did we see the development of villages during medieval times? It is easy to hark back to the Iron Age and the Bronze Age and say that because our forefathers lived in groups at that period, then it was natural for them to live in groups later on. This, however, is not good enough. A farmer does not necessarily need neighbours; in fact, there are advantages in placing your farmhouse in the middle of your land.

There are two essential reasons why villages became popular. First the increased structure put into the society by the arrival of the Normans in the late 11th century meant that there was a requirement placed by the lords who held the land from the king upon the subtenants of the land. There was a need for them to till the land of the lord, and this required that they be relatively near the manor lands. The lord also provided certain equipment for the common use of the villagers.

The main reason for subsequent village development was the pressure brought by increased population to till the land more efficiently. Agreements had to be made over who tilled pieces of land which were held in common.

Villages in the early Middle Ages were not as static as they are today. For a number of reasons, as we shall see later, the houses were not built to the same permanent standard as

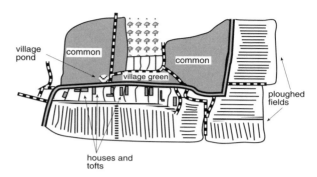

Medieval houses gather round the village street

today, so that after some years it became appropriate to move out and build alongside. We therefore see a gradual, shifting village pattern which became more static as the period moved on. There was an apparent reduction in building standards as the end of the eleventh century was passed, and some historians have argued that this represented a decline in standards of acceptability. Another view is that only after this time did it become possible for the villagers to grow enough crops to be able to employ relatively expensive tradesmen to construct proper timber-framed buildings, which were seen as desirable and long-lasting. Built on stone pads or dwarf stone walls, these houses may have been simple and dirty in many cases, but they at least provided a definite and long-term security against the weather.

The general arrangement of a typical village is shown in the diagram above. You can see a group of farmhouses separated from their neighbours by a farmyard, here of the simplest kind, the barn or cowshed being the same building as the house itself. This yard is known as the toft and served as a secure

area to keep animals when required, a repair yard, a general storage yard and for any other purpose that a farmyard serves. Towards the end of the medieval period when the climate began to worsen, we begin to see the foundations of drying kilns where crops could be prepared for winter storage. The toft held a particular significance for the family that ran it, and archaeologists sometimes find the sad remains of young children and babies buried here in the immediate vicinity of the house.

You can see that the tofts are grouped around a wide access road, while further away from the centre of the village are the enclosed areas called crofts. Here crops were grown specifically for the family. You can think of these crofts as large kitchen gardens, where peas, beans and other root vegetables (but not potatoes!) were grown. These crofts were walled, just as the earlier Bronze Age enclosures were, to dissuade marauding farm animals from supplementing their diet with vegetables intended for the table.

In the middle of the village were the chapel and the manor. On relatively unsophisticated sites like Houndtor, there was no manor or church, but that was because of a lack of resources rather than a lack of a wish on the part of the villagers to have their own amenities close by.

Next to the village were two vital areas. First there was an area of common land where, up to a certain limit, animals could graze and fallen wood be collected. Larger and later villages gave privileges to the villagers in the form of the rights to collect peat from the common beds (called turbary), and to gather food for themselves and their pigs in the woods, a right known as pannage. Second, the common fields lay away from the village. These were cultivated strips, each of a size that a man and an ox team could till with the assistance of quite an effective plough known as a mould-board plough, since it pushed a slice of earth sideways, upwards and over as the oxen drove the share through the earth. The depth of the ploughing was critical and was controlled either by a wheel at the front or by a sledge arrangement. The most successful type, however, was the free plough, the depth of which could be controlled only by the skill of the ploughman. The cultivation of these strip fields shows itself today because of the manner in which they were ploughed. On the first and second passes of the plough the farmer would lay two strips of upturned earth one against the other, by ploughing first up and then down the centre of the strip. He then continued ploughing around and around this ridge. This produced a

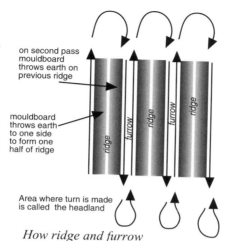

on second pass mouldboard throws earth on previous ridge

mouldboard throws earth to one side to form one half of ridge

ridge furrow ridge furrow ridge

Area where turn is made is called the headland

How ridge and furrow marks are formed

very distinctive mark in the ground which is visible even today. Where the plough and team were turned at the end of the row was an unploughed area known as the headland. You can see all these features on the ground today where there has been no substantial building, and many such sites are marked on the Ordnance Survey maps as ridge and furrow.

Some villages had a pond. This was there for the purpose of growing coarse fish for eating, such as carp, rudd and dace, these providing a very valuable form of protein for the villagers.

Medieval Tools and Implements

The progress of farming methods from the Iron Age until the 16th century is shown by a gradual introduction of implements enabling animal power, as opposed to man-power, to be applied to the land.

Much of the agricultural improvement which archaeologists and historians can detect during this period were a direct result of these innovations.

So, what was the motive power for these ploughs, harrows and carts? In the eastern two-thirds of England the dominant beast of burden was the horse, generally a large shire-horse with no great speed but immense pulling power. Intelligent and robust, these animals provided an excellent power source which could move relatively quickly over good ground.

In the western third of England, however, which includes Dartmoor, the ground was generally steeper and less well drained. Here the more old-fashioned ox-drawn vehicles were more popular, as the oxen could pull heavier loads here, albeit more slowly. Both the oxen and the horse were shod with iron, although generally speaking the ploughing horses were shod on their front feet only.

There were three types of plough, the swing plough, the foot plough and the wheeled plough. It is important in ploughing to maintain a fairly constant depth of cut. The blade or share of the plough is driven into the ground by the forward motion of the oxen, while the ploughman controls the direction. As the plough moves through the earth, a mouldboard behind the share (the cutting edge) turns the earth over to one side, thus burying the top surface and aerating the soil. The most developed type of plough was the wheeled type. A wheel was fitted to the front so that the depth of cut was steady. There was a problem, however, because the wheel could get clogged up in heavy soil. In the foot plough the wheel was replaced by an iron foot, which skidded over the ground. This had the advantage that it cleaned itself and did not become clogged. The most skilful ploughmen could dispense with both wheel and foot, and controlled the depth by their own effort; this allowed good ploughing even in the most rocky and uneven soil. This swing plough gets its name from the quick way in which it could be manoeuvred by a good ploughman. Generally speaking, wheeled ploughs were used on Dartmoor, although in the rocky marginal areas swing ploughs were also used.

After ploughing, the ground had to be further broken up by the use of a harrow. These days harrows are often linked arrays of spiky chains dragged behind a tractor, but in the Middle Ages they were made of wooden beams or bulls with iron teeth, attached to great wooden cross-members and dragged by oxen. There was also an unsophisticated type of harrow, known as the bush harrow where thorn bushes, weighed down by large logs, were dragged behind the horse or ox.

In the in-country, the outer fringe of cultivated land around Dartmoor, carts or tumbrels were used to transport fodder and manure. The wheels of the horse-drawn vehicles were spoked and those of the ox-drawn variety were made solidly. In the high moor, however, it was very practical to use sledges, which were particularly suitable for the transport of peat and other heavy material over the wet and sludgy high peat bogs. You can see examples of these and of the hand tools used in late

medieval times in the Museum of Dartmoor Life at Okehampton.

The variety of medieval hand tools is always entertaining. There were cutting tools, such as hooks and mattocks, tools for moving fodder and bedding, such as pitchforks and three-tined forks, and buckets for dairy work and carrying water. In spite of the use of animals as motive power for the preparation of the ground for planting, much of the work had to be done by hand, using axes and hatchets to clear virgin ground, and spades, forks and mallets to break up the ground, either before or after the plough had passed. The physical labour was intense, but no greater than on farms in many parts of the world today.

Seeding was done by the broadcast method where a seedlip or seeding bag was carried over the ground, the seed being cast in a regular manner by hand. When the seed had germinated weeding began, and depending on the crop, either a hook and stick or tongs were used. This was effective but labour intensive.

Harvesting required a scythe and sickle, a rake and a fork for making sheaves. The preparation of grain needed flails, sieves, a riddle and sacks, and later the grain was ground using a quern or hand-mill. Apples, which provided the basis for the all-important cider production, required the special cider press which you can some-times see in the farmyards around. This consists of a heavy stone disc running in a grooved basin,

into which the apples were put. Water was not necessarily good to drink in the Middle Ages and so alcoholic drinks, which were necessarily sterilized, were drunk much more widely than today. Even a medieval nun had an allowance of ten pints of beer a day!

Where dairy work was done, a multitude of buckets, pails, cheese presses, jugs and churns were needed, all made of wooden staves bound with iron bands. You can see these being made today at Buckland Abbey by the craftsmen in residence. Lastly came the odd implements needed for the general work of the farm, such as wheelbarrows, hammers, chisels, traps and nets, combs, shears, and many others.

VAB

Medieval farmer with scythe

Walk 26 – Hound Tor Medieval Farmstead

Distance
About 4 miles.

Main Features

Hound Tor	743790
Medieval Village	746789
Greator Rocks	748786
Holwell Lawn	745783
Bonehill Rocks	742775
Jay's Grave	732799

Difficulty
None at all. You still need a map, compass and waterproofs, though. Some of the ground lower down can be a bit wet, so good footwear is essential.

Description of Walk
From the car-park at Swallerton Gate (**739791**) make your way towards **Hound Tor**. Do not climb to the top of it but rather work your way round to the left on a grassy track. You should pass about 50 yards from a prominent rock pillar. As you follow the track, which runs just under the lower rocks, you will see the distinctive mass of **Greator Rocks** ahead of you. The **medieval village** is between Hound Tor and Greator Rocks, and you will soon pick out a branch of the path which leads downhill towards the easily visible walls of the village.

When you have finished examining the remains, go up to the right-hand end of Greator Rocks. Climb to the top if you wish – there are superb views back towards Hound

Tor and you can get an overall impression of the layout of the medieval fields, with the very prominent farm boundary wall running away towards Hound Tor until it turns back to the right, downslope.

From the end of Greator Rocks, put your back to Hound Tor and turn right. You should be facing a track which makes its way slightly upslope towards a gate into Holwell Lawn. You will meet the medieval farm wall near the track directly from Hound Tor to the gate, which joins you from the right.

Go through the gate into **Holwell Lawn**, and follow the sign pointing to Bonehill Down. The path curves gently right and goes through a gateway. Downslope you will see a signpost. Go to it and follow the direction again towards **Bonehill Rocks**. Make for the stile and gate on the road (**739781**), skirting round

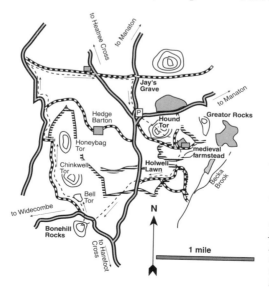

a marshy area, which you leave on your left.

When you reach the road turn left and go to the cattle grid a few hundred yards along the general line of the wall. You will soon see the triangular shape of Bell Tor (**731778**) peering through the trees. Make your way towards it, keeping to the left of the marshy ground near the wall.

From the top of Bell Tor go upslope to the two cairns on Chinkwell Tor. From here Honeybag Tor is easily seen along the ridge.

From Honeybag Tor make your way carefully down the steep slopes to the west, until you come to the track which runs along the edge of the larch wood between Honeybag Tor and Hameldon Down, opposite. On reaching the track turn right and follow it into a double-walled track which reaches the road quite soon (**725788**). Here turn right and walk along the road until it turns sharp left. About 15 yards further on is a sign on the right. Cut across the field here and rejoin the road.

Continue uphill past Lower and Higher Natsworthy Farms, and when the road levels off and a track joins from the moorland on the left, look for a bridle-way off to the right (**721801**), signposted to Hayne Down. This leads eventually to the gate near which you will find **Jay's Grave**, where you turn right and walk down the public road back to gain the car-park at Swallerton Gate.

163

Houndtor Medieval Village

The relatively fertile slopes of Hound Tor, between it and Greator, were attractive to a number of early farmers. There is evidence nearer to Hound Tor of both prehistoric and early medieval farming, at what is known as Houndtor East Settlement, but we are concerned here with the spectacular and superbly preserved remains of Houndtor medieval village itself.

It all began around AD800, when an unknown farmer decided to take his chance in this area by building a single-roomed longhouse, now submerged under the later buildings, in which he and his cattle lived in malodorous intimacy. The longhouse was built and rebuilt many times, with the low stone footings, which supported a rough wooden and turf wall, being reused. The roof was heather and turf thatch and was held up by stakes, the holes of which have been found in the excavation of the later buildings. Nothing of these early buildings can be seen today.

The Domesday Book of 1086 records the existence of Houndtor

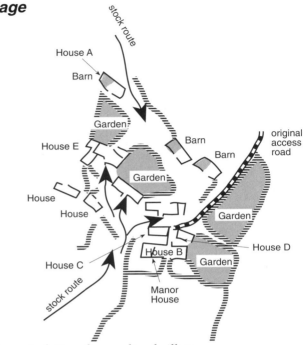

Layout of Houndtor medieval village

village, which at the time was owned by Tavistock Abbey. It was deemed to be worth twenty shillings, and supported six villagers, the lord and all their families. That makes about twenty people. Like all medieval villages it laid claim to a certain amount of meadow land and to some

View to Hound Tor from Great Tor

Hound Tor medieval village

woodland, from which game, wood and fruits and berries provided important additions to the cultivated produce. It supported seven cattle, twenty-eight sheep and eighteen goats, not many animals even for such a small village.

The first house (House A) you come to in walking down from Hound Tor is one of the later ones, and, even more confusingly, is not a house at all but a corn-drying barn. In the 13th century the climate deteriorated sharply, meaning that the subsistence of these relatively high-altitude farms was threatened unless they were prepared to dry their corn for keeping through the winter.

The best way to understand the site is to go straight to House B. This is generally understood to be the manor house, where the local landlord, the lord of the manor, lived with his family. Because he could extract taxes from the whole village he was a more wealthy man, but nevertheless lived fairly near

subsistence level in today's terms. If you stand in the upper part of House B you can gain an impression of the layout. The upper family room with its hearth looks down into the byre, distinguished by the drain gully in the centre, and separated from it by a rough wooden wall and stone foundation. The living room is separated into two, with two steps leading up to an inner room, a bedroom in all probability. The other room contains a hearth. Look at the northern doorway, where you can see a rough paving and the remains of a passageway into a paddock. Houses C and D were built as barns, but were converted into dwelling houses at some later time. If you look down from the upper room of House B towards the byre, you are looking over the farmyard or toft, where implements and cattle were kept close to the house when necessary.

All of the other houses have had different uses during the life of the village, being converted from barn

to house or from outhouse to barn. House E is a complicated building, having a good internal structure and an outhouse or penthouse built on the outside for extra storage. The porch of House E is still substantial, and you can see the drain in the centre of the lower part, the byre, where the animal waste drained down through a hole in the wall.

Note the way in which the village walls were laid out to allow the animals access to the byres attached to the houses without trampling over the food crops in the gardens.

The diagram shows the field layout of sheltered cultivated land on which produce could be grown. Further out is a system of fields with ploughing marks, walled by what are known as corn-ditches. These consisted of a wall and ditch, with the earth heaped up at the back of the wall. Most corn-ditches have now been destroyed by the weather, but in certain lights you can see the field boundaries and the ploughing marks.

Greator Rocks

View from Greator Rocks over medieval fields back towards Hound Tor

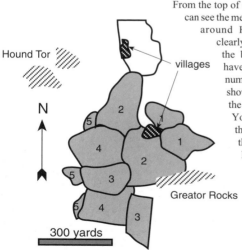

The fields of Houndtor village were built at different times

From the top of Greator Rocks you can see the medieval field system around Hound Tor quite clearly, particularly when the bracken and grass have died down. The numbers on the diagram show the order in which the fields were created. You can see that after the establishment of the gardens near the houses, an intake of land was made quite near the village, and the succeeding intakes naturally had to move further away from the village. By the time the fields marked 5 were taken in, the land was

becoming limited in use as the ground further away from the village was more rocky. (See the photograph above, taken from the top of Greator.) Shortly after these fields were taken in, the village ran in to disuse.

A climb to the top of Greator Rocks gives a splendid panorama of the whole area, with wonderful views over both Hound Tor and across to the huge mass of Hay Tor and to Smallacombe Rocks on the other side of a deep valley. The steep slopes of the tor are covered in rowan trees, heather and grass, and the way in which the granite sheets fall down to the sward of the medieval fields makes it, I think, a very evocative place. Just sit quietly here in the late afternoon and imagine the fields filled with the noise of cattle, and the smoke rising from the houses of the peaceful village below you.

The Duke Stones

The manor of Natsworthy near this walk has existed since Saxon times, and is one of the houses of the Dukes of Somerset. In the middle of the 19th century, the 11th Duke of Somerset decided that the boundaries of his land should be marked out and he arranged for a set of boundary stones to be put up. Some of these have strange names that commemorate places in the vicinity, such as Two Burrows, and Broad Burrow, and also individuals, such as Prince of Wales and Old Jack. My favourite, on the other side of Hameldown from Honeybag Tor is called Wm. Stone. Quite appropriate really!

Down by Natsworthy is another commemorative stone with three fishes on it.

Greator Rocks

Bonehill Down

There was once a landowner in this area who became curious as to how his tenants viewed him, so he went walkabout, making out that he was a stranger. He met an old woman who didn't know him, so he asked her who owned the estates. 'Mr X,' she replied. The man asked her what sort of man this Mr X was. 'Don't rightly know,' she replied, ' Never seen him. But we call him the old darnin' needle round here.'

Eavesdroppers never hear good of themselves!

Holwell Lawn

The other side of Greator is a lovely grassy area on which a show-jumping course has been laid out. It has been popular with settlers since prehistoric times; there are ancient remains nearby. Stories also tell of the pixies using it but unusually there are no stories of people being turned to stone or never seeing their families again. Perhaps the down is too pleasant for that. It is private land; please comply with the restrictions.

Ned Hacker

To your left as you approach Jay's Grave down the bridle-path, you see the edge of Cripdon Down. This hillside is the site of the strange visitation of the fairies to one Ned Hacker of Natsworthy. Ned arrived late for work one day, looking pale and ill, at the farm where he worked in Natsworthy. His explanation was that he had been up on Cripdon Down the previous evening when he chanced upon a pool where some small people were dancing. The sheer beauty of these little people kept him entranced until, when they finally waved goodbye to him, the entire night had passed unnoticed. He had spent the whole night literally entranced by the fairies. As soon as he was released from his trance he came straight to work, as the dutiful labourer he was.

All went well until that afternoon when the owner of the Half Moon Inn at Manaton arrived to claim the money for the slate Ned had run up the night before. He had got lost on his way home from the pub, and, drunk as a skunk, had fallen into a hedge near Cripdon Down. History does not record what happened when his gaffer found out.

Walk 27 – Early Farmhouses Near Chagford

Distance
About 6 miles.

Difficulty
Although much of the walk is on good tracks, you should take water-proofs and stout footwear because the first and last sections are on open moorland. A map is essential because of the confusing nature of the small Devon byways you will be using, as is a compass to ensure that you complete the final section back to Bennett's Cross without event.

Main Features

Bennet's Cross	680817
Heath Stone	670838
Yardworthy	679652
Hurston Farmhouse	686842
Jurston Farmhouse	696844

Description of Walk
Bennet's Cross is on the edge of a car-parking area to the north-west of Warren House Inn on the B3212. Leave your car here, and secure it.

From the cross walk at right angles to the road (which you cross); you will soon see the dark green swathe of Fernworthy Forest ahead and to your left. You are making for the point where the forest meets the road – in other words, the right hand edge of the forest – but you would be well served to skirt round the head of the North Wallabrook to the left. When you have negotiated this, make directly for the point where the forest meets the road.

You will find the **Heath Stone** to your right in a line of other stones, about a hundred yards before you reach the road. It is a large gravestone-shaped menhir with some 20th-century religious graffiti on it.

From the Heath Stone turn right along the line of the road past Metherall Farm and through a cattle grid. On your left you will see the track opening and sign for **Yardworthy**. There is a walk of about 200 yards to the medieval barn at Yardworthy, and if you wish to view it, you should turn left up the track. The footpath leaves Yardworthy cottage to the right, and is well

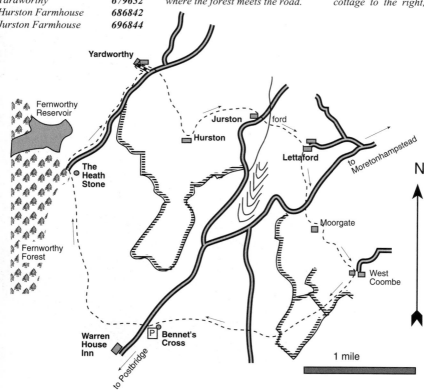

Hurston and the Heath Stone

signposted. Go through the gate into the field beyond the cottage and the medieval barn is just over the wall to your right. Do not stray from the footpath. When you have had your fill, return to the public road, and look for a ladder stile in the wall opposite the track exit. This leads you to **Hurston** *and is indicated as being part of the Mariners' Way.*

You emerge from the track at Hurston, with the beautifully restored longhouse on your left. Walk down the road and look for a sign on your right indicating the track to **Jurston.**

At Jurston turn left onto the metalled road and then immediately right again onto the signed track to Moorgate. Jurston longhouse is on your left on the public road.

Soon you will arrive at the busy metropolis of Lettaford. Do not walk down the public road on your left as you emerge, but instead walk to the gateway opposite where you will find a signpost indicating the route to Moorgate.

The track continues through Moorgate to West Coombe, where you will emerge onto a lane with the hamlet on your left. Do not turn down the lane, but go up and to the right. This is the Two Moors' Way, which here breaks away from the waymarks of the Mariners' Way which you have become used to. Follow this track on to the open moor, and you will soon come to the road. Cross the road and continue on the same line until you meet the B3212, either at Bennet's Cross, or slightly to the right of it. In the latter case turn left and walk down the road towards the Warren House Inn until you meet your car.

The Heath Stone of this walk is now a stunted piece of roughly worked rock, with some irritating modern graffiti on it, but its name has an interesting history. It started life as a menhir, erected in the late Stone Age or early Bronze Age as a ritual monument. The word menhir, meaning long stone, originated in the Iron Age, *maen* being the Celtic for stone and *hir* being the word for long. Eventually the Celtic was adopted into the early English and the stone became the hir-stone, then the heth-stone, until it gained its present-day name of the Heath Stone.

The ridge under which the stone sits is called the Heath Stone Ridge, except that this is corrupted to Hurston Ridge, which in turn gives its name to the picturesque farm which you pass on your way to Yardworthy.

The Heath Stone was was well known to early map-makers. It appears on one of the earliest maps of Devon, produced by Ebden. A later map of 1713 shows only the Heath Stone on the whole of Dartmoor. It was mentioned by name in 1702 by a William French of Widecombe.

The Heath Stone

169

Yardworthy Farm and Medieval Yard

If you have chosen to go up the short detour to Yardworthy you will pass through the outer yard of the present farm, with the cottages on your right, and then through the gate into the field beyond. There is a footpath here, and you can just see the excellent medieval barn in the upper yard. There is not much to see, but what there is is very well preserved. In particular, you can see the massive doorway and porch which stood over the barn. The scene is easily imagined, with the present disarray of the farmyard representing quite well the medieval toft. You can imagine the beasts in winter being fed with valuable foodstuffs gathered in the summer and autumn. You can hear, if you wish, the broad tones of the farmers, with their different words still expressed in the same broad accents of the older Devon folk today. In medieval times the English language was much more divided than it is today, and the dialect of the south-west was largely unintelligible to someone from the north-east. We can hear in the accents of Devonians today, and, indeed in the accents of hill folk in the United States, something of the original speech of Dartmoor.

In medieval times the farmyard was an important place of stability in the often oppressed lives of the tenant farmers. The remains of small children are often found buried in the toft, which indicates that it was very much a family territory, and the oppressions of the landowners were kept at bay by the family's control of its own backyard.

Medieval houses were not as flimsy as we used to think. It appears that they consisted of a substantial substructure and foundation on which was placed a wooden structure and a wattle and daub walling. We can see the substantial nature of the building here at Yardworthy, where the megalithic porch stands out from the old walls. It is easy to imagine the filthy conditions in which man and beast lived in the 12th century.

Medieval stone porch at Yardworthy

Warren House Inn

This lonely hostelry sits high on the road which runs from Postbridge to Moretonhampstead. It has been said that it is the oldest house on the moor, but this is untrue for two reasons. First, the hut circles all around show the antiquity of human dwelling on the high moor, and second, it is well known that the Warren House Inn replaced a building on the other side of the road, called Newhouse Inn. This latter inn has a number of stories associated with it. It was owned at one time by a Dartmoor poet called Jonas Coaker. One evening he was settling down to service his usual clientele from the mines around, when a group of travelling miners arrived, and threw him out on to the moor, where he had to sit and watch while they demolished his stock.

There used to be a little rhyme over the hearth at Newhouse (although some authorities say it was, in fact at Headland), which said

'Jan Roberts lives here,
Sells cider and beer,
Your hearts for to cheer;
And if you want meat
To make up a treat
Here be rabbits to eat.'

The name Warren Inn, of course, refers to the warrens in the area. These were basically rabbit farms, so the local people became very good at cooking rabbit in different ways.

Another story you will hear is that the fire in the inn has never gone out since it was first lit. It must be said that even in the summer there is always a fire going. I once asked the owner how they swept the chimney when there was this fire down below. His answer? 'Very carefully!'

The best story, however, is the one about the traveller who made his way in deepest winter over the high moors. As he crawled up the slope towards the Warren House he could see the lights glinting on the deep snow. No tracks could be seen in front of him, just the snow crystals twinkling in the moonlight. Eventually the traveller reached the welcome door, with its light creeping around the jamb. He was soon ensconced with the cheery owner in the parlour, the only guest to have arrived for ten days.

Late at night, with the silence of the snow all around the inn, the traveller crept whistling and humming into the room allocated to him, his candle fluttering in the draught of his movement. He opened the door and walked to the bed. Putting the candle down he began to take off his outer clothes, and as he pulled off his jerkin over his head his eye was caught by the other bed in the room. He immediately stopped whistling, realizing that there was a second guest in the house. Surprisingly the other guest had not stirred. In fact, there was not a sound coming from the other bed.

Taking his candle in his hand once more, the man crept over to the other side of the room. The candlelight glinted on the white face of the occupant, who lay there fast asleep, eyes closed and hardly breathing. In fact not breathing at all. It was soon clear that the occupant of the bed would rise no more. The white corpse gently glistened in the cold and candlelight, staring terminally at the inside of his eyelids. The traveller was petrified. The man must have been killed in his bed in the inn during the snows. For all he knew the innkeeper himself must have

The traveller meets the other guest!

been the murderer, because otherwise he would have mentioned the gruesome event.

The traveller spent a wakeful night, torn between the horrible face of the corpse in the bed next to him and the doorway, through which he expected the innkeeper to creep, with an intent expression on his face and a long knife in his hand.

Dawn came to find the traveller perfectly safe. Still he did not budge from the room, convinced that the innkeeper was going to dispatch him and fill the other bed. Eventually, the smell of breakfast cooking and a

woman's voice from below calling him to eat made him make his way carefully downstairs. He was persuaded to have some breakfast before he went on his way.

It was at the breakfast table that the woman asked the innkeeper how his father was keeping. 'Ah,' said the innkeeper, 'the poor old man passed away this week past. We had to salt the old fellow down to keep him from going off until the Lich party arrived through the snows. I dare say this gentleman has already made his acquaintance.' With that, the coffin party arrived ready to take the corpse off to Lydford for burial!

Venville and Jurston Farm

Bennet's Cross

Jurston Farm is one of the oldest settlements on Dartmoor (not counting the Bronze Age settlements, of course). It has valuable rights attached to it which date back before the establishment of Dartmoor as a forest.

Before the afforestation of Dartmoor, the villages around the area had rights of pasturage and turf-cutting which were very common in medieval times. Generally speaking, the animals which could be pastured were only equal in number to the capacity of the farm to overwinter them. The beasts could only be pastured on the common lands during daytime at first and it was only later that the right of 'night-rest' was allowed. The tenants were also allowed considerable privileges in the forest when it was set up, to the extent that they could take anything from the

forest other than green oak and venison. The penalty for poaching was death. These rights were not given for nothing, and the rent which the villages or 'vills' had to pay to the king was known as venville, from the Latin *fines villarum*.

The owners of the old farms, the venville lands, are regarded as particular tenants of the Crown. They used to have to perform certain duties, particularly the rounding up of beasts on the moor at a summer meeting known as a drift. These duties are a direct throwback to the medieval feudal requirements of a man who held land from a lord to do service to that lord as well as pay the rent. It was in this way, by a kind of pyramid of duties and services, that land was passed down from the king, and service trickled upwards, so that a national army could be called up from the grassroots.

This twisted and slanting cross is a favourite. Standing on the line of the road from Moretonhampstead to Warren House, it marks the line of the ancient track on which the modern road was built at the end of the 18th century. On the cross you will find the letters WB, which are said to stand for Warren Bounds. The cross has a dual purpose, because it marks both the track and the boundary of the parishes of Chagford and North Bovey. Two mines also used it as their boundary marker, namely Vitifer and Headland Warren.

We do not know who Bennet was. It is a Norman name, meaning blessed, and there was a Bennet mentioned in the rolls of the Tinners' Parliament as early as 1509, when he represented Chagford at the assembly at Crockern. The cross has been known as Bennet's Cross for at least the past 200 years.

Lettaford

Jan Reynolds and the Devil

Near Bennet's Cross you can see the unusually shaped enclosures known locally as the Four Aces. They do indeed look like the aces in a pack of cards, and they are the property of one Jan Reynolds, who made a pact with the Devil.

Jan was a poor man who had worked all his young life as a farmer's lad. The work was hard, the hours were long and the wages were small. Jan dreamed of leaving the moor and making his fortune in the wide world. One day he was leaning on his shovel and wishing that he could dig up a treasure among the turnips, when an elegant man dressed in black poked his head around the big stone wall. Jan stopped dreaming and looked at the man. He was tall and good looking with a mischievous glint in his eye and the sound of silver in his pocket. The man asked him what his name was, and offered to show him

Widecombe Church

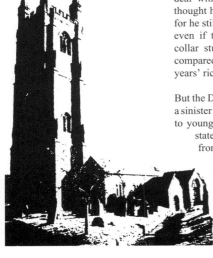

where he could find riches. Jan was suspicious, but when the man assured him that this was no market-place three-card trick, and that there was a deal to be done, Jan was reassured. After talking about business deals and how money could be made, the man made Jan an offer. If, after seven years, Jan would let him have the use of one little thing that he possessed, of the man's choosing, he would provide Jan with all he wanted during that time. Jan immediately saw this for the great deal that it was, and figured that since he possessed almost nothing anyway, the man in black could hardly choose anything that Jan would miss. So he agreed. The man could pick whatever he liked of Jan's possessions to keep, but only after seven years. They shook hands.

Immediately, there was a filthy smell of sulphur in the air and the man's handsome countenance took on a fearsome and grisly appearance. Jan was scared, and even more so when he figured out (for he was certainly slow-witted) that he had made a deal with the Devil. Even so he thought he had struck a good deal, for he still had almost nothing, and even if the Devil took his silver collar studs it would be no loss compared with the gain of seven years' riches.

But the Devil had other ideas. With a sinister smile he said his goodbyes to young Jan, and left him with a statement of his awful choice from all of Jan's possessions with which he wished to be repaid after seven years. The foolish Jan had lost his very immortal soul to the Devil. Nevertheless, as is the case with this

frequently signed contract (remember Doctor Faustus who did a similar thing?), everything went well until the seven years was up. Jan found that things went well for him at the card table. If he needed an ace to complete his hand, one would appear at the next turn. He found that he could make a comfortable living betting on everything from horse races to hymn numbers. In fact, he made such a comfortable living that he hardly needed to work, but even his idle picking at the farm labouring that had kept him until he met the Devil that fateful day went well for him. In spite of doing little, the pigs in his charge thrived and his cows gave milk by the gallon.

As far as socializing went, Jan seemed to be able to do no wrong with the local girls. His new-found easy wealth and self-confidence meant he was never at a loss for a partner to spend a lazy afternoon in the hayloft or a boisterous evening at the pub. Jan forgot all about his contract, and put his success down to his own native ability and hard work – the seven years flashed past. However, he was soon to be reminded of his obligations. On the appointed day, seven years after the contract, Jan was dozing fitfully in the back pew of Widecombe Church in his Sunday finery, safe from any thought that the Devil would come and get him.

He was wrong. Under cover of a tremendous thunderstorm the Devil broke into Widecombe Church and chased Jan out of the church and over the moors. Just before the Devil caught him, Jan dropped the cards which had made his fortune during his seven years of good luck. The aces turned to stone, forming the enclosures you see today.

The Mariners' Way

On this walk you are following part of a very old track which passes between Bideford on the north coast of Devon, and Dartmouth on the south coast. The track was used by sailors who tended to be paid off their ships on the opposite coast to where they lived. They therefore established a track which passed over the high parts of the moor, a rather dangerous place in earlier days.

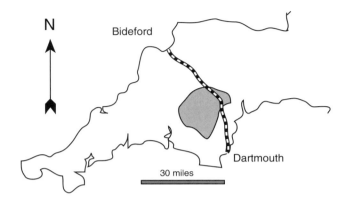

The exact line of the track is unknown but we can be sure that it passed off the moor at Throwleigh, and then went down Deave Lane, marked on the map today. From here it went to Gidleigh, and then worked its way through the farms of Yardworthy, Hurston and Jurston, and Littaford, and continuing to Coombe. From here the track went off to Widecombe and then down into the South Hams and Dartmouth.

The track passes right through a house at Coombe and this has led some historians to surmise that these farmhouses provided rooms and food for travellers.

Although I have picked out this particular track, all the main roads on Dartmoor are based on ancient tracks, so every time you get in your car to go from Tavistock to Widecombe, say, you are following an old track. The tracks were used as the basis for the roads following an act of Parliament in 1772, which established the main roads in the region. Some of the walks in the final chapter follow these tracks.

Vitifer and Birch Tor Mines

As you walk back towards Bennet's Cross you pass quite near to some of the most important mining works on Dartmoor. During the 1820s, because of the exhaustion of the surface ore and the falling price of tin, the Vitifer and Birch Tor mines were two of only three large mines still producing. By the 1850s Vitifer was employing more than a hundred men, some working underground in winning the ore, others preparing it for smelting. The works were quite deep, the lowest shafts being about 450 feet below the surface. Vitifer ceased working in 1870 as the demand and price of tin altered, and it remained closed until about 1900 when new machinery was installed,

a new leat was built, and twenty men were employed until 1914. The mine produced not only tin, but usable quantities of iron at times, too.

At its height Vitifer was as important as the mines at Hexworthy, which you visit in the next chapter. Most of the men came from the surrounding villages, but some came from further away. These workers either stayed in the local farmhouses or in the mining buildings, and brought a week's food with them on their backs, arriving on a Sunday night and leaving on a Saturday. You can imagine that the nearby Warren House Inn was a well-frequented drinking hole and from all the tales

of fights and quarrels, a pretty lively night out. It prides itself on having a fire that has never been out since the house was built, and you can see why that should be so when you consider the likely state of a miner who worked more than ten hours underground in very wet and uncomfortable conditions in the mines over which you walk. The work was also tiring and extremely dangerous.

On one occasion around 1855, the men had only just come out of the mine for their mid-morning snack when a huge flood burst in. No one was hurt on that occasion, although it had been a near run thing indeed.

Walk 28 – Pizwell Farm, Cator, Sherwell and Babeny

Distance
About 6 miles.

Difficulty
None whatsoever. The walk is along clear paths and tracks, except for a very short section up to Bellever Tor and down to Kraps Ring. A map is useful, however, because some of the roads can be most confusing. Don't forget your waterproofs!

Main Features
Pizwell Farm	**668785**
The Cators	**683770**
Sherwell	**679749**
Babeny	**672751**
Bellever Tor	**645764**
Kraps Ring	**645781**

Description of Walk
Leave your car at the information centre at Postbridge. Make sure that you secure it from thieves. Go out of the car-park and turn left on to the main road, passing the

the bottom. Follow the wall on your left until you go through a gateway. The wall is now on the right of the path. Continue along the path until you meet a gate into an enclosure. The track appears on the other side of the paddock, rising up the slope opposite. Go through the waymarked gate and at the top of the slope turn right at the signpost. Follow the track along, with the old wall on your left. Soon you will come to a wall across the track. Go through

the gate. Note a hogget hole in the wall on the left after the gate.

Where the track turns right sharply down the slope towards the ford, there is a superb example of a 'wooden stone' gate, with new bars across it.

*Go down to the ford, cross it as best you can (it is usually better on the right), and climb up the slope opposite towards **Pizwell Farm**. There is an excellent drystone wall near the farm gate,*

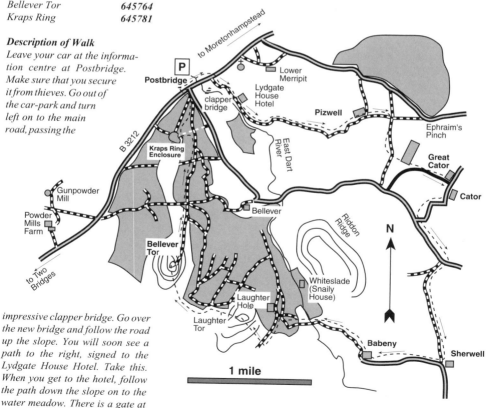

impressive clapper bridge. Go over the new bridge and follow the road up the slope. You will soon see a path to the right, signed to the Lydgate House Hotel. Take this. When you get to the hotel, follow the path down the slope on to the water meadow. There is a gate at

Pizwell Farm

with a beautiful chevron pattern. Take the opportunity to examine the medieval layout of the farm, and then pass between the farm proper and the cottages. As you approach the bottom ford, look to your right and on the wall of the lowest building you will see the inverted triangle of the arms of the Duke of Cornwall. From the ford, follow the clear track up the slope. Soon you will come to a clearly marked bridle-way to the right. Take this across Cator Common. Shortly after a track joins you from the left, look upslope and you will see a path marker inviting you to draw further to the right to join it. Keep along the line of the existing wide green track and make for the double line of oak trees ahead of you. Follow the track through these. It will bend first right and then left, guiding you into the funnel of two enclosure walls which will eventually lead you to the double-walled track of Great Cator. As the track joins the small metalled road, look to right and left to see **Cator Court** and **Great Cator**.

From here turn right on the public road and pass **Cator** and **Higher Cator**. There is a superb rude arch over the doorway of the thatched cottage here, and an excellent example of broad and narrow work.

Follow the road up the steep slope to Cator Green Cross. The standing stone on the right appears to be a gatepost, and certainly does not have any indication of a cross on it. Turn left at the T-junction.

You will soon come to a moor gate and, a little further on, to the left you will see a milk-churn collection structure built into the wall. Turn right there and follow the obvious track away from the road. Very soon

a green track leaves the vehicular track, which continues down the slope toward the farm. Take the green track marked 'Footpath– Sherill–Dartmeet'.

Follow the track across the moor until you reach a gate in the wall. Do not go through the gate, marked 'Private', but turn left up the slope until you meet the corner of the enclosure walls. There is a signpost here turning you to the right. Follow the wall until you come to the buildings at **Sherwell**, or Sherill.

Turn right here on the public road, passing Rogue's Roost on your right, and cross the river. Pass through the white gates towards **Babeny** farm. A sign directs you up the slope, to leave the farm on your left, onto the moorland above. Ahead you will see the suburban dwelling of Laughter Hole House. Drop down and cross the river by the impressive stepping-stones. The path continues up the slope through a gate, passing a stile (which you ignore) on the left after Laughter Hole House. This track will lead you up through the logged forest until you reach the four-way junction under Laughter Hole Farm.

At this point turn left and follow the track until you can head uphill and reach the top of Laughter Tor.

From here it is an easy walk along the edge of the forest until you reach the top of **Bellever Tor**.

From Bellever Tor make your way into the deep gap in the forest and follow this until you reach the Bronze Age enclosure of **Kraps Ring**. From here an obvious track leads to the main road, where you turn right to return to Postbridge.

The farm at Pizwell is one of the ancient tenements of the forest. The tenants of these farms, which were established before the moor was afforested, had special privileges, notably the right to collect peat and wood from the moor. They could also pasture animals and collect stone from the surface of the moor.

The tenements are held by right of the court roll, which establishes their rights from the duchy courts, the legal body of the Duke of Cornwall. The duchy of Cornwall has bought out a number of these tenements, and you can see the Duke of Cornwall's arms, an inverted triangle filled with golden balls, on the walls of both Pizwell and Babeny on this walk.

The tenants are obliged to do service at the duchy court and help at certain collective events, such as the census of animals on the moor. It used to be the case, up until 1796, that tenants could enclose a further 8 acres of land (called a newtake) on the change of tenancy, if the new tenant's father and grandfather had also held the tenancy to the farm in succession.

Pizwell is a superb example of a tiny medieval hamlet, with the larger house sitting above a collection of smaller cottages nearer the ford. You pass between these smaller cottages and a good example of a medieval barn. You can see very clearly, without straying from the footpath, the layout of the outer croft-type paddocks and the inner toft or farmyard. Look at the architecture of the buildings and you can see the distinctive details of the farm buildings in this area, with their substantial stone-work around the windows, and the outshots, or out-houses which were added at a later date. Many of the other farms in the area tend to show the development of the Dartmoor house rather more clearly. Pizwell does have the advantage, however, that because it is away from the road, and because you approach it over the farm lands, you can easily get a good idea of the appearance of the medieval farm, which is perhaps rather more difficult to visualize at farms such as Jurston and Yardworthy, which lie nearer to roads.

The name of the tenement appears in 1300 as Pishull, and a little later one James de Tresympel, a custodian of the forest, reported that Pishull had 'a clawe of land containing eight acres ...'. This refers to a new enclosure of land, as described above.

Pizwell in medieval times

'Wooden Stone' Gates

On the approach to Natsworthy is a superbly restored and maintained slotted gatepost, which you can see in the photograph. You will find it before the ford as you approach the slight rise up towards Pizwell Farm proper.

The medieval farmers used whatever materials were to hand. The stone which lay around so conveniently on the moorside was ideal for gateposts and walling, and there were a number of different ways of using it. One example, which is quite rare, is the holed stone, where a horizontal stone with a depression or hole in it is used as a hinge stone for a conventional type of gate.

Much more common is the type you see here, where slots are cut in two vertical gateposts so that horizontal bars can be fitted into them. This has the advantage that it is extremely cheap to run, quick to set up and, moreover, can be arranged as a sheep press, so that sheep can be driven through one at a time for cutting out.

On page 195 you can see how the stone was cut along a fracture line created by chiselling a groove in its surface and then banging wedge-shaped devices into it.

The description of this type of gateway, 'wooden stone', comes from a corruption of the phrase 'wood and stone'. It refers more

Refurbished 'wooden stone' gate

correctly to the first type of gate described above, but is applied to the slotted type too.

Peat Cutting

One of the most important rights which the commoners hold is that of turbary, or peat-cutting. All over the moor you can see the sites at which the peat is cut, each tenancy having its own particular area. The diagram shows the layout. First, the top layer of grassy soil is removed and laid aside. Two spits or spade depths are cut into the solid, chocolatey peat below, with the aid of a long spade which has a right-angled piece attached to make the narrow edge of the peat block. When the end of the run is reached, another two spits are made and the process repeated.

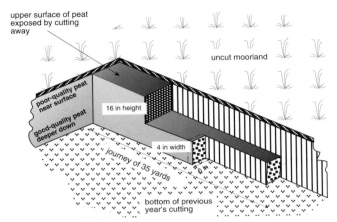

Dartmoor style of cutting peat

The peat blocks are left to dry in long pyramid-shaped piles until they have dried out and are ready to be transported back to the house. When dry the peat blocks burn readily, giving a scented smoke which locals say never makes your eyes water as does the smoke from wood or coal. The incendiary qualities of peat would have been discovered naturally, probably by Bronze Age folk, as peat sometimes burns of its own accord during very hot and dry summers.

You can think of peat as the raw material for coal. In the Devonian period of the Earth's history (about 400 million years ago) great swamps of peat were created from the primitive vegetation and these peat beds were later compressed to produce the huge sheets of coal and the pockets of oil and gas which we have exploited over the past few hundred years. When you walk over the peaty uplands today you could well be walking over the coal seams of the future.

The Cators

As you come off the open moor having passed through the strips of trees, you will come to the hamlet of Cator. Higher and Lower Cator (or Catrowe as it was known) are two of the five vills of Widecombe, mentioned in the Domesday Book, two of the others being Sherwell (or Sherill) and Grendon. The fifth vill is unrecorded.

This whole area used to hold its land under rent from Lydford, which may not seem so far away today, but in the 13th century 8 miles was a very long way indeed by foot over the wild moor, the distance being almost doubled when there were floods that made the fords unusable. As a result, in 1260 the inhabitants of the tenements of Babeny and Pizwell petitioned Bishop Bronescombe (after whom the rock called Branscombe's Loaf is named), that they should be allowed to pay their tithes to Widecombe rather than to Lydford. I suspect there was also the underlying motive that Lydford was becoming a somewhat rough old town at the time, with a high traffic in tin and its associated social activities taking place. Tinners were not known for their cultured manners and good behaviour.

Some of the architecture of Cator's ancient buildings is interesting as you walk down through the peaceful little hamlet. Notice the doorway of the cottage on the left as you turn down the road, having passed between the large, upper houses. It is a splendid example of a stone arch.

Normally the arches in the east of the moor are semicircular in shape, like the very well-known ones in Widecombe itself, whereas in the north and west of the moor the more complicated four-centred arch is a more popular design.

Bellever Tor

This is a splendid viewpoint. From here you can look out over the vast green wilderness of the moor towards Powder Mills and Littaford Tor, standing on the majestic line of tors which ends deep in the northern moor at Higher White Tor. You can see the shapes of the great tors the other side of Two Bridges as they guard the way north from Princetown. Beneath Bellever Tor or Bellaford Tor, as it was known, lies the great forest between you and Postbridge. The hill on which the forest sits, between you and Kraps

Ring at the end of the forest ride driving deep into the woodland, is called Lakehead Hill. The local hunting community mispronounce it as Naked Hill. Quite what they have on their mind when they ride I have no idea!

There is one of those rather sad stories involving the pixies told about Bellever Tor. It appears that a man called Tom White was courting a young woman near Huccaby, and felt the need to visit her frequently during the week to make sure that he remained in her affections. Late one afternoon he set off after work towards the top of Bellever Tor and near the top he came across a huge family of the little nuisances dancing in the late sunlight. He was forced to stop to watch them for a while but they soon noticed him, dragged him into the ring and whisked him around until sunset. The sad part of the story is that he was so upset by his experience that he never went to Huccaby again, and his young woman married another.

Kraps Ring

From 1930 the trees of the forest began to advance over the unspoilt moor of Lakehead Hill. In so doing they covered up a large number of antiquities which were not even recorded in many instances. It is both the planting of the trees and their roots which cause damage, and the fact that the antiquities on Dartmoor lie on the surface, in the main part, makes them both easy to see and easy to disturb.

Kraps Ring, a Bronze Age pound with a dozen or so hut circles in it has survived, however, because it is so prominent. It is about 60 yards across and like all these pounds has a retaining wall. The wall is somewhat dilapidated but it would have been about 5 feet high when in good condition. The pounds were used to create a paddock in which the farmers could grow crops safe from their stock. There is another theory that they were used to keep the stock safe from predators, and I guess the truth lies somewhere between the two ideas.

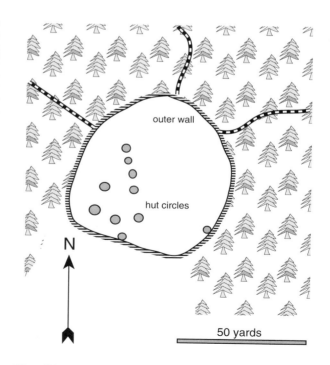

Plan of Kraps Ring near Bellever Tor

179

Walk 29 – Iron Age Forts and Castle Drogo

Distance
5 miles.

Difficulties
None; the paths are well marked and the going is generally good. The steep climb back up to Cranbrook will set you puffing, though.

Main Features

Cranbrook Castle	**738890**
Prestonbury Castle	**747900**
Teign Valley	**73.89.**
Castle Drogo	**723902**
Fingle Bridge	**742899**

Description of Walk
Leave your car on the road near **Cranbrook Castle**, which lies to the north-west of Moreton-hampstead and is clearly marked on the OS map. There are a number of suitable parking places, but do not obstruct the road.

Walk up the track to Cranbrook Castle and enjoy the view over the valley. Look over towards **Prestonbury Castle** on the right of the gorge opposite, as it sits up on the hill-side overlooking the **Teign Valley**. On the east side of the castle is an entrance which leads to the foot-path goes south-east back to the road, but you can also go down the slope on a pack-horse track which wiggles its way downhill eventually reaching the car-park at **Fingle Bridge**. Here you should cross the bridge to the other side of the Teign and walk up the gentle slope. You

will soon notice on your left a footpath sign to Hunting Gate, and towards Sharp Tor. Before you get to Sharp Tor (it's actually worth a visit even if you have to retrace your steps) you take the track to the right (**732899**) which is signposted to Drewsteignton, and eventually pop out on the road near the village. If you wish to visit Drewsteignton, turn right into the village.

To get to **Castle Drogo** turn left from the track (right if you've visited Drewsteignton) and walk west until you come to a road junction (**727908**) after the track to Cross Farm. Turn left at the junction, and the entrance

to Castle Drogo (**726906**) will soon become obvious. Follow the signs and walk up the driveway to the house.

After enjoying the superb building and its estates, you should return down the driveway and turn left. The road descends and you will soon pick up the path on the left of the road which leads to Hunter's Tor. Do not climb up to the tor, as you will be walking instead along the valley floor on the north bank of the Teign until you reach Fingle Bridge. The way is very clear. From Fingle Bridge head back up the pack-horse track to Cranbrook and your car.

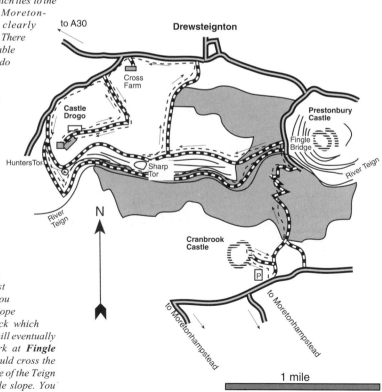

180

Fingle Bridge

The Teign Castles

Fingle Bridge is the bridge that goes nowhere, at least so the advertising material says. In fact it was an important feature on a pack-horse route which wiggles its way up the sharp slope opposite and comes out near Cranbrook Castle.

Fingle Bridge has three arches, and on spring, autumn and winter days it is a wonderful place to walk and generally dawdle about. In summer, however, the woodland scene is transformed. The road from Drewsteignton to the bridge is invariably full of cars and the crowds at the bridge can be oppressive. It does, however, have certain advantages. There is a good tea shop and a good pub here, the Angler's Rest. It's not often on Dartmoor that you have the chance to stop for a drink on a hot day in the middle of a walk, but this is one.

The bridge has recesses in it so that if you met a pack-horse you could stand aside until it passed. You may think this rather excessive, but as a fully loaded pack-horse looked like a hay cart with produce hanging off every corner of the animal it seems a wise precaution to me.

Fingle Bridge and the River Teign

Cranbrook Castle is one of four major forts in this valley. It commands the junction between the Teign and the valley in which Fingle Bridge sits, and is positioned extremely well, both for military effect and for efficiency of construction. On the south and west sides there is a wall, with a ditch on the outside for defensive purposes. On the north side there is no need for a wall and vallum, as it is called, because the ground just drops away into the valley. The castle is roughly circular in plan. It would have been well nigh impossible to attack effectively from the valley bottom, and so the only defences necessary were on the easier graded south and west portions. There appear to have been two phases of construction, one of which was never finished, and the castle is unusual in that it is connected with a series of reaves, so that it must have had an informal administrative purpose as well as the obvious military one.

On the other side of the valley is Prestonbury Castle. It is also well placed and commands the valley opposite Cranbrook. It is much bigger than Cranbrook in extent. Each would have had not just a defensive purpose in the troubled times after the Celtic incursions, but would have provided a trading centre, together with extensive religious sites.

The Celts had what was called a chthonic religion, whereby deities which lived in the ground were worshipped. They developed cults which had as their religious sites series of holes in the ground where animals as large as cows were sacrificed and left to rot. The smell alone must have been strong enough to take the paint off the chariots!

Castle Drogo

*Castle Drogo
seen from the
Teign Valley*

The contrast between the early Iron Age castles in the Teign Valley and Castle Drogo is stunning. Both sit high above the entrances and approaches to the central wooded cleft, both are the result of substantial work and imagination and both declare the builder's right to control the lands around. Architecturally, however, we are seeing two extremes. The Iron Age forts are curved in outline, functional in appearance, naturally rounded in appearance; Castle Drogo is rectangular, stark, forbidding and intimidating. The latter sits on the wooded hill at the end of the valley in a beautiful arrogance, created by two men of vision and obsession: Julius Drewe, the owner, and Edwin Lutyens, the architect.

Julius Drewe was a grocer. He built up the hugely successful grocery complex of the Home and Colonial stores from nothing, and retired at the age of 33 in 1889, a very rich man. As was often the case in Victorian (and indeed succeeding) society, his new money was no guarantee of recognition. The ability to make money from trade was, rather, a disbarment from society, and Drewe was largely unaccepted by the class of English society he wished to enter. So he turned to history to make his new money old.

In 1910 Drewe bought the Drogo estate in Drewsteignton, having researched his family history and identified with a Drogo de Teign who lived in the 12th century. It is true that Drewsteignton takes its name from Drogo, but rather less certain that the Drewe family stemmed from that particular shoot. There was enough proof for Julius Drewe, however, and he became entrapped in a vision of the Drewe family seat overlooking the beautiful lands which he had acquired by his energies and talents. Such a castle would, with his new found ancestry, surely allow him entry into fashionable society.

The best known architect in the land at the time was Edwin Lutyens, who was later to design and build the great colonial capital of New Delhi. Lutyens had already completed a number of prominent and successful projects, not least of which was the refurbishment of Lindisfarne Castle in Northumberland, similar in some ways in aspect to the site of the new Castle Drogo.

Lutyens was given the enormous budget of £60,000, and in one of his diaries expresses a mixture of feelings about a sum of money which may have been minuscule in the context of a large municipal project, but which for a family home was huge. He clearly saw the conflict between the ambitions of Drewe and the feasibility of the project.

The original plans for the castle were for a huge and monumental building. If World War I had not intervened, we would have seen the huge double-winged symmetrical house which had originally been planned. As it is today we see only (!) the single granite wing and the central portion of the behemoth. Lutyens, to his great embarrassment, forgot to apply for planning permission in 1911, so that the start was somewhat

> *The planned layout of the castle is shown (approximately) in the upper figure. This was cut back to the relatively modest building which exists today. Stand in the courtyard and imagine the size of the original proposal!*

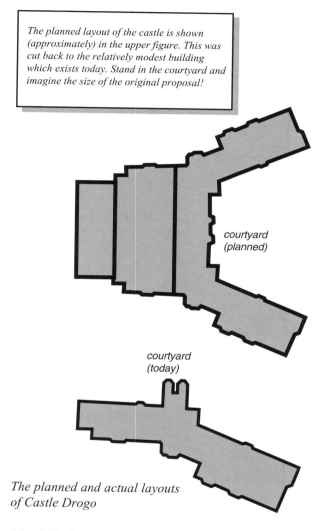

courtyard
(planned)

courtyard
(today)

The planned and actual layouts of Castle Drogo

The layout of the castle changed dramatically during its construction, starting off as a central keep with two huge splayed wings enclosing a central courtyard. The central keep overlooked the slopes of the valley, and the courtyard is more or less where you enter the house today. The symmetrical arrangement was abandoned later and the present two-winged arrangement emerged.

The two men were both strong-minded and authoritative, and the relationship between them was stormy. At one point Lutyens lambasted his employer for wanting to continue the rough-hewn granite which Drewe associated with castles and baronial homes, right up to the top. Lutyens wanted it to be faced in dressed stone, and compromised with an elevation which had the undressed stone only at the foot of the wall. He referred to the Drewe arrangement as 'a barbaric building worthy of a small municipal corporation,' which must have stung Drewe in the light of his desire to obtain a position in society. At one point during the very dry summer of 1913, Lutyens had to build a complete timber exterior in order to obtain some stability in the design.

The house was effectively finished in 1925, but Drewe had suffered a stroke in 1924 and was not to survive to enjoy his spectacular new home for long. He died in 1931 in Torquay and is buried under a simple granite tombstone, designed by Lutyens, in Drewsteignton churchyard.

Castle Drogo is a monument to Julius Drewe and his desire for roots in history, but it is also a monument to the energy of the Victorian entrepreneurs who enabled the work of gifted men such as Edwin Lutyens.

delayed. The foundation stone was laid on 4 April 1911, but the project was not to be finished until 22 December 1925, when the last stone was put on the castle. It was not possible to live in the castle until some two years later. During this time the architect was engaged in one of the most prestigious projects in the western world, the building of New Delhi, and the nation was occupied with the Great War, both of which clearly disrupted progress, but the scale of the project occupied around a hundred men during most of that time.

Tinning & Quarrying

Of all the human activities undertaken on Dartmoor, it is the mining of tin which has made most impact on the countryside. Wherever you go on the moor you will be walking at some point where the miners themselves walked. On the banks of every significant stream you will see the great mounds of stone they built up as they dug out the beds looking for the black gold of the ore, which was washed down from the lodes of tin that lay upstream.

In some places the mines are even more visible. At Eylesbarrow, for example, the last mine to be worked on Dartmoor, you can see extensive buildings still standing roofless, as well as a shaft. Other workings still to be seen include the stones which used to hold up an interesting system of transferring power around the site using a flat-rod system.

Many of the upper valleys contain tinners' mills where the ore was crushed and worked, the sand and light material washed out, and then the residue put into a furnace to be smelted. These medieval factories can still be seen in remarkably good order on many of the walks in this chapter. From earlier times still, you can see the faint traces of the 12th-century tin streamers, who lived for periods of time in harsh conditions in rude huts high above the river valleys to win the valuable ore.

This chapter takes you to the remains of both early and late tin-working and gives you an insight into the way of life of these hard men and the way they made their money from the ground.

In the walks of this chapter we will also see the quarries that lie scattered over the Dartmoor landscape. The stone from these has gone to produce everything from humble gateposts to great buildings. You will be able to see the spectacular walls abandoned by the quarrymen, and the deserted and poignant buildings which they were forced to leave behind them. Occasionally on the walks you will see the half-finished remains of the work, left, like the *Marie Celeste*, as if a sudden silent deadly plague had mysteriously taken away the workers.

Lastly, you will be able to see at Haytor the superb granite tramway, with its track made from solid granite. It was along this that tramcars used to transport the stone to the outside world.

Origins of Tin

You will have read in the Geography & Geology chapter how the granite of Dartmoor welled up from the earth's molten body to form a bubble under the sedimentary rocks which originally lay over the area. Granite itself is formed from parts of the Earth's surface which are driven deep underground into the hot centre as parts of the Earth's crust fold and move over one another. This material from the Earth's surface melts and rises as it is less dense than the material into which it has been driven.

The material from the Earth's surface contains many different metals and compounds formed during the formation of the Earth itself. If conditions are right, metals can form vapours which gradually diffuse and flow through the very structure of the rocks. Just as water vapour formed in your living room, the vapours are created when temperatures are high, and are driven out when the warm humid air reaches a cold surface. If you are lucky it is the outside of a cold beer glass in the garden; if you're not, it's the cold inside surface of your windows, where it reforms as water and flows down the glass. In the same way, metallic vapours will be formed when temperatures are very hot, and the metal will move around in the rock until it meets a colder area where it reforms as solid metal or metal compounds.

In the case of tin, the metal is closely bound to oxygen, even at quite high temperatures, so that the most common form in which the metal appears is as tin oxide or cassiterite. This is a dense black ore which appears in relatively localized veins or lodes within the tin-bearing granite.

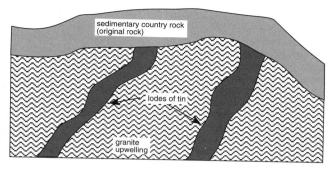

Tin lodes form as metallic vapours recondense

Distribution of Tin

Once formed the Dartmoor tin lay trapped in veins in the granite under the sedimentary layer. As we have seen before, the sedimentary rock was gradually worn away by river erosion, and by a certain amount of chemical corrosion. When the rivers reached the veins of cassiterite, the ore was broken up and carried downstream by the force of the water.

Water can only carry a certain amount of material but as the speed of flow increases it can carry more

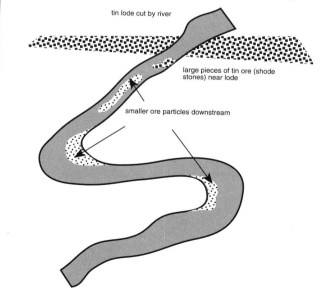

Large pieces of ore show where the river cuts the lode

Tin-Streaming

material. If you look on the inside of the bends of a river you will see that a lot of material is deposited here, since the water flows more slowly on the inside of the bend compared with the outside. Similarly, if you look at the bed of the river after a flood, when the water was moving very quickly, you will see that it has been able to carry quite large boulders a short distance while the flood was high, depositing them on the bed when the flow dropped.

The result of this effect is that the larger pieces of cassiterite were left high up the stream. Where smaller pieces were carried downstream (as they were to a great degree) they were then covered with finer material that was carried more easily and more frequently downstream.

The old tinners, therefore, knew where to find the tin: on the inside of river bends under the alluvial material carried down from above, and high up in the stream beds wherever the stream had intersected a vein of material. The stream had already done much of the work for the tinners in digging out the cassiterite from the vein.

The process by which the medieval tinners (from about 1150 until about 1700) won the tin was essentially simple. Like gold-miners panning for gold they would work their way upstream looking for the characteristic dark, heavy material of the cassiterite. The layers of deposited material would be heaped up on the sides of the river, and the tin-bearing ore dug out from the bed of the river would be deposited behind it ready for further treatment. You can see the walls of stones which prevented the ore from falling back into the river in very many places on the moor. They are distinguished from the drystone walls of the region by their rather disorganized look.

As they worked their way upstream the pieces of ore became larger, indicating that they were near the source of the tin, but at first the tin-streamers restricted their activities to the stream bed. These larger pieces of tin ore were called shode stones.

Soon even these simple methods produced a quantity of tin greater than that of any country in Europe, and Dartmoor became a highly strategic centre for tin production. The subsequent rapid denuding of the stream beds meant that the lodes had to be followed away from the shode stones into the banks of the river and so the process of shoading began.

The lode was followed away from the river by digging down from the surface with picks and shovels until it was located. Then the surface material could be removed by the use of water. This water came either from a higher portion of the river or a pool would be dug and rain, of which Dartmoor is not exactly short, would be collected. The water would then be released along the line of the lode to wash away the material. Leats were also used to wash away the lighter overlying material, these often bringing in water from quite long distances away.

These early miners were restricted in their winning of the tin not by their skill and courage so much as the simple fact of the wetness of Dartmoor. Unless they could remove the water from the underground workings they could not mine. There were limited works where the lodes were followed into the ground, and at times the digging was done under the live earth, with supports and beams put in to give some protection, but in the main part the work was open to the air.

These early miners must have been hard men indeed. Living for weeks in the harsh conditions, delving tirelessly in wet and dangerous workings, and with the hardest of hard labour for company, the tin-miner is a man to be admired, although, as we shall see elsewhere, some of the collective antics of these men were not so admirable.

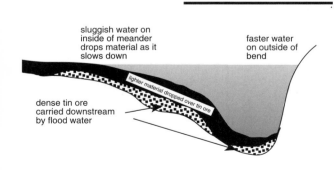

Deposition of tin on bends

Tin Processing

Tin in the form of cassiterite is unusable. The oxygen has to be removed by a process which chemists call reduction. The best practical way to do this is by heating the tin in an environment where the oxygen contained in the oxide (cassiterite) is more attracted to something else than to the tin. It therefore leaves the tin, which is made into a pure metal, usable for all manner of things from making pewter and solder, to coating the outside of other metals to preserve them.

The early methods did not use this reducing method except by accident. The tin was piled into a depression in the ground, and a fire was lit on top. There was little oxygen in the base of the fire, and so the oxide was reduced, dripping into the ashes at the bottom. When the fire had cooled, the pieces of grubby metallic tin were picked out. This was known as the first smelting, which still produced a black tin, as opposed to the more effective later methods which produced pure metallic (white) tin directly.

Soon a more effective method was invented, where the tin, having been crushed by hammers and hand-mills, was placed over a fire in a clay cone in the ground. The molten tin could then be drained off from the bottom.

During the 14th century tinners' mills began to be built, so that instead of smelting tin in small quantities near the source, it was purified further downstream. The buildings are often called either crazing i.e. crushing mills, stamping mills or blowing houses. The stamping mills were for crushing the ore; heavy stamps moved up and down to pound the ore on a mortar stone. When the stone became worn it was simply turned over and used again. You will see examples of the mortar stones with their characteristic depressions in most blowing houses. The crazing mill was a sort of circular mill with stones which ground the ore rather than crushed it. Today the term tinners' mills is preferred because many of the sites were used for double purposes. The important factor was that suddenly the tinners could use water power to supplement

their own muscles. Ore could be processed further before being smelted, since it could be broken into smaller granules, and any further washing from leat water could drive away the lighter particles, to leave a purer input of ore to the furnace. Moreover the furnace could be brought to a higher temperature, because bellows could be driven by water power. This made the whole process more efficient. In part, this increase in efficiency came about because the tinners worked their way back into the lodes, the tin which they won there being less pure than that found in the river beds.

In the tinners' mills the tin was layered with charcoal and placed on a furnace floor made of stone rafters. The molten tin could be drawn off into a reservoir below and then into a mould, where it cooled in a known shape whose weight was already established rather accurately. The mould-stones usually contained about 200 pounds of smelted tin. A sample was taken of the smelting quality in a small mould often found on the side of the large mould-stone.

One side of the tinners' mills contained a water-wheel in a channel or race. Most of the wheels were about 15 feet in diameter, although some were bigger than this. You can usually see the wheel-pit in the mill today.

The leats which powered these mills were often quite substantial, and their remains can be seen all over the moor today. This is in contrast with the leats of the early miners, whose water channels were much less substantial and more temporary in nature.

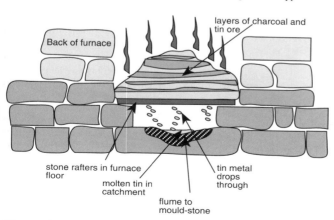

Tin smelting in a furnace

layers of charcoal and tin ore

Back of furnace

stone rafters in furnace floor

molten tin in catchment

tin metal drops through

flume to mould-stone

Later Mining Methods

Dartmoor's tin production was rather variable. During the middle of the 14th century, when the Black Death was weaving its sinister and frightening web around Europe, the production of tin was very low. During the early part of the 16th century, however, great quantities of tin were being produced.

During the time of the English Civil War, in the middle of the 17th century, production stopped, and after a few fitful starts only restarted again at the height of the Industrial Revolution at the end of the 18th century. There was then a relatively intense period of production, but by the early years of this century the cost of Dartmoor's tin had priced it out of the market; the increased ease of transportation made it uneconomical to use Devon tin, and metal from south-east Asia became more commonly used.

This last period of tin-working involved using new methods of mining, since the 'old men', as the early miners were referred to, had been very effective in winning the most easily removable ore. The later miners used a system of shafts and adits to work the seams underground. Dartmoor is a relatively amenable country in which to use this type of mining, since, although there is a lot of water around both above and below ground, the country is ridged, so that the lodes can be followed in a horizontal fashion fairly easily. The early miners left few shafts, but

their Victorian successors built them freely. Any shafts which you see today, for example at Eylesbarrow, will therefore be from the later period.

The system used to access the lode was simple. Vertical shafts were used to provide ventilation and near-horizontal adits were used to provide access into the lode and to give drainage. Where the shafts were driven down below the level of the bottom adit, no natural drainage could be used, and so water from the bottom of the shaft had to be lifted. This was done by water power or by steam, after the invention of the steam pump by James Watt, first used in Cornwall. The lode was worked in a step-wise fashion, in what were called stopes, with each miner working a step back into the lode. Sometimes the stopes would work their way out into the open hillside, forming a gunnis. Often these would appear at old surface workings.

The later period of mining also brought improved methods of preparing the ore. The ore mined in this period was smelted off the moor. At Hexworthy you will see two great circular washing beds, where water separates the heavy ore from the lighter sand and gravel. Buddles were also used at this time, and you will occasionally see the circular bed of one with its distinctive beehive-shaped centre.

Be careful walking among these old workings. Although farmers have filled in the workings to stop their sheep falling into them, there is still the risk that if you go exploring you may get more excitement than you bargained for!

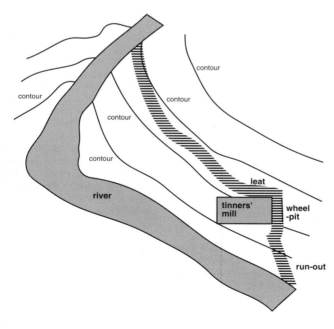

The blowing house and leat

Stannary Law and the Tinners

The earliest tinners in the West Country are lost in the darkest depths of uncertain prehistory. Legends tell of Phoenician craft trading with Cornwall before the Roman invasion, but these amount to little more than folk-tales. More attention was paid to the moor as a production centre for tin in Saxon times, but the tin-streaming was done on an individual basis, and the trading was carried out without the support of law.

It was the Normans who first started the development of Dartmoor as a tin-mining area. They brought little in the way of new techniques, but the importance of the metal as an economic material was not lost on them. At this time the tin industries of Dartmoor and Cornwall were intimately connected. The first reference to the tin industry of Devon and Cornwall is a document drawn up by Richard I, appointing a custodian of the industry. There is a return documented in 1198 by the Sheriff of Devon and Cornwall to the Archbishop of Canterbury, who had given him the position of Warden of the Stannaries in succession to one Geoffrey Fitzpeter. We know then that the stannaries were in existence some time before 1198. In 1201, during the reign of King John, the first stannary charter was granted. In 1305, during the reign of Edward I, they became separately allowed for in law, by a charter, with the establishment of the stannaries around the edge of the moor. These were Ashburton, Chagford and Tavistock in 1305, but after a successful petitioning by Plympton in 1328, Tavistock was displaced temporarily, regaining its position later to leave four stannaries. The most important change in the status of the tinners, however, was that the

charter established stannary courts, which administered a set of laws allowing considerable freedom of action to the tinners in pursuing their trade. In the mid-15th century these were added to by the establishment of a stannary parliament which met at Crockern Tor near Two Bridges. You can still see the tables and seats hewn from the rock for the use of the officials during sessions.

Prior to this time the tinners were already in a relatively privileged position, standing aside from the feudal structure which made so many into slaves of the land and the lord. The tinners could exist without the permanent use of the land and this gave them a freedom to earn a living, albeit a meagre one. But when the stannary laws came into force, their power locally became very great. They were allowed to enter any private land for the purpose of winning the ore, and were immune from the interference of non-tinners, with whom they often dealt harshly. Such non-tinners were frequently taken to the hard stannary prison at Lydford, whose court and jail were known throughout the land as harsh and summary. The tinners were allowed to divert streams, take peat and collect wood. The freedom of the tinners to go about their business was confirmed in 1305 by the bailiff of Blackmore, when as a precedent he reports that before 1305...

'They always used to work and seek for tin in waste ground and also in the prince's sovereign ways to carry and recarry their several works for the purifying of their tin having liberty likewise to dig mine search, make shafts, pitch bounds, and for tin work in places to their most advantages, excepting and reserving only all sanctuary grounds

churchyard, mills bakehouses, and gardens, paying and yielding only to the prince or lord of the soil, the 15th part for the toll of their tin to farm. Providing always that if it chanced the said tinners in their mining to subvert or work up any man's house to fall or else any highway whereby it may cause the house to fall or one that travels to be troubled in his journey, then the tinners ... should to their own expenses make ... the house or highway ... as they were.'

Such a grant of freedom caused untold problems to the farmers and landowners, both from the disruptions of the tinners' workings and through the loss of wood and other gleanings from the moor.

Economically, too, the tin industry was important. In the second half of the 15th century, production doubled, and by 1524 it was at its peak, with an output of nearly 300 tons of tin. This was a considerable addition to the treasury, and so the strength of the tinners increased. Taxes on the tin were, of course, related to the price of the tin and control of the prices was administered in what today we would find an unusual way. The tin of the first smelting – in other words the first processing high in the moor – was transported down to the stannary towns where it was smelted again and tax charged on it according to weight. In 1198 the tax was set at 'thirty pence per thousand weight'. The tin of the first smelting was less valuable than the tin of the second smelting for three reasons. First, tax had to be paid on the latter. Second, it had to be transported to the stannary town (which cost money) and third, some weight was lost in the second smelting as the impurities were driven out. Instead of altering the price as such, differently marked weights were provided, so that the tin of the first smelting was weighed using weights marked as 16 ounces but which actually weighed 18 ounces. So, you got more tin for your money, albeit of poorer quality. In Cornwall the ratio was 7:8 rather than the 8:9 used in Devon.

The most striking example of the power of the tinners is the story of Richard Strode, the MP for Plymouth at the height of the powers of the stannary court, who complained about the activities of the tinners.

It appears that the estuary at Plympton was being silted up by the vast quantities of light material washed away from the ore in the first processing on the moor. The tin ore at this stage was subjected to pounding and washing to concentrate the dense ore before smelting. This made it difficult for Strode's constituents to earn their livings as ferrymen and fishermen, and the MP had the temerity to let it be known that he did not approve of the cavalier attitude of the tinners to other folks' livelihoods.

The result of his protests was his arrest and abduction by the tinners. He was placed in Lydford Prison without trial and was only released on a grace and favour basis on the understanding that he would not attempt to restrain the activities of the tinners in the future. And this was the way they treated a member of Parliament!

The text of the 1305 charter of Edward I is reproduced opposite. Note how stringent it is in giving 'the tynners' immunity from prosecution by the crown officials.

The text of Edward I's Charter of 1305

The text below is from the charter granted by Edward I to the tinners. The letter 'y' at this time stood for 'th' so that the word yt would be read as 'that'.

Note the extensive rights granted to tinners. They could cut peat and wood and divert streams at will. Moreover, on most charges they could only be brought before the tinners' court, and even when arraigned for serious felonies had to be heard by a jury at least half of which were tinners.

'... Know ye yt we... have granted for us and our heires that all tinners aforesaid working in the Stannaries wch are our demesnes so long as they work in the same stannaryes be free and quite from all pleas of villanies & from all pleas and plaints of our Court... so yt they shal not answeare before any oure justices or ministers or of our heires for any plea or plaint growing within our Stannaries aforesaid for the tyme being (pleas of land liffe or lym excepted) nor yt they depart from their works by somons of any of the officers of us or our Heires but by the smons of our said warden. And yt they be quite from all tallages Tolles Staflages Ayds & other Customs whatsoever for theire aune proper goods in the tounes portes and faires & markets wthn the County aforsaid. We have graunted also to the same tynners yt they may dig tyn & turves for melting of tyn everywhere in our lands moores and wastes & of all other persons whatsoever in ye County aforesaid. And the waters & water courses for the works of the Stannaryes aforesaid to turn where & as often as need shall be & to buy bushement for the melting of tyn as of old tyme hath b'm accustomed to be done without let ... And yt our warden aforesaid or his leiftenant hold al pleas growing betwene the tyners aforesaid also betwene them and other foreners of all trepasses plaints & contracts made in places wherein tyn works within the stannaries aforesaid likewise arising. And yt the same warden have free powre to Justifie the tynners aforsd & other foreyners in such places & to do Justice to the pties as right requireth & as heretofore in the sd Stannayes hath bin accustomed. And if any of the sd tynners in any thing shall offend whereby they ought to be imprisoned yt they be arrested by the warden & in our prison of Lostwithiall & not els where be kept & detayned untill they be delivered according to the law & custom of our Realme. ... one halfe of the jurors of the enquest shall be of the tynners aforsaid and thother half of forenors.'

Walk 30 – Blowing Houses and Foggintor Quarry

Distance
9 miles.

Difficulty
The climb up from Ward Bridge is a stiff one, and very young children may find it difficult. Otherwise, there are no problems, as the walk is along well-defined paths and tracks.

Main Features

Potato Market	556750
Walkham Valley	
Blowing Houses	553763
	553755
Merrivale Quarry	546753
Heckwood Tor	538738
Foggintor Quarry	566736

Description of Walk
Leave the car at Four Winds on the Princetown–Merrivale road (561749). Walk out of the car-park and cross the main road. Turn left

towards Merrivale and walk along the edge of the road until you can see the field wall which joins the road from the right as it bends to the left. Here you will find the northern half of the Merrivale hut circles called the **Potato Market**. From the hut circles follow the wall until you reach a stile over it. Cross the stile and make a beeline for Shillapark Farm on the other side of the River Walkham. Do not go right down to the river, but keep about 100 yards away from it. Turn right (upstream) and make for the bank of a miniature cleave a few hundred yards upstream. Go along the top of the bank and follow the course of the

river upstream. You will soon see the point where the uppermost wall of the Shillapark enclosures run down to the river. Make for this point. You will probably meet the remains of the two medieval farmsteads first, but in any case the **middle blowing house** is clearly visible on the steep side of the river bank about 60 yards from the river, on the opposite side from the Shillapark enclosure wall, and about 200 yards downstream from where the wall meets the river.

Turn back downstream, staying up on the bank to avoid the swampy ground, and make your way

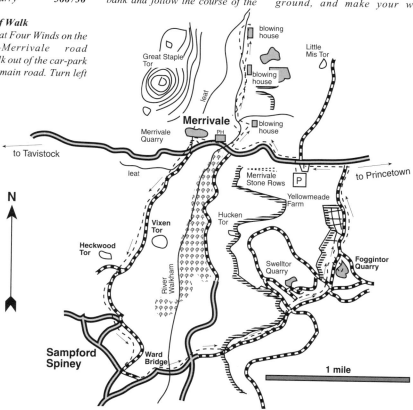

downstream until you see the river. Make a sharp turn to the left. The banks come near the river just downstream from here, and you will find the **lower blowing house** set into the bank just where the River Walkham takes a second 45-degree turn to the right.

Climb up the bank and follow the path roughly downstream. You will soon see a superb pillow mound on the left of the path.

From the pillow mound, turn up-slope and cross the wall at the stile which is near the fenced stock enclosure. Take care if there is traffic on the road. Turn down the slope towards Merrivale.

A few hundred yards down the slope you will see, on the other side of the road, a boundary stone marked A on one side and T on the other. Walk past the Dartmoor Inn.

Walk up the slope until you see the entrance to **Merrivale Quarry**. Cross to the south side of the road and you will find a leat. Follow the leat until it begins to break away to the right away from the line of the wall, then follow the wall. As the wall breaks sharply to the left, Vixen Tor appears. Walk to the wall opposite, which is the boundary wall of Vixen Tor, and you will see a stile of steps in the wall. If you want to visit the tor, take this stile and leave the enclosure to the south by another stile. If not, carry on round the wall, keeping Vixen Tor always on your left, and cross the swampy region up to **Heckwood Tor**. You walk past a boundary stone marked SSP on the way up to the tor.

Soon you will see a track joining you from the right. Follow this track

right over the ridge. As you get to the top you will see on the right of the track a superb example of the quarryman's skill, a dressed stone sitting ready to be transported when the quarry was shut down.

Continue to follow the track. Pu Tor will come in sight, and you continue to follow the very clear track until you reach the vehicle track near Pewtor Cottage. Follow the metalled track down to the road junction, where you follow the 'path' sign for a few yards until you reach the public road again. Note on your left after a few yards a little clapper bridge near the entrance to one of the houses.

Just before the sharp right turn in the road, turn into the farm yard of Gees Farm (**536727**), and make your way to the gate on the right at the back of the outer yard. The way is signposted, and you cross the meadow diagonally to the left-hand gateway at the top. All the gateways are marked with a yellow blob in this section. Continue on the same line to the gateway diagonally opposite. There is a stile here. Turn to the right and you will see a ladder stile over the old wall. Cross this and follow the wall on the right (do not go through the gateway on your right but keep the wall on your right hand), and you will come to a five-bar gate into a double walled pathway. Follow the pathway down to the public road.

Here turn immediately left and follow the rough track down until you meet the road again, where you turn left and eventually come to Ward Bridge (**542720**), with its strange hole. Follow the road up the steep slope until you come to Criptor Cross, where you continue up the

slope towards Criptor. Follow the road until it peters out into a rough track at the moorland edge. Continue along the continuation path towards the farm of Criptor.

Where the sign forbids you to proceed any further, a green track takes off to the right. Look carefully for the blue spots of the waymarks, and make your way roughly along the line of the river until you reach the ford, where you cross. Continue to follow the blue spots until you reach the wall of the farm enclosures up the slope. Turn right and follow the line of the wall, again following the blue spots until, after climbing steeply, you meet the disused railway track near Swelltor Quarry.

Turn right along the track, and you will soon come to a five-bar gate on you right. Turn left up the slope, following the wall. The track dog-legs right and then left at the top of the wall. Continue up-slope until you come to another disused railway track near **Foggintor Quarry**. Cross over the track, and take the first right branch into the quarry itself.

You will find the crane base to the right of the entrance side of the quarry, towards the back. Make your way as best you can to the other end of the quarry, using the stepping-stones if you need to, and rejoin the track after going through the narrow gap at the north end of the quarry. After examining the ruined buildings, turn right towards Yellowmead Farm, which you leave on the left, and, having passed the farm, either make your way directly to Four Winds over the moor, or go along the Yellowmead track to the main road. Turn left on the Tavistock road to regain your car.

Merrivale Quarry

Merrivale Quarry from the Plague Market

The quarry at Merrivale is the last on Dartmoor to produce stone commercially. It is owned today by Tarmac. It produces very high quality granite used for the facings of buildings. When polished, granite has a glossy, speckled appearance because of the presence of feldspar crystals in the structure of the hard igneous rock.

Tor Quarry, as it was originally known, was started by William Duke in 1875. The quarry expanded greatly in the early years of this centur, and then passed to his son, and ownership changed to CL Duke & Co. It was naturally in competition with the nearby quarries of Heckwood, Swelltor and Foggintor, and was remarkably successful,

employing some 150 men in the very early years of the 20th century. In 1903 it produced a record 1,600 tons of granite in a single blasting, for the purposes of building parts of London Bridge.

The great promontory of spoil which you can see for many miles is part of an abandoned plan to connect the quarry with the Princetown railway. Originally the stone was transported by road to Tavistock and the canal, but later traction engines were used, much to the annoyance of the Council who had to keep repairing the roads damaged by the iron tyres.

Stone from Merrivale Quarry was used to construct the war memorial in the Falkland Islands.

The Merrivale Fisherman

The lower blowing house was the site of an unfortunate encounter by a fisherman whose hook went into an enormous fish. He pulled and reeled, as the fish made its way downstream towards him. When it broke surface, however, he observed that it was the body of a middle-aged man, drowned in the river. It was taken to the Dartmoor Inn.

The verdict of the coroner's jury was that the unfortunate had 'died by the visitation of the Almighty, brought on by crossing the river when it was flooded'.

Pillow Mounds

As you leave the lower blowing house by the Walkham you will walk past a large, vaguely geological mound like a drumlin, at the top of the slope. It is not, in fact, geological, but is a rabbit farm.

The tinners spent long periods up on the moor, and fresh provisions were scarce. In order to provide a ready source of fresh meat they built comfortable mounds for the rabbits, who preferred them to the damp, marshy ground generally available. You can see these pillow mounds near many of the main tinning sites.

The tinners identified strongly with the rabbits, and their symbol is three rabbits, seen on many of the churches in the area. The miners obviously viewed themselves as burrowing and industrious just like the rabbits. It didn't stop them eating the rabbits though!

Walkham Valley Blowing Houses

There are three blowing houses in the Walkham Valley, of which you visit two in this walk. This shows what a busy industrial centre it was during the height of tinning on Dartmoor, from about 1500 to 1550. During this period Dartmoor was producing about 20 tons of processed tin per year. By 1600, however, the region was producing only about 6 tonnes per year.

The Walkham houses were part of this substantial industry, and represented at the time a very sophisticated industrial process. The furnaces which you can see, particularly in the lower house (the second which you visit), is of the blast-furnace type, where a forced draught can create really quite high temperatures for the smelting process. The process of smelting is described in the late 18th century by Pryce, the author of *Mineralogia Cornubensis*.

He says that the charcoal and ore are laid layer on layer on one another. The bellows, fixed in position by a wrought iron hasp at the bottom of the furnace then 'throw in a steady and powerful air into the castle, which, at the same time that it smelts the tin, forces it out also through a hole in the bottom of the castle ... into a moorstone trough ... called a float'. You can see the remains of the float in the lower blowing house.

In each of the houses you can see a wheel-pit, a mould-stone and the remains of the furnace. On the edge of the mould-stones is a sample mould, a small square depression which allowed a sample of the smelting to be taken and checked for finish. Both tin-houses are about 30 feet by 15 feet in area, and the leat system supplying them with the power for the stamp and bellows can clearly be traced.

Mould-stones in the Walkham Valley tinners' mills

Heckwood Quarry

Heckwood Quarry, perched on the tor overlooking Vixen Tor and Pu Tor, is a 19th-century quarry which provided much of the stone for the Plymouth breakwater. The stone was transported from here down the track which you have just climbed and then down to Tavistock, from where it was put into lighters on the canal to Morwellham, and then down the River Tamar.

By the side of the track you can see an excellent example of the worked stone which also came out of this quarry. You will notice that the large piece of stone has been dressed roughly over its main part, while the edges are cut quite true. It will be clear to you that in constructing a large building, it is the trueness of the edges and bearing faces which are important, rather than the outer and inner faces. When Julius Drewe wanted to use roughly hewn granite as the facings of his beautiful if distinctive Castle Drogo, his architect, Lutyens, would not condone it, not because it made building difficult, but because it was considered tasteless. Nevertheless, rough-faced stone is used all over the country for suitable surfaces, such as railway bridges and sea walls, where appearance is secondary to the cost.

The dressed stone you see before you is a relatively sophisticated product, the moorstone, or surface granite on the moor, being finished by rougher means. Up until about 1800, a method known as wedge and groove was used, whereby a groove was cut down the desired break-line and, as it deepened, wedges were inserted and banged in. Eventually the granite would crack along the stress line produced. Later the better known feather and

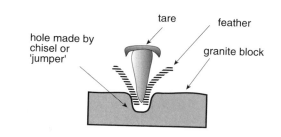

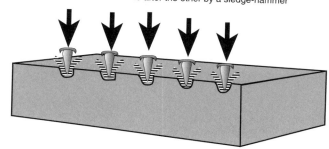

tares are struck one after the other by a sledge-hammer

The tare and feather method of granite-cutting

tare method was used. You can see the results of this on very many of the tors, and on the open moor where there is surface stone. In this method a series of holes were cut into the stone in a straight line by means of a long-shanked chisel called a jumper. Into these holes, about 3 inches in depth and 6 inches or so apart, were placed rounded bearing pieces called feathers into which a wedge-shaped tare was fitted. This was then gradually driven into the granite until the stresses drove a crack along the desired path. This was more efficient than the wedge and groove method, as it required less work to produce the crack. After cutting, the moorstone was generally used undressed as construction material and as gateposts. You can see many examples of such undressed stone in the farms around the edge of the moor.

Sampford Spiney

The village takes its name from its original lord, Robert de Spinet, but was known at one time as Sampford Spanley. It was under this name that it was mentioned in documents as a vill, or a farmstead having certain rights and privileges in the Forest of Dartmoor.

The village has a lively church with pinnacles rising from the corners of its square tower. The parish used to be under the control of Plympton Priory, whose arms (two crossed keys) can be found on the south face of the tower. Near the church is the manor house, which at one time was in the possession of the same Drake family that produced Sir Francis.

Foggintor and Swelltor Quarries

The deserted buildings of Foggintor Quarry

The common on which these two quarries sit has been a source of stone for major building projects since 1785. In that year large amounts were taken by Thomas Tyrwhitt, the eventual builder of Dartmoor Prison at Princetown, for the building of the large houses at Princetown, and Tor Royal in particular. A little later the stone for the prison was taken from the same area.

The quarries began production in earnest around 1820, when the Princetown and Plymouth and Dartmoor Railways were built. The map of the walk shows the close relationship between the railway and the quarrying. Fortunately for the quarry-owners, the railway was more or less forced to proceed in the big loop, passing the valuable quarry sites.

Foggintor was the first to start, closely followed by Swelltor. Production of the roughly finished stone continued until about 1900 at

Foggintor, then called Royal Oak Quarry. Swelltor finished working in 1921, but restarted again in 1937 when both quarries were opened to provide stone for the county road programme. The stone from the

quarries was used for Nelson's Column in Trafalgar Square.

Of the two I prefer Foggintor, with its great high cliffs and the clear lake in the centre, both formed as stone was won from the ground. In the corner of the quarry is a crane base, which was used to lift stones on to trucks for transportation. Across the quarry is a set of stepping-stones which leads to a track above the little lake. Look back and you will see the huge promontory left sticking out of the hillside. There can be a tremendous sense of peace here even on a hot Sunday in summer, which, bearing in mind its nearness to a good track, is unusual.

For the photographer, the cliffs and the ruined buildings outside the quarry itself are very attractive. Atmospheric scenes of the daily workplace of scores of men now form a favourite subject in the right light.

Foggintor Quarry

Walk 31 – Hooten Weals and Skir Gut

Distance
About 5 miles.

Difficulty
No great problems. Carry a map and compass, because the country around the foot of Skir Gut can be confusing. Take waterproofs and stout footwear.

Main Features

Week Ford Stepping Stones	662725
Blowing Houses	662724
Hooten Weals Mine	655708
Skir Gut	646705

Description of Walk
Leave your car at the bridge north of the Forest Inn in Hexworthy. Walk up the road until you are opposite the entrance to Huccaby Farm (**664730**). On the opposite side of the road you will see the track which leads down to the Dart at Week Ford, where there are some impressive **stepping stones**.

You will find the two **blowing houses** at Week Ford 100 yards or so from the river above a swampy section of ground.

At the end of the stepping-stones turn left and cross the wooden bridge. There is a path junction here. You should head up-hill with the O Brook on your right. At the top of the slope you will reach the public road at Saddle Bridge (**665719**). Continue up the O Brook with it on your right. As the brook turns right there is some evidence of tin-streaming. Keep up on the bank to avoid the swamp near the little river. Soon you will come to a leat take-off. This is Horse Ford (**663711**).

From Horse Ford continue up the brook, climbing up to the old leat. If you look back you can see two old leats making their way over towards Combestone Tor.

After a while the brook turns right where a subsidiary stream joins it from the left at a marshy flat area. This smaller brook is called Dry Lake. You may notice a cross high on the opposite bank. This is part of the Monks' Way, which goes from Horn's Cross towards and beyond Skir Ford, which you will visit. Take the branch of the brook to the right. You will very soon see the three spoil heaps of **Hooten Weals** ahead of you. Make your way to them.

From Hooten Weals go back down to the O Brook and continue upstream. You will eventually come

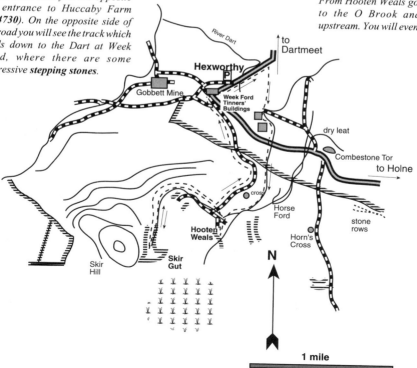

197

Week Ford

Week Ford stepping-stones

*to a ford, with an indistinct path crossing the small brook. Continue to follow the river upstream. It swings left and can be seen to emerge from what appears to be a small tin-working. Continue upstream and you will find yourself in the impressive workings of **Skir Gut**. It is worth carrying on until the very top, where a complicated set of gullies ends in a pair of springs and pools. Return to Skir Ford.*

On the right bank of the O Brook, under the tinners' banks, you will find a tinners's hut about 200 yards down from the ford.

Continue back down the brook, until you come to the bridge over the O Brook near Hooten Weals. Cross over and continue along the track back towards Hexworthy. The path will take you past another mine which you might have noticed from Dry Lake, and also past the cross. The track will lead you to the Forest Inn. Continue down the road and you will soon come to the bridge and your car.

Everyone who takes the trouble to walk down the paths to Week Ford through the deep woods on either side is enchanted by the setting. The River Dart here runs away out of the cleave and over a shallow ford in which a set of excellent stepping-stones now sit to allow walkers to pass dry-footed. If it's raining you need to be a little careful or you will achieve an intimate knowledge of the River Dart that you could do without. You will find the blowing houses on the south side of the ford, about 300–400 yards away up the slope and on the side of some rather swampy ground. They are well-preserved and the mould-stones and wheel-pits are clearly visible, although some trees have grown through the walls over the years. You can get around to them by going upstream, but I cannot vouch for any right of way.

Hexworthy

The ancient tenement of Hexworthy was known by an amazing variety of names: Hexworthy, Hextworthy, Hextenworth, and once even Bisouthexworthi. The locals pronounce it Hexary. In 1344 there is a mention of a Robert de Hextenworth as a tenant of the forest.

There is an old inn here, the Forest Inn, and a number of farms on the opposite side of the river, called the Byes, of which Huccaby is an example. Below Hexworthy the Dart flows through Cleave Combe and down into Week Ford, which we will cross on the walk.

In the summer Hexworthy attracts rather too many car-borne tourists for its own peace and quiet, but outside these few weeks it is an attractive place. In the past it was not so quiet, since it was a centre for the provisioning and entertainment of local miners.

Week Ford Blowing Houses

The two blowing houses at Week Ford are very picturesque, with rowan trees growing through the old walls. The upper blowing house has a very well-preserved wheel-pit, from which you can get a good idea of the size of the wheel necessary to drive the stamps that pounded the ore and to drive the bellows. There is a fairly complete furnace here, and you can see a nice mortar stone. The inside of the upper house is relatively clear, so that you can get a good idea of the layout when it was working.

The lower house was driven by the water which had passed through the pit of the upper. There is a good door-jamb here, and you can find a well-preserved mould-stone and a number of three-holed mortar stones, upon which the ore was pounded.

Mortar-stone at Week Ford tinners' mill

Huccaby

Huccaby, Hokecaby or Hookerby is one of the ancient tenements of the forest. There were originally thirty-five of these, all of which had particular rights and privileges on the moor, notably pasturage, peat-cutting and wood-gathering. You can read more about the rights of the ancient tenements, as they are known, in the chapter on Ancient Farms & People.

Just below Huccaby Cottage lies Jolly Lane Cot, which was one of the last dwellings to be built in its own enclosure towards the end of the last century, under an old law which allowed land to be claimed if it could be enclosed between the hours of sunrise and sunset, and a dwelling built in the enclosure on the same day.

Saddle Bridge

The bridge crosses the O Brook here and marks the beginning of a delightful walk up to Dry Lake and Horse Ford, with the brook babbling on your right over steep steps and through the roots of rowan trees. In the autumn the scene is breathtaking, when the bright red berries of the rowans hang like bunches of small grapes over the rushing stream. It is worth leaving the path and getting close in to the stream as it leaps into pools and over small cascades. There used to be a wooden pack-horse bridge here, but it was taken down a long time ago because it was unsafe, and it has been replaced by the stone bridge which you see today. Crossing reports the interesting fact that Prince Albert caught his first trout here. I assume he used a fly and not a worm.

O Brook

The O Brook is also called the Wo Brook and the Oke Brook. The names come apparently from a Saxon word meaning crooked or windy. It flows down under Henroost and Hooten Weals, past Horse Ford and under Saddle Bridge, and falls into the Dart at Week Ford. It is part of the boundary of the forest and is mentioned in the perambulations as such. Horse Ford is a paved crossing over the O Brook and lies on an ancient way from Buckland to the east part of the moor, that passes through Holne. If you look on either side you will see the crosses which lead travellers to this useful crossing place. Near Horse Ford is the Holne Moor Leat which runs for many miles, skirting round Combestone Tor. It is marked clearly on the Ordnance Survey map.

Hooten Weals Mine

Hooten Weals was worked as a mine from around the 16th century, and must have been a relatively large centre in those early times of tin-streaming. It contains one of the two shafts on Dartmoor dating from this time, the other being at Vitifer near Warren House Inn. It was rather difficult for these early tinners to build shafts, because of the problem of draining them. It was only after the introduction of the adit and shaft system in the 19th century that this became generally possible.

The circular buddles below Hooten Weals mine

The visible workings here date from the 1890s, when work was started on top of the previous workings. The commercial decision to start a mine on Dartmoor was always a difficult one since the more accessible ore had already been taken by 'the old men', as the medieval miners were called. This was the case with Hooten Weals and its associated working, Henroost. Work soon stopped in spite of the fact that the mine produced tin of very high quality.

Around 1901, however, the economic conditions changed, and a very modern mining operation began, electricity being supplied from a high-pressure wheel at Saddle Bridge. There were extensive arrangements for stamping and dressing, and as you climb up to the workings you should note on your left the circular beds of the dressing floors, the lowest of three such floors. Here were the stamping machines which crushed the ore in the first instance, and the armature of one of the large electrical machines can be seen lying by the side. The circular beds which you can see in the illustration are called buddles. At the height of its operation the mine employed about thirty men, who lived in the surrounding villages and farms. The mine continued production until about 1922.

The remains are confusing. The deep gullies which you can see from the top are both the result of the early mining techniques of following lodes up from the river, and from the later mining.

In the later period dressed ore was taken down to Dry Lake by a tramway, and there it was further treated using the power of a wheel 45 feet in diameter, whose seating you can see above Dry Lake on the walk. Water taken from the O Brook below the Hooten Weals workings flowed over an aqueduct to service the wheel.

The Henroost and Skir Gut

These two workings are an extension of the Hooten Weals mine, and are also the result of both early (medieval) and late tin-workings. You can see as you walk up the workings of Skir Gut that they followed the lines of the lodes and you can trace these roughly if you stand on the top of the ridges and follow their lines. Paradoxically, the lode ore was not as pure as the river or alluvial ore because the latter had already been subject to the washing process by the river in whose bed it lay. Large quantities of ore had to be removed from Henroost and Skir Gut (or Gert) to the dressing floors further down the valley. At the top of the workings Skir Gut splits into two as the lode split, and in each you can find a peaceful pool, admittedly with somewhat waterlogged edges, where you can sit and eat your sandwiches with only the curlews on Skir Hill above you and the voices of the tin-miners in your mind for company.

Walk 32 – Haytor Granite Quarry

Distance
A mile or so.

Difficulty
None at all.

Main Features
Haytor Quarry   759774
Haytor Granite Tramway 75.77.
Holwell Quarry   752777

Description of Walk
Leave your car at the top car-park above Haytor Vale (758767). From the car-park walk up to the right of the right-most mound of Hay Tor. From here you can see, depending on your exact position either two or three granite spoil mounds below you to your right. Make your way

down towards these on the obvious path, and you will soon find on your left a wire fence which marks the upper edge of **Haytor Quarry**. A little further down from this spot there is a gate in the fence.

If you go into the quarry you will find it a peaceful place amidst the bustle of tourists around you. For some reason few people enter it, imagining I suppose, that it is a dark and dangerous place. There is a pool with water lilies and a natural tranquillity that belies its original industrial purpose.

Leave the quarry by the same gate and go down to the lowest spoil tip by continuing along the same path.

You will find a branch of the **Haytor Granite Tramway** immediately below the spoil heap.

Follow the tramlines away from Hay Tor until it meets the main line in a set of granite points. Turn left here and follow it around to the left until it offers you a path down to **Holwell Quarry** or a more level path curving around back under Hay Tor. Go down to Holwell Quarry.

At the end of the tramlines you will pass over a decrepit embankment. Beyond this you will see where a piece of the tramway was under construction, and you can examine the components from which the tramlines were constructed.

Turn back to go up the slope where the shire horses used to pull the wagons. Before you leave the embankment area look on the left down the slope to see a beehive-shaped quarrymen's hut down below tramline level.

Make your way back to the main line and turn right to follow the tracks up towards Hay Tor and into the last of the three quarries. You enter this via a narrow defile into a rather uninteresting small quarry area. From here climb up the steep path to the right and make your way to the left of the right-most outcrop of Hay Tor, which towers above you as you pass by it. Follow the wall of rock around until you can see the car-park ahead of you on the other side of the main road.

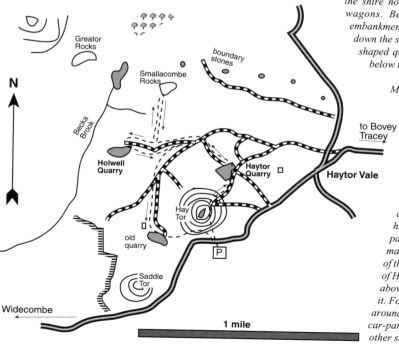

201

Haytor Quarry

The quarry on Hay Tor is the best known on Dartmoor for two reasons. First, it has a fascinating example of a stone-tracked tramway, which we talk about elsewhere, and second, it provided stone for London Bridge.

The quarry was started in 1819 by George Templer of Stover. Vital to the success of Templer's operation was the opening of the tramway to connect the quarry with the canal at Teigngrace and hence to his markets to the east. There are a number of quarries, three main ones, in fact, all of them busy until about 1860, except for a gap in the 1840s. Around 1865 Cornish granite gained a significant cost advantage, and the Dartmoor quarries all fell largely into disuse. Haytor was no exception. The main basis on which the quarry was expanded was the winning of the contract in 1825 for the provision of stone for London Bridge, and later for the British Museum.

By 1825 the quarry was being worked by the Devon Haytor Granite Company, and by 1829 it was in the hands of the Duke of Somerset, who retained control right into the early years of this century when it was leased by J Easton & Son. By this time, however, the tramway was no longer used, and the stone was transported to Bovey Tracey by boring old tractor power.

I enjoy the old quarries here immensely. They contain quite a few interesting industrial relics, including a derrick which looks like a pair of sheerlegs, and which was used to swing huge blocks of granite around. There is also an interesting winch rusting gently in the lower quarry. Of course, when the quarry was working there would have been even more equipment in use, such as

Haytor Quarry

flatbed horse-drawn waggons and trucks for use on the tramway itself. The scene would have been one of considerable bustle and industry as the stone was pulled out from the walls of the quarry and manhandled around into position for the rough dressing it received before being carried away downhill. Although it is peaceful today the noise of work would have been substantial, as the masons and the quarrymen performed their noisy tasks.

Now the lower parts of the quarries are flooded, leaving a fairy tale scene in summer of water lilies and calm

amidst the bustle of the tourists. Swallows swoop low over the water and blackbirds sing contentedly. As long as you don't climb on the walls, the quarries are perfectly safe and are well worth a visit. If you look around in the quarry you can find any number of bolts, rings and footings which will allow you to work out how the quarry worked. At one point there were about 100 men working at Haytor, so you can sit in the old quarry and imagine the scene of bustle and the noise of labour which you would have heard a century ago as the men worked and moved the stone.

Hay Tor

View of Hay Tor from the south-west

There is no doubt about it, as you climb up to Hay Tor you are looking at a very substantial piece of granite. It overlooks the whole of the eastern half of Dartmoor, looming like the superstructure of a battleship, ploughing its way over the stormy seas of the eastern valleys.

Hay Tor is immensely popular and immensely well known. For many years it was the only thing on Dartmoor that ever appeared on small-scale maps. Countless thousands of tourists clamber up to the plateau on which it sits, and a large fraction of them clamber up to the top of the granite mass. From here enormous views can be had over Dartmoor down to the bays and coves of the coast, down to Salcombe, and towards Plymouth Sound over the South Hams, the parishes directly to the south of Dartmoor. In the middle of the last century an iron stairway was built, arousing the wrath of a William Croker, who wrote of 'the unsightly stair step to enable the enervated and pinguedinous scions of humanity of this wonderful nineteenth century to gain its summit'.

The rise of Victorian tourism latched on to Hay Tor as archetypal of the Dartmoor wilderness, and thereby ensured that all one had to do to claim that one had 'done' Dartmoor was to climb it. Much the same view prevails today, with the inevitable inclusion of Hay Tor on the itinerary of any coach tour, along with Becky Falls and the prison. At least the 1905 plan to build a coal-powered electric tramway to take people to the summit was never realized!

Hay Tor gets its name from being the higher of the two outcrops on its hilly base. The Dartmoor speech modifies higher to 'hayer' and hence to Hay Tor.

You will often see climbers on the steeper of the two sides, where there are a number of climbs of quite demanding grades. Surprisingly, it is not the highest cliff face in the area, since the innocuous-looking Vixen Tor holds that prize. Do not go climbing on any of these faces, or you may become a more permanent part of Dartmoor than you might have wished.

Holwell Quarry

It is worth walking down to the quarry at Holwell, since there are a few interesting remains of its quarrying days that can be seen.

On the right as you reach the bottom is a beehive hut, built by the quarrymen. It is a corbelled construction, somewhat squalid inside, but interesting none the less. The hut lies slightly below the level of the main track.

On the left as you get to the bottom of the slope are the high cliffs of the stone working, and if you continue along the line of the track you will find it soon peters out after crossing a gully. Here you can see good examples of unworn tramway sections, lying at odd angles. The views across to Smallacombe are worthwhile, too. Often in the summer you can look across the valley to the brackeny slopes opposite to see a farmer pulling out small granite outcrops and savaging the bracken in an attempt to try to improve the grazing for his sheep.

Haytor Tramway

The main problem with quarrying as a way of making a living is that stone is heavy. The cost of transportation is therefore a fundamental consideration for the owner. The reaction of the owner of Haytor Quarry, George Templer in 1820 was to ignore the expensive iron rails which were then available and use a much cheaper local alternative, namely stone.

From the bottom of the lower quarry walk down to the tramway and have a look at the rails. You will find them to be about 14 inches in section with a wide, lengthways groove cut out of them to make them into a rail-shaped section. Most are under 6 feet in length, but a few are longer. Clearly, if the pieces were longer they would tend to crack in the middle under the weight of a 3 ton wagon. The tram tracks are about 4 feet apart, but this is a very rough estimate, since there was no way that the stone rails could be stabilized over a long period.

The most interesting part of the tramway are the clever points. In some places there were moving parts to the points, but generally speaking a hefty heave was required on the side of the wagon to ensure that it went the right way at the junction. Nevertheless, the points were rather clever, and, moreover, almost made themselves, since the curving of the tracks was produced in no small measure by the friction of the wagon wheels.

Granite points on the tramway

The wagons were drawn by horses which worked in teams of eighteen in order to crawl up the steady incline from Holwell Quarry. Twelve trucks, bearing a total of 35 tons were drawn up each time. The wheels of the wagons were without flanges, were about 26 inches in diameter, and carried a flat bed, the front ones usually having shafts.

The tramway ran from Holwell Quarry where you can see the end of its construction, where there are some excellent unfinished examples of the stone rails, and then drew up the horse-drawn slope, swinging to the right and then to the left below the spoil promontories at the lower quarry. From there it ran away down towards Hay Tor Down, eventually reaching what is now the Newton Abbott – Moretonhampstead railway before terminating at Teigngrace.

Walk 33 – Lee Moor Clay Works and the Dewerstone

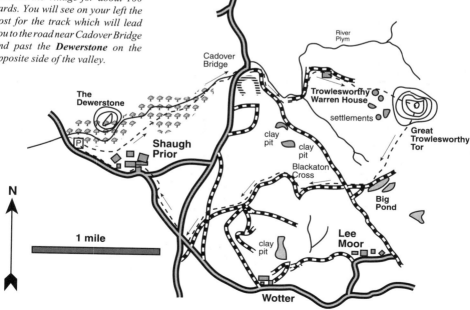

Distance
6 miles.

Difficulties
Map and compass should be carried as you will be going onto the open moor near Trowlesworthy. The tracks over the clay workings can be confusing. Wear stout footwear and take waterproofs.

Main Features

The Dewerstone	537638
Cadover Bridge	555646
Trowlesworthy Warren	567648
Trowlesworthy Tors	578644
Big Pond and Lee Moor Clay Workings	570625

Description of Walk
Leave your car at the car-park near the bridge below Shaugh Prior. You can leave your car in the village but there is generally more room down at the bridge. Walk back up the road towards the village for about 100 yards. You will see on your left the post for the track which will lead you to the road near Cadover Bridge and past the **Dewerstone** on the opposite side of the valley.

When you reach the road, turn left and make your way down past the car-park and **Cadover Bridge**. Just before the bridge is a metalled road to the right. Walk up this road.

Where the road makes a definite right turn, there is a clear gravel track off to the left. This leads you to the area of **Trowlesworthy Warren Farm**. Before you get to the farm turn right over the open moorland towards **Little Trowlesworthy Tor**. (There is a Bronze Age settlement near here.)

Proceed up to **Great Trowlesworthy Tor**. From the top of Great Trowlesworthy locate the lakes at Big Pond. Make your way in a straight line just to the right of the lakes and above the white **clay-workings** of Lee Moor to their right. There is a wood at Lee Moor House, and you should aim for its right-hand edge. Soon you will see Blackaton Cross by the roadside. Fifty yards further on after you pass it you will see a track to the left which heads on over Saddlesborough, with its trig point. You will see more than enough of the clay workings on your route. After Saddlesborough you cross a track, and at the next junction, where a track crosses your route obliquely, take a 45-degree turn to the right and join the road again near Beatland Corner, which you reach by turning right onto the road. From here back to Shaugh Prior the route is clearly signposted. Walk back down to the bridge.

The Devilish Dewerstone

Dewer is the local name for the Devil. The story has it that the Devil and his hounds run around the moor at night looking for unrepentant sinners, and hounding them over the cliffs at the Dewerstone. Leaving their home in Wistman's Wood near Two Bridges, they scour the uplands, until they locate the poor unfortunate. They then drive him closer and closer to the cliffs, never physically pushing the victim over, but waiting until the terror of the red eyes of the evil wisht hounds drives him to hurl himself over the cliff on to the rocks below.

On a stormy night you can hear the cries of the unfortunates as they relive their horrible deaths on the bed of the Plym. On dark winter's nights it is best not to dawdle on the paths near the Dewerstone, because they are haunted by a huge black dog with evil red eyes. No one who sees it survives. I wonder how we know about it then?

You can read more of the legends of Dartmoor in the Myths & Legends chapter.

The Dewerstone area is a favourite one for families from Plymouth and the surrounding towns and villages who come out here on summer's days to play in the Plym below, and ramble around the picturesque paths and tracks. It is a very good place for photography, but as the best time is early morning and evening, it is best to bring a tripod.

The river below the Dewerstone flows over large boulders, leaping and babbling its way eventually under a road bridge below Shaugh Prior. This is a beautiful area to spend half an hour just relaxing.

Trowlesworthy Tors

Great and Little Trowlesworthy Tors give good views out over the Plym and down towards the clay workings over which you will be walking later. There has been a lot of stone-working in this area, and you should be able to find a large number of partly finished artefacts. Most of these are boring rectangular lumps of stone, but on Little Trowlesworthy you can find a huge cylinder of granite, hewn from the rock in the 1820s to be the base for an enormous flagstaff for Devonport. By the time it was finished the project had evaporated.

The area has been inhabited for thousands of years. There are both Bronze Age hut circles and a relatively modern Dartmoor farmhouse at Trowlesworthy Warren.

Cadover Bridge and the Plym

Both the Plym and Cadover Bridge are named in a charter of 1291. The Plym is referred to as 'Plymma', from a Celtic word, *pilim*, meaning to roll. Although some people would have you believe that the river below Cadover Bridge is called the Cad, it is called the Plym all along its length. This is a misreading of the old word for Cadover, namely Cadaford, some people concluding that it was the bridge over the Cad. In fact, it was called 'ponte de Cada worth' in the 1291 document, and the name probably derives from the word *cad*, meaning a skirmish, so the nearby settlement was probably built on the site of a local battle. The whole area here is infested with Celtic place-names; Dewerstone may well derive from the welsh word *dwr*, meaning water.

Blackaton Cross

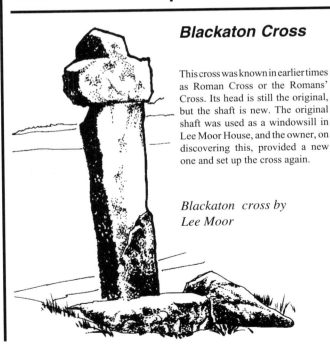

Blackaton cross by Lee Moor

This cross was known in earlier times as Roman Cross or the Romans' Cross. Its head is still the original, but the shaft is new. The original shaft was used as a windowsill in Lee Moor House, and the owner, on discovering this, provided a new one and set up the cross again.

China Clay Processing

As we discussed in the Geography & Geology chapter, granite looks hard and tough, but is, in fact, very unstable when subject to attack from weather and corrosive influences. Under the influence of weathering it produces its broken down form of growan, the grey material of which most of the worn tracks on Dartmoor are made.

When granite is subject to a particular form of corrosion, however, it breaks down to form kaolin, or china clay, which is useful not just in the making of pottery, but above all in the paper industry, which takes about 80 per cent of the production. When the granite forms it creates three component parts, namely feldspar, mica and quartz. The feldspar is susceptible to attack chemically by acids because of its

Lee Moor clay workings

make-up. During granite's formation, very hot and acidic vapours, originating from the source rocks, rise up from the underlying rocks and condense in the cool granite above. This combination only needs the addition of water from above to provide the environment in which the feldspar can be converted into a slightly simpler compound called kaolinite. It is this kaolinite which is the china clay. For those with a knowledge of GCSE chemistry, the feldspar gains two water molecules, and loses three silica molecules and all its potash, while retaining three silica molecules and its alumina core.

After all this frantic chemical activity has taken place we are left with a spongy matrix of quartz and mica, and a high-value surrounding mass of kaolin. This kaolin can be separated out by virtue of its fineness, since the suspension of the fine particles in water will last longer than that of the other two components, quartz and mica (called the dross). The latter tends to occur in bigger lumps, to use a technical term.

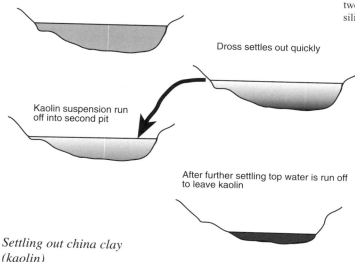

Kaolin suspension and heavier dross run into settling pit

Dross settles out quickly

Kaolin suspension run off into second pit

After further settling top water is run off to leave kaolin

Settling out china clay (kaolin)

Lee Moor Clay Works

I suppose these works are a rather strange place to recommend people to go walking on Dartmoor. Almost everywhere else is more beautiful and almost everywhere else has more interest in terms of natural history, prehistory or scenery. Yet it is still worthwhile going to look at an industry that is as much part of Dartmoor as is Fur Tor or Dartmeet or Princetown Prison. China clay has been won and processed on Dartmoor since 1930, just after it was recognized for the important natural resource that it is. In that year John Dickens and John Cawley leased land from the Earl of Morley in order to start the exploitation of the area. The business was soon sold to William Phillips, who was joined, two years later in 1853, by his son John. Within a short time the family was producing rudimentary artefacts such as fire-bricks for furnaces at the site.

In 1862 the Martin brothers took over the works. The site had expanded dramatically in the intervening years, and there were now subsidiary workings at Wotter. There were no fewer than nine separate ventures operating in the immediate vicinity of Lee Moor. By this time the village of Lee Moor itself, manned initially by Cornishmen, had grown too, and it soon gained the reputation of being a god-fearing town, minding its own business in the main part. There was little need for the inhabitants to go outside the boundaries before the advent of the motor car, and the villagers had a reputation for looking after their own. There was a strong Methodist undercurrent, and even today there is no pub in Lee Moor. Like all the moor villages it is under pressure from the larger towns in the area and the ease of transport; there

is now no school in the village and the young people look elsewhere than clay working for their futures.

The original method of winning the china clay was straightforward. The turf was cleared away from the under-lying kaolin, which was dug out. Then, either water was caused to flow over the dug clay or the clay was removed to a more convenient place where it could be mixed with water so that the kaolin itself would go into suspension. This left the larger particles of mica and quartz temporarily in suspension too, as the mixing process took place. The mixture was then allowed to settle in a lake, and the denser, larger particles dropped out of suspension much more quickly than the fine kaolin. The overlying suspension con-taining the china clay could then be run off into another pit where it was left to settle for a considerable time. The fine particles eventually dropped to the bottom to form a grey-white stiff mud. When the overlying water was relatively clear it too was drawn off, and the clay on the bottom was cut into manageable cubes, which were then dried.

The water for this process was taken from the Plym along a leat starting at Ditsworthy Weir, and was returned to the river downstream through a tunnel.

Today the clay is won using high-pressure hoses, cutting directly into the clay from the side. Because of

Course of supply leat

the instability of the clay, there is no way at present of getting at the clay which lies deep underground, and indeed, at present, no one is exactly sure how deep the clay goes in places. The pits which you see as you walk over the works are a combination of the working pits, dormant areas and settling pools.

Some of the other sites on the moor were used to transport the clay in suspension for some miles. An example of this is the transportation of kaolin suspension from the Red Lake area down to Shipley Bridge, where it was settled out. With the abundance of water on Dartmoor, this was a most effective way of transporting the clay.

You can see the same process in operation today as you walk over the lunar scenery of the Lee Moor works. These are owned today by *English China Clays International*, a name that fully reflects the importance of china clay to many industries outside Dartmoor.

Walk 34 – Yealm Steps and Blowing Houses

Distance
About 4 miles.

Difficulty
None. A straightforward walk for all the family. Take waterproofs and a map and compass, nevertheless.

Main Features

Enclosures	**620635**
Yealm Steps	**616636**
Blowing Houses	**617635**
	616639
Stalldown Moor Stone	
Rows	**632623**

Description of Walk
From Cornwood take the road to Torr, signposted opposite the Cornwood Inn. Go over the Wisdome Bridge (called Vicarage Bridge on the signpost), and go straight on up the little hill. At the top turn left and then take the first right. At the top of the slope the road to the right is signposted 'Yadworthy Farm Only'. Do not take this, but rather go straight on, and you will find yourself on the road to the water treatment works (**629612**) marked on the map. Go through the gate and park near it.

On the left just past the gate is a signpost to the left, marked 'Permitted Path to the Moor'. Take this and follow the enclosure wall out on to the moor until you reach the end of the small wood (**624618**). Up the slope from here you should be able to see a stone row. Walk to this, at about forty-five degrees to the track, and then follow it along to the west. The wall breaks off left, and at the brow of the hill the stone row curves left also, at about forty-five degrees and down the slope. Follow it for a few hundred yards. You will now be able to see the enclosure to your right. It is between

the two small hawthorn trees, and it cuts across the stream running from right to left over your path. The huts in this enclosure are small but good, and some of them have well-defined doorways.

The enclosure continues on the other side of the stream, which you should cross. Continue on the same level and towards the right-hand side of the forest which you can see ahead. Continue to follow this, bearing right as more of the forest comes into view. As you breast the hill you will see the beautiful valley of the Yealm open up ahead of you, with **Yealm Steps** being the

cascade just visible in the rocky section in the cleft of the valley. Note the two large enclosures to your right and up on the opposite bank of Ranny Brook, because you will be walking to them on your return. Go down to the Ranny Brook, where you will observe extensive tin-workings, and make your way up the right-hand side of the Yealm.

The **lower blowing house** is on the right-hand side of the Yealm, 100 yards or so further up and on the opposite side from the forest corner.

From the lower blowing house continue up to the lovely waterfalls and cascades. Cross to the left-hand bank where you can and continue up the

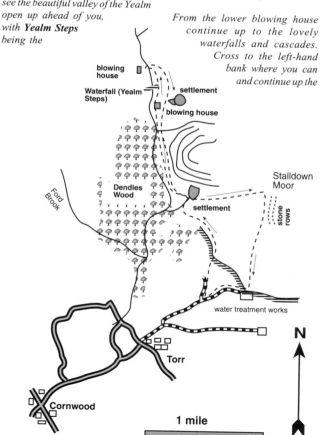

209

Yealm Steps

stream. The **upper blowing house** is about 400 yards above the top of Yealm Steps on the left-hand bank.

From the upper blowing house you should cross the Yealm again and contour round at the same level as this house (slightly above the top of Yealm Steps). Above and to your left you will soon see the low wall of the enclosure. Examine the huts and the central wall, and then continue to the opposite wall of the other enclosure. Look back towards the upper blowing house and you will see a prominent outcrop of rock. Put your back towards this and look ahead. You will see a lower hill to your right, whose slope you breasted in going down to Ranny Brook, and another, higher hill to its left. Between you and this higher hill you will see some tin-workings. Make your way towards these, where there is a ford (**624633**). Cross the ford and continue up the slope in the same direction.

You should be travelling directly away from the outcrop above the upper blowing house. Continue up over a boggy section, and over a false summit. You will soon notice a summit outcrop, which you should make for. Continue up the slope and only a few yards from the outcrop you will see four prominent standing stones. These form part of the **Stalldown Moor Stone Rows**.

Turn right along the row and continue down to the last stones. On the same line you will see a low cairn. Make your way to that, and when you reach it turn slightly to the right and walk down the slight slope towards the wall. In the wall is a gate. Pass through this, gain the concrete track and turn right to regain your car after 200 yards.

This lovely waterfall is better seen than described. It lies between the lower and upper blowing houses on the Yealm, and slightly upstream from the double pound marked on the map. The waterfalls are a set of beautiful cascades rather than, say, the single large drop of the East Dart waterfall, but are well worth a visit. The water falls over and between huge granite boulders rounded out of their usual angular shapes by the constant gentle abrasion. Near the top is a cave over which the water dribbles, and next to this is a huge ivy, falling over the rocks as if mirroring the cascade of water. This is a delightful place to have your lunch, but be careful you don't come a cropper on the slippery boulders.

The huge boulders of Yealm Steps

Yealm Blowing Houses

Mould-stone in lower Yealm blowing house

There are two blowing houses on the Yealm, one below the cascade known as Yealm Steps and the other above it. The lower one is on the right-hand bank as you look upstream, and the other is on the opposite bank above the cascades.

The lower house is a good example of this type of early industrial building, with a prominent wheel-pit in which the waterwheel sat to drive the bellows for the furnace, which can also be seen. The wheel was driven by water from a leat which was taken off upstream from the house, contoured round and led into the wheel-pit. In the lower blowing house you can also see two mould-stones into which the tin was poured after smelting. In one of the stones there is a sample mould, which was used to test the quality of the smelting. The ingot of tin was cast with a hole through it by which it could be manoeuvred. An ingot made in this way would weigh about 100 pounds depending on the exact size of the mould-stone.

The upper house is better preserved, but is not quite so interesting. It has two mould-stones, but, like the lower house, no mortar-stones. The latter were used to provide a base on which to pummel the ore to break it up, the better to smelt it.

The setting of the lower house in particular is very attractive yet rarely visited. It is difficult to imagine this peaceful valley submerged under the weight of industry that it would have seen in the 16th century. Try to imagine the bustle as the ore was brought in, the noise of the wheel turning and the roar of the furnace. Imagine the cries of the men as they manoeuvred the hot, heavy ingots around in the small house and as they carried the peat charcoal for the furnace.

Dendles Wood

The piece of land on which Dendles Wood now sits used to be called 'Hawns and Dendles'. Dendles is a corruption of 'Daniels'. The two names come from the two original owners of the land. The land used to be open to the public on occasion, but today, although it is owned by the Woodland Trust, it is not accessible to the public at all.

The wood extends up the valley of the Yealm now, in a beautiful blue-green spread of conifers banked by broad-leaved trees. Normally I would not be enthusiastic about any conifer plantation – I find Fernworthy a particularly intrusive example – but this one seems to fit the valley well, and its deep blue-green cover sits attractively against the brown of the dying bracken in autumn.

211

Walks

In this section are collected a number of walks which do not have the sustained interest of the walks in the main chapters, but which are nevertheless worth considering. They vary enormously in length and difficulty, and you should be very careful to get out the map and look at the route before you set off. If you find that you cannot follow the descriptions on the Ordnance Survey map then you probably should not be attempting the walks, as the more difficult routes have the most sparse descriptions. Do not forget the safety advice given in the introductory chapter.

These additional walks are described in much less detail than the main walks, and assume that you are thoroughly familiar with the use of a map and compass. The key topics are indicated only, but if you have followed many of the walks in the main part you should have no difficulty in recognizing the features when they occur here.

Some of the walks here are included because they cover sections of the Lich Way and the Abbot's Way (or Jobbers' Path). The Lich Way was a route from the central eastern part of the moor, around Postbridge and Widecombe, which was used by the parishioners to transport corpses for burial. They were obliged until fairly recent times to go to Lydford for such religious purposes, and it was only by special pleading that they were eventually allowed to forego the 8 mile journey, doubled in wet weather, to bury their dead.

The Abbot's Way is a route between Buckfastleigh in the south-east of the moor to Tavistock Priory and to Buckland Abbey in the west of the moor. It is also known as the Jobbers' Path because of its use as a route for transporting wool from one end of the moor to the other. The Abbot's Way traverses the most remote parts of the southern moor, and takes you over wet upland and picturesque valleys, notably that of the Plym, before coming out into the in-country of the western moor.

The last walks in this chapter are unlike the other walks in this book, as they are one-way routes only, and are simply my own recommendations of the best and most practical ways of traversing the moor from south to north and east to west (or vice versa). Two of these latter routes follow the two main branches of the Abbot's Way. Do bear in mind that these are not meant to be full walk descriptions but are merely indications of a recommended route to follow.

Walk 35 – Belstone, Irishman's Wall and Cosdon Hill

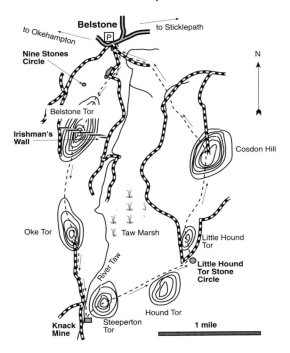

Leave your car at Belstone near the church (**619935**), and walk down towards Resugga (**617929**). Belstone Tor (**614922**) is obvious from here. Make your way to it, and then along the crest of the ridge to Oke Tor (**613901**). You will cross Irishman's Wall, which is a monument to a local farmer who employed some Irishmen to enclose part of the moor. The track on the south side of Oke Tor leads you to Knack Mine (**614885**), now deserted.

Cross the River Taw and head up the steep side of Steeperton Tor. From the top of Steeperton (**618887**) head off towards Little Hound Tor, leaving Hound Tor to the right. Just before you get to Little Hound Tor, look for the excellent stone circle to the south-east of it (**633896**). From the stone circle climb the tor and make for Cosdon Hill (**636915**), from which Belstone is (usually) easily visible.

Walk 36 – Old Farmhouses near Chagford

From the town centre of Chagford make your way on the B3206 towards Easton. Turn off left towards the north and cross the river at Rushford Bridge (**705883**). Turn left here on to a track which follows the river up to Chagford Bridge (**694879**), where the track dog-legs right and then left. Here a track leads to Murchington. Go through the village and turn left at **684883** towards Leigh. The track continues to the end of the public road (**683877**), but you turn right to Teigncombe (**673872**). Here you join the Mariners' Way which leads to Great Frenchbeer and Yardworthy. At the public road beyond Yardworthy (**681850**) turn left and follow the road, eventually leaving it at the junction at **690858** up on to Meldon Hill. From the top of Meldon (**696862**) continue towards Chagford and locate the exit track on Padley Common (**699873**), leading back to town.

213

Walk 37 – Beardown Man and the Lich Way

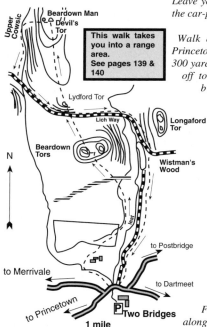

This walk takes you into a range area.
See pages 139 & 140

Leave your car at Two Bridges in the car-park opposite the hotel.

Walk along the road towards Princetown until you see after about 300 yards a signed track (**607599**) off to the right indicated with bright yellow markers. Follow this track up past Beardown Farm until you turn right on to the Devonport Leat. Follow the leat through the forest until you come out on to open moorland. At a clapper bridge (**608767**) turn left up the track marked on the map to the top of Beardown Tors. From here walk down the slope to Lydford Tor (**599782**), crossing the Lich Way along the route.

From Lydford Tor walk along the ridge until you reach Devil's Tor (**597797**). There is a false summit part of the way along, but the real Devil's Tor can be identified easily by the huge spike of Beardown Man to its left. Make your way to this.

From Beardown Man turn left (west) and walk down into the valley of the Cowsic. Turn left at the bottom of this beautiful upland valley (**592797**) and walk down to Broad Hole (**592786**).

From Broad Hole turn left back up towards Lydford Tor along the Lich Way. Climb up towards Lydford Tor, but leave it to your left, in the broad valley between it and Beardown (**600781**). Continue down the other side until you reach the weir over which the Lich Way crosses the West Dart above Wistman's Wood (**606781**). Turn right here and pass above the wood, where you will pick up a path which leads you down past Crockern Farmhouse (**610756**) and eventually to the car-park at Two Bridges.

Walk 38 – Crock of Gold and Nun's Cross Farm

From the centre of Princetown walk towards Two Bridges until you pick up a footpath to Bachelor's Hall which leaves the road at **593736**. Turn right here to Bullpark, and follow the track out on to the open moor at **604733**. The Crock of Gold, a cist, is on the left-hand side of the track just before the fourth stile on the left at **614731**. Leave the track here and go to the top of Royal Hill (**617726**), from where you walk in a roughly south-easterly direction until the angle of the enclosure at **618718**. Cross by the stile, and walk south to the track which leads you right into Whiteworks. From Whiteworks walk west towards Nun's Cross Farm, and then walk north over South Hessary Tor (**597723**) on the old section of the Abbot's Way until you reach the outskirts of Princetown.

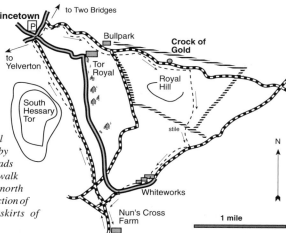

Walk 39 – High Willhays, Lints Tor and Black-a-tor Copse

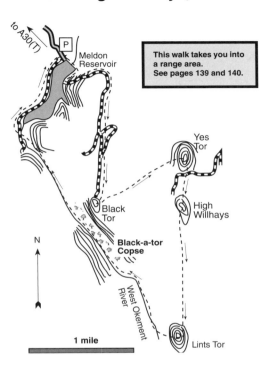

Park your car at the end of the access road to Meldon Reservoir (**563917**). From here walk down to the dam and cross to the other side. There is a track here which goes along the side of the reservoir for a way and then turns left up the side of Longstone Hill (**563913**). As the slope begins to ease off, follow the track due south until you reach the outcrop of Black Tor (**567895**). The view from here into the valley is superb. In the valley are the wrecks of a number of aircraft lost here in World War II as they failed to make altitude to cross the rising ground when they came in from the west. From Black Tor make your way over the rocky slope up on to Yes Tor (**581902**), and from there go along the broad ridge until you get to High Willhays (**579895**). Due south from High Willhays is Lints Tor (**580875**), from where the West Okement river can be gained. Take the north bank and go downstream until you reach the ancient wood of Black-a-tor Copse (**571884**). This is a wood like Wistman's Wood in the valley of the East Dart, where the oak trees have become stunted into a natural bonsai-type formation by the poor soil and wind. Continue downstream, passing Shelstone Island, and cross the river at the footbridge at **555906**. From here a footpath leads on the south-west side of the reservoir back to the car park.

Walk 40 – Lustleigh, Hound Tor Wood, Hunter's Tor

Park your vehicle in Lustleigh and make your way past Rudge Farm. Continue up the slope and at the road turn left and immediately right on to a path that winds its way down past Gradner Rocks, eventually gaining the weir at **800780**. Cross the river and follow the large path to the right and up until you reach the road near Water (**756806**). The next track on the right will take you through Water and Letchole Plantation, eventually reaching Foxworthy Bridge (**757821**). Cross the river and take the track towards Peck Farm and up the steep slope to Hunter's Tor. The track on the top of the slope leads you back towards Lustleigh, join-

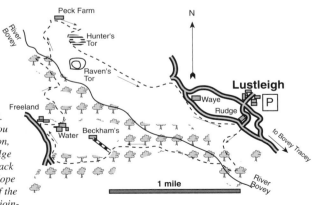

ing the road at **775816**, although you can carry out another loop which avoids the lovely Waye Farm and rejoins the road at Pethybridge (**779809**). Here take the track north back into Lustleigh.

215

Walk 41 – Black Lane, Duck's Pool and Abbot's Way

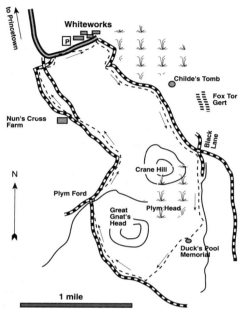

*Whiteworks (**613710**) is a convenient place to leave your car. A clear path works its way through Fox Tor Mires, the site of Sir Arthur Conan Doyle's story The Hound of the Baskervilles. Do not stray from the track, particularly in wet weather. The path goes past Childe's Tomb and up the slopes of Fox Tor until it reaches Black Lane (**626693**), a peat-cutters' track, near Crane Hill. Cater's Beam marked on the map is in fact a railway sleeper on Black Lane at (**627690**), so do not expect to see it on the marked track. It is a marker in the peat, and was mistaken by early map-makers for the name of a hill. The track turns south (**631690**) and follows the eastern side of a depression in which sits the Blacklane brook. Duck's Pool (**626679**), with its distinctive brick-built base, will be seen on the opposite side of the depression. From the memorial to William Crossing, walk in a south-westerly direction until you meet the track between Erme Pits and Broad Rock at about **622670**. This is a section of the Abbot's Way which passes near to the head of the River Erme, this working its way south from here. You are on the watershed of the south moor. Turn right on the Abbot's Way and follow it around and below Great Gnat's Head until you reach the ford over the River Plym at **610684**. Cross the river and follow the track to Nun's Cross Farm (**606698**), from where the route to White-works via the road at **606707** is obvious.*

Walk 42 – Widgery Cross, Dick's Well and Sourton Tors

*Leave your car near the Fox and Hounds Cross at **525867**, and follow the track to Nodden Gate (**530863**). You can see Brat Tor and Widgery Cross ahead. Climb up to this (**539856**). Regain the track and continue to Dick's Well, a spring at **553861** which supplies the Doe Tor brook. The track continues round to the left and leads to Bleak House at **559864**. From here continue on the track and then over moorland to Hunt Tor (**556876**), from whence one of a number of tracks will lead you to Sourton Tors, on the top of which you can see the pits which were used to make ice commercially. From Sourton Tors retrace your steps on the track until you come to the complex junction of tracks at **543881**. Here you take pot luck and follow any (or all!) of the tracks back to Nodden Gate, passing in the shadow of Great Nodden on the way.*

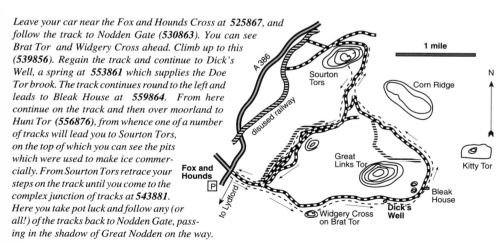

Walk 43 – Princetown Railway

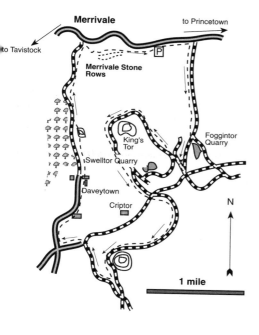

There is an excellent car-park (*561749*) on the road between Princetown and Merrivale. Leave your car here. Walk back towards Princetown and take the obvious track at *567749* south past Yellowmead Farm. This will lead you to the magnificent Foggintor Quarries. Here you can pick up the railway built by Tyrwhitt which swings around to the north, past King's Tor and then back under Swelltor Quarries. Both sets of quarries are worth an investigation; they produced the stone to build Princetown Prison (also built by Thomas Tyrwhitt), and for many prominent buildings in London. The railway on which you are walking was built to allow cheaper passage for the stone to Tavistock and beyond. The railway carries on round to Ingra Tor, and shortly after this a track leads you north again from Routrundle (*555717*) to the little road at *549723*, where you turn left and then right at the public road which will lead you to Daveytown (*549733*). Here a track leads north through the beautiful Walkham Valley until you reach the B3357 near Merrivale. Turn right here (*550750*) and follow the line of the road back to the car-park. The stone rows at Merrivale are well worth the slight detour. After climbing the steep slope once you have joined the road near Merrivale, walk along the line of the road about 300 yards away from it. You will soon see the magnificent and world-famous Bronze Age ritual monuments.

Walk 44 – Bittaford Tramway, Western Beacon, Cuckoo Ball

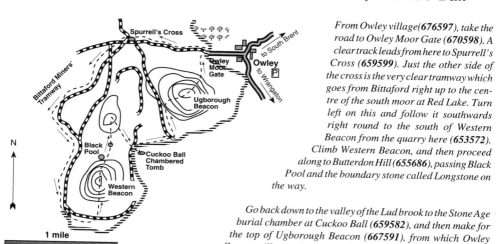

From Owley village(*676597*), take the road to Owley Moor Gate (*670598*). A clear track leads from here to Spurrell's Cross (*659599*). Just the other side of the cross is the very clear tramway which goes from Bittaford right up to the centre of the south moor at Red Lake. Turn left on this and follow it southwards right round to the south of Western Beacon from the quarry here (*653572*). Climb Western Beacon, and then proceed along to Butterdon Hill (*655686*), passing Black Pool and the boundary stone called Longstone on the way.

Go back down to the valley of the Lud brook to the Stone Age burial chamber at Cuckoo Ball (*659582*), and then make for the top of Ugborough Beacon (*667591*), from which Owley Corner will come into view again.

Walk 45 – Sheepstor, Drizzlecombe and Nun's Cross

Park at Norsworthy Bridge (**567695**). This a favourite spot for thieves, so secure everything. Walk around the reservoir to the south until you see the track at **566688**. Take this, and when you come out on to the open moor make for the top of Sheeps Tor, from which the views are superb. Make directly for the little village of Sheepstor, and on reaching the road at **562676** turn left and walk along it until you reach the ford and scout hut at **581673**. At Ditsworthy Warren House (**583662**) turn towards Drizzlecombe along the track and follow the Plym up to Plym Ford (**610684**). A good track leads from here to Nun's Cross Farm, where you take the track to Older Bridge (**598706**). Walk along the leat for a while until the track diverges from it to take you past Newleycombe Lake and eventually on to the edge of the Raddick Plantation at **578701**. Follow the edge of the forest until it eventually reaches the road at Norsworthy Bridge.

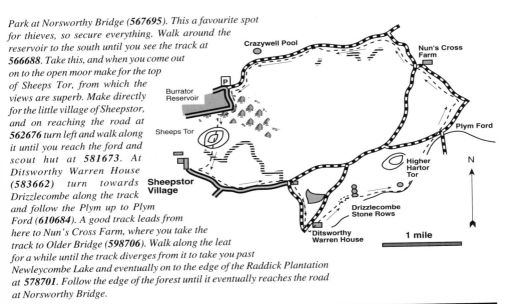

Walk 46 – Huntingdon Cross, Abbot's Way

From the car-park in Holne, walk along the road towards Michelcombe. From here a track known as Sandy Way leads on to the moor (**696689**). Follow this right out on to the moor until you reach the old tin-workings of Hapstead (**670692**). From here make for the top of Ryder's Hill, on top of which is a cairn and a trig point (**659690**). Huntingdon Warren is due south of here, and in walking to it you will be traversing the tinning area known as Snowdon. Huntingdon Cross lies at the junction of the two valleys at **664663**. From Huntingdon Warren top you are best going to the east in order to strike the valley of the Western Wallabrook. From the cross follow the obvious route of the Abbot's Way to the east over Lamb's Down until you reach the ford at **698666**, and the road beyond. Turn left here and follow the road until Two Oaks at **702674**, where you can take a track to Hawson Cross at **710682**. Turn left here and go straight on at the junction, past Hawson and eventually entering Holne, where the Church House Inn is an excellent place to stop.

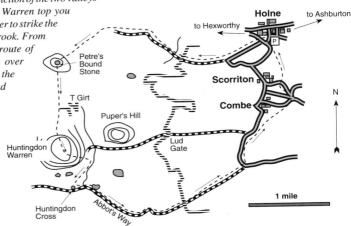

218

Walk 47 – East–West Walk

A convenient place to start an east–west route across the north moor is Chagford. Remember that you will be walking some 15 miles or more over some of the wildest country in Britain. You will need all the safety equipment mentioned in the introductory chapter, including food, waterproofs, map and compass. The section between Sittaford Tor and Tavy Cleave requires good navigation, particularly in mist, and if you are not completely confident about your navigation do not attempt this walk.

There are plenty more walks in this book of an easier standard.

From Chagford you can follow any number of routes along roads and past the old farmhouses towards Fernworthy Reservoir. From Sandeman Bridge at Fernworthy (*657836*), follow the tracks through the forest until you reach the open moor (*647831*) near Grey Wethers circles. Go to the top of Sittaford Tor (*633831*) and then to the ruined tinner's hut at Statt's House (*622825*). From here plod through the upland bogs to reach Kit Rocks on the East Dart at *613827*, and then up the even wetter route to Cut Hill (*599827*) and on to Fur Tor (*588831*). From Fur Tor make for Sandy Ford on the Tavy (*572834*). The Tavy runs down through the cleave until a point under Ger Tor, where a leat is taken off on the north side (*549829*). Follow the leat until you see the car park at Willsworthy (*537824*). From here there are a number of routes leading back to Tavistock, all clearly marked on the OS map.

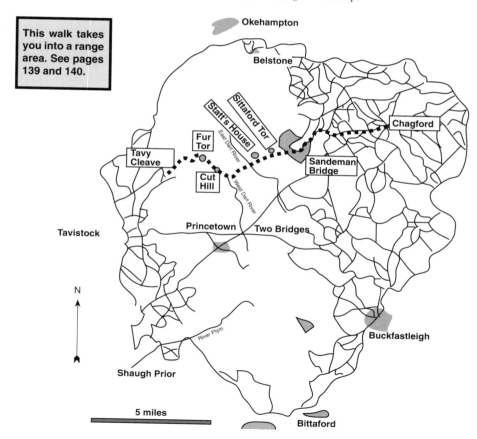

This walk takes you into a range area. See pages 139 and 140.

Walk 48 – East–West on the Northern Abbot's Way

This a substantial walk of easily 15 miles (depending where you start and finish) over the wildest part of the south moor. You should be prepared for bad weather and take waterproofs, food, map and compass. The section between the Avon reservoir and Princetown needs care, particularly in misty weather. That being said, it is a very worthwhile experience to have traversed Dartmoor on the route of the old monks. You should be able to do the walk in one day, although it is a pleasant two-day back-packing trip. An alternative to public transport is to arrange to leave a car at each end, not forgetting to swap keys when you meet at, say, Nun's Cross Farm.

The northern branch of the Abbot's Way linked Tavistock and Buckfastleigh. Take the small roads from the Abbey past Hockmoor and Parklands Farm, reaching the open moor just south of Cross Furzes (**698668**). The Abbot's Way crosses Dean Moor and works its way along the north bank of the Avon Reservoir until you reach Huntingdon Cross (**664661**). Continue in the same general direction skirting to the left around the top of the reservoir, and cross the miners' tramway at **647659**. Make for Red Lake Ford, with the cone of spoil from Red Lake works to your right. From here you need to take care in crossing the centre of the southern moor via Erme Pits and Broad Rock (**618672**). The

track is well used, however, and with the judicious use of your compass you should find Plym Ford fairly easily. Take care in misty conditions over this stretch.

Cross the Plym at Plym Ford (**610684**) and then proceed to Nun's Cross Farm (**606698**). From here there is a straight track marked all the way to Princetown, from where you gain the main road at Rundlestone (**574749**) via North Hessary Tor (**577742**). Walk along the side of the main road until you are past Merrivale and then leave on the track at **541750** towards Moortown (**526738**). Walk to Tavistock by way of Warren's Cross and the golf course road.

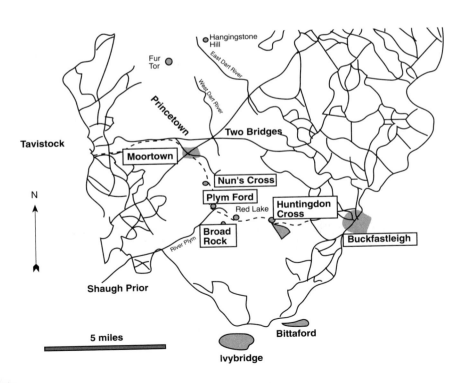

220

Walk 49 – East–West on the Southern Abbot's Way

This alternative southern route of the Abbot's Way is probably the better known of the two. It linked Buckfastleigh and Buckland Abbey, which was owned at one time by Sir Francis Drake, and is now open to the public. The times of opening are variable, so you will need to check with the National Trust.

It is a walk of at least 15 miles which crosses some of the wildest country in the south moor. Many people will tell you that it is only the north moor which is dangerous. Do not be fooled, it is just as easy to lose yourself south of Princetown as it is to the north. You will need to be well-equipped with food, waterproofs, map and compass. The section between Huntingdon Cross near the Avon reservoir and Plym Ford needs particular care in mist.

Follow the route for the northern branch described in Walk 48 from Buckfastleigh Abbey, past Red Lake and Broad Rock, until you reach Plym Ford. Turn left here into the valley of the Plym, and then follow either bank down in a south-westerly direction past Ditsworthy Warren and Trowlesworthy until you reach Cadover Bridge at **555646**. There are a number of antiquities on either side, including a number of large Bronze Age enclosures, but in particular, if you take the northern bank, you will pass directly by the Drizzlecombe menhirs (**592670**). At Cadover Bridge turn left on to the road and walk a few hundred yards up the slope until you see a signpost on the right which leads you down beautiful wooded tracks past the Dewerstone, reaching the road again at Shaugh Bridge. There are various routes, all on the road and all clearly marked on the map, which lead you from here to Buckland Abbey.

Transport back is always a problem, but one alternative is to leave a car at each end. Don't forget to meet and exchange car keys in the middle somewhere, or you will have a very long walk back! You could also make it the basis of a two-day walk, returning by a different route.

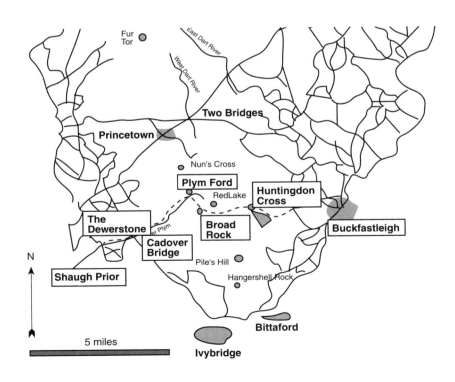

Walk 50 – North–South Walk

This is a two or three day walk which takes you into the heart of both north and south moors. Be prepared accordingly. You will need all the equipment mentioned in the introduction and you should take particular care in winter. Then the middle of both south and north moors can provide a chastening experience for poorly equipped walkers, particularly those whose navigation is weak. William Crossing, the great writer on Dartmoor, used to walk this route regularly in a single day,

but with a heavy pack you should allow two stops, since if you do not you will miss all the sights along the way.

Stowford Bridge (*642568*) near Ivybridge is the start of the Two Moors Way which you follow along the Bittaford Miners' Track until Red Lake Ford (*643665*). From here it is best to follow the Abbots' Way north branch (see Walk 48) until Princetown, where you make for Two Bridges along the road. From

the hotel at Two Bridges go north past Wistman's Wood. Continue up the West Dart and make for Flat Tor (*609817*). From here squelch your way to Cut Hill (*599827*) and then to Fur Tor (*588831*). Three peat passes (at *591842*, *896855* and *602869*) then allow you access to Okement Hill where you can use the military roads to reach Oke Tor (*612901*) and eventually Belstone Hill (*615922*), the route from the summit leading easily down into Belstone village.

This walk takes you into a range area. See pages 139 and 140.

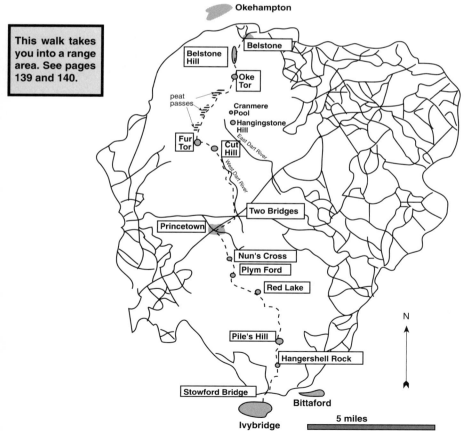

222

Index

224